AN INTRODUCTION TO THE MODERN GULF OF GUINEA

People, History, Political Economy & Strategic Future

AN INTRODUCTION TO THE MODERN GULF OF GUINEA

People, History, Political Economy & Strategic Future

Otoabasi Akpan

Published by
Adonis & Abbey Publishers Ltd

United Kingdom
P.O. Box 43418
London
SE11 4XZ
http://www.adonis-abbey.com

Nigeria:
No. 3, Akanu Ibiam Str
Asokoro,
P.O. Box 1056, Abuja.

Year of Publication 2013

Copyright © Otoabasi Akpan
British Library Cataloguing-in-Publication Data
A catalogue record for this book is available from the British Library

ISBN: 978-1-909112-35-3

The moral right of the author has been asserted all rights reserved. No part of this book may be reproduced, stored in a retrieval system or transmitted at any time or by any means without the prior permission of the publisher

Dedication

- Otoabasi
- Victoria
- Sekerema
- Affiong
- Ediomoabasi

Contents

Dedication..iv
Contents...v
List of maps..ix
Acknowledgements..x
Preface...xi

Introduction

The Strategic Significance of the Gulf of Guinea to Modern Civilization...15

Section I: The Outline of the Gulf of Guinea

Chapter One
The Ancient History of the Gulf of Guinea..............................29

Chapter Two
The Modern History of the Gulf of Guinea..............................45

Chapter Three
The Political Economy of the Gulf of Guinea..........................61

Chapter Four
Politics in the Gulf of Guinea...90

Section II: The Countries of the Gulf of Guinea in the Central African Sub-Region

Chapter Five
Cameroon..109

Chapter Six
Democratic Republic of the Congo...........................119

Chapter Seven
The Republic of the Congo.......................................131

Chapter Eight
Equatorial Guinea..139

Chapter Nine
Gabon..145

Chapter Ten
São Tomé and Principe..151

Section III: The Country of the Gulf of Guinea in Southern Africa

Chapter Eleven
Angola...158

Section IV: The countries of the Gulf of Guinea in the West African Sub-Region

Chapter Twelve
Benin...167

Chapter Thirteen
Cape Verde..175

Chapter Fourteen
Cote d'Ivoire..181

Chapter Fifteen
The Gambia..189

Chapter Sixteen
Ghana...195

Chapter Seventeen
Guinea..204

Chapter Eighteen
Guinea-Bissau..211

Chapter Nineteen
Liberia..217

Chapter Twenty
Nigeria...223

Chapter Twenty-One
Senegal...237

Chapter Twenty-Two
Sierra Leone...243

Chapter Twenty-Three
Togo...251

Section V: Making Africa Visible Actor in the International System

Chapter Twenty-Four
The Strategic Future of the Gulf of Guinea.................................259

Chapter Twenty-Five
History, Geo-Politics and the African Desideratum....................276

References...307

Index...312

LIST OF MAPS

Political Map of Africa...xiv
Fig. 5.1: Political Map of Cameroon......................................111
Fig. 6.1: Political Map of the Domocratic
          Republic of the Congo..121
Fig. 7.1: Political Map of Republic of the Congo..................133
Fig. 8.1: Political Map of Equatorial Guinea.........................141
Fig. 9.1: Political Map of Gabon...148
Fig. 10.1: Political Map of São Tomé and Principe..................155
Fig. 11.1: Political Map of Angola...162
Fig. 12.1: Political Map of Benin...172
Fig. 13.1: Political Map of Cape Verde..................................180
Fig. 14.1: Political Map of Cote d'Ivoire................................186
Fig. 15.1: Political Map of the Gambia..................................194
Fig. 16.1: Political Map of Ghana..200
Fig. 17.1: Political Map of Guinea...209
Fig. 18.1: Political Map of Guinea Bissau..............................216
Fig. 19.1: Political Map of Liberia...222
Fig. 20.1: Political Map of Nigeria..229
Fig. 21.1: Political Map of Senegal..243
Fig. 22.1: Political Map of Sierra Leone................................249
Fig. 23.1: Political Map of Togo..256

Acknowledgements

No one ever writes a book alone, and this one is no exception. I have benefited from the information, opinions, encouragement and support of many people-so many, in fact, that it is impossible to thank them all individually. But there are several without whom this book would never have come to be what it is, and I would like to register my gratitude in print.

In the first place, there are my colleagues in the Department of History and International Studies of the University of Uyo, who have been my constant companions in our quest to sustain the Uyo School of Historiography. These include Professors Okon Uya, Monday Abasiattai, Anthony Nwabughuogu, Koko Ete Ina and Eno Ikpe; Drs Sylvester Eka, Joseph Robert Bassey, Dominic Akpan, Udida Undiyaundeye, Ekong Demson, Nkereuwem Edemekong, Ini Etuk, Anietie Inyang and Mfon Akwang. Ubong Umoh, my protégé in the field of International Security Studies (ISS), provided a wealth of insights and information. In writing a book like this, while I have relied on my own experiences, these were rightly amplified by these colleagues and, indeed, my post-graduate students.

Secondly, my wife, Victoria, supplied the editorial work and personal encouragement, while Dr. Charles Udosen of the Department of Geography and Regional Planning of the University of Uyo provided all the maps used in the book. Inemesit Ukpeyeh of the Department of History and International Studies of the University of Uyo was extremely helpful in organizing the final draft. Aniefiok A. Iniunam did the final editorial work while Ekemini Akpan designed the cover of the book. However, none of my colleagues or assistants is accountable for any short-comings in the book, which are my sole responsibility.

Preface

The purpose of this book is to examine the salient features of the Gulf of Guinea which conspire to make it a strategic region in world politics. It should be noted from the outset that this work is not an exhaustive study of the Gulf of Guinea, but mere outline of its history.

The Gulf of Guinea is located on the Atlantic Ocean off the Western African coast and it extends from Senegal in the north to Angola in the south.The region is often referred to as the geographic centre of the earth because of its zero degrees longitude and latitude.

The countries that make up the region are 19, and they are: Angola, Benin, Cameroon, Cape Verde, Cote d'Ivoire, DR Congo, Equatorial Guinea, Gabon, Gambia, Ghana, Guinea, Guinea Bissau, Liberia, Nigeria, Republic of Congo, São Tomé and Principe, Senegal, Sierra Leone and Togo. Some scholars have included the Central African Republic (CAR) as one of the states of the Gulf of Guinea, but, strictly speaking, the CAR should not be included because its coastline neither ends in, nor joins the Atlantic Ocean. In fact, the CAR is a land-locked state and to that extent is not qualified to belong to the states of the Gulf of Guinea whose coastlines are washed directly by the Atlantic Ocean.

The book uses both thematic and idiographic approaches to examine the Gulf of Guinea as a region and the individual states within it. The major themes include the strategic significance of the Gulf of Guinea and features of its ancient history, modern history, political economy, politics and strategic future. The idiographic approach provides the lens to view the states of the Gulf as distinct and unique self-contained political systems. Therefore, focus on their ethnic compositions, history, politics and structure of governance, economy and foreign relations illuminate the more the particulars of the Gulf of Guinea.

In specific terms, the book has five sections made up of 25 chapters. Section one which treats the broad themes of the outline of the Gulf of Guinea comprises the first four chapters of the book.

Chapters five to twenty three examine individually the features of the nineteen states of the Gulf through the prisms of the people, history, politics and structure of governance, economy and foreign relations. These chapters are grouped under three sections coterminous with three geo-political regions in Africa where the states are located as Follows:

GULF OF GUINEA STATES IN CENTRAL AFRICA	GULF OF GUINEA STATE IN SOUTHERN AFRICA	GULF OF GUINEA STATES IN WEST AFRICA
Cameroon DR Congo Equatorial Guinea Gabon Republic of Congo São Tomé And Principe	Angola	Benin Cape Verde Cote d'Ivoire Gambia Ghana Guinea Guinea Bissau Liberia Nigeria Senegal Sierra Leone Togo

The last section which is entitled; ***making Africa Visible Actor in the International System*** contains the last two chapters which treats the themes of the strategic future and geo-politics of the Gulf of Guinea.

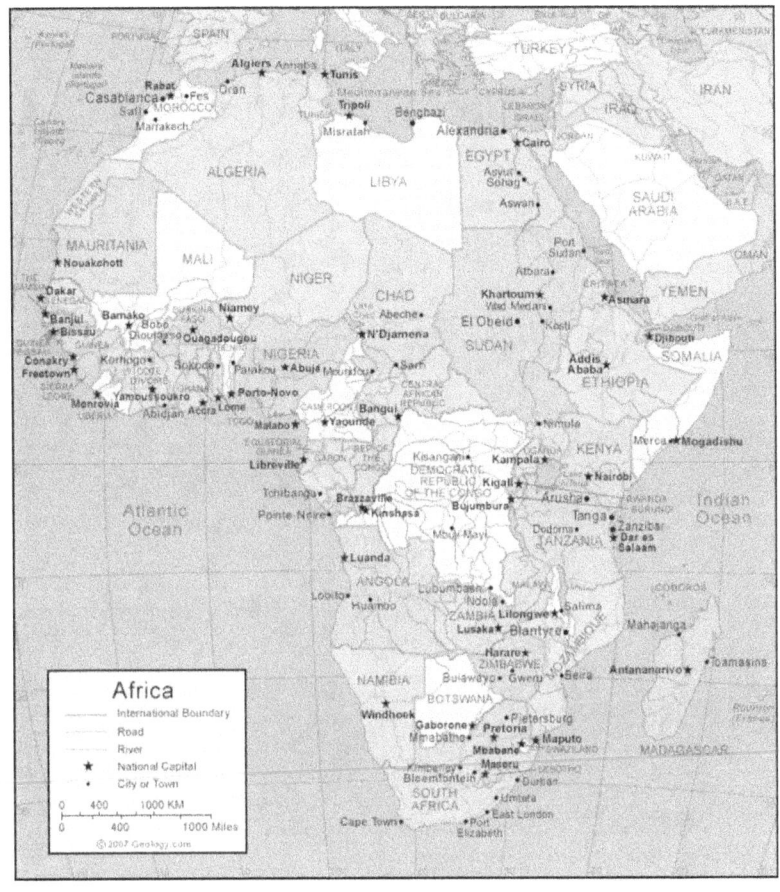

Political Map of Africa

INTRODUCTION

The Strategic Significance of the Gulf Of Guinea to Modern Civilization

Location

Guinea is the forest and coastal region of West Africa between the tropic of Cancer and the Equator. The name Guinea is derived from the Berber word *aguinaw* or *gwana*, meaning *black man*, hence, *akal n-igiunamen* or land of the black men. The name was first adopted by the Portuguese and it was variously known as *Guinuia, Ginya, Gheneoa* and *Ghinea* which also appeared as such on European maps from the fourteenth century onward. In fact, at a time the West Coast of Africa was called Guinea. A description of Guinea and the Guinea Coast is provided thus by the Encyclopaedia Britannica (1999:802):

> Guinea is a term used originally for the coastlands and adjacent forests of western Africa between the Republic of Guinea on the west and Equatorial Guinea on the east, including the whole, or the southern parts, of Guinea-Bissau, Sierra Leone, Liberia, Cote d'Ivoire, Ghana, Togo, Benin, Nigeria and Cameroon. There have been conflicting accounts of the derivation of the name Guinea, but it would seem to be a version of the Berber word **aguinaw**, or **gnawa**, meaning "black man" or "Negro".

Giving a further description of Guinea and the sources of its attraction to the ancient world of Europe, W. D. Hussey (1977:66) writes:

> The word 'Guinea' is derived from the 'Ghana' or 'Gheneoa' of the medieval Arab geographers, who used it to describe a rich kingdom which, with Timbuktu as its capital, was thought to exist on the headwaters of an imaginary western branch of the River Nile. The Portuguese transferred the name to the coastline from the River Senegal to Cape St Catherine ... the sea-captains of Prince Henry had discovered this coast as far as Sierra Leone and had brought back the first gold dust and slaves. Trading voyages soon started, and in 1448 a number of merchants from the Portuguese port of Lagos set up a factory on Arguin Island. Their trade was in gold dust, slaves, ostrich feathers and gum and it was a very profitable trade.

Introduction

The Gulf of Guinea (GoG) is a part of the Atlantic Ocean adjacent to the coastal region. It extends from Cape Lopez near the equator to Cape Palmas at 7°west. Its major tributaries are the Casamance, Volta and River Niger. The coastline on the Gulf of Guinea includes the Bight of Biafra and the Bight of Benin.

Historically, the GoG as a region is the sprawling area that the Portuguese held sway and had significant influence in West Africa between the fifteenth and the seventeenth centuries. This extended from Senegal in the North to Angola in the South. This was, indeed, the Portuguese sphere of influence in West Africa and it consisted of two areas: the Upper Guinea and Lower Guinea. The former extends from Cape Blanco in Senegal to the Shebro Island in Sierra Leone. Lower Guinea stretches from Shebro Island to the eastern end of the GoG in the Niger Delta. By the end of the fifteenth century, the Portuguese had traced the coastal line of Western Africa to Angola from where they pushed on round Africa to India in the East.

Sections of the coast of Guinea, especially the area of the Lower Guinea, were known by the chief commodities they produced. For example, the area from Cape Mesurado to Cape Palmas, along present-day Liberia, was known as the Grain Coast principally because it was the source of the ***grains of paradise*** (Guinea pepper; xylopia aethiopica). The Ivory Coast stretched from Cape Palmas to Cape Three Points; the Gold Coast was located east of the Cape Three Points, and the Slave Coast was between the Volta River and the Niger Delta in Nigeria.

Today, the states of the GoG traverse three of the five sub-regions in Africa-Central Africa, Southern Africa and West Africa. The Gulf states are: Cameroun, the Democratic Republic of Congo, Equatorial Guinea, Gabon, Republic of Congo and São Tomé and Principe (Central Africa); Angola (Southern Africa) and Benin Republic, Cape Verde, Cote d'Ivoire, the Gambia, Ghana, Guinea, Guinea-Bissau, Liberia, Nigeria, Senegal, Sierra Leone and Togo (West Africa). These are the states located on the Atlantic Ocean and the arm of it which is the GoG. The Gulf States constitute four (European) language groups: Anglophone, Francophone, Hispanophone and Lusophone. All of them were created and colonized by European countries namely; Britain,

France, Germany, Portugal and Spain. The region has a population and, indeed, market size of 300 million people.

Earliest Contacts with the Outside World

From the earliest times, the GoG had been quite strategic to powers outside the region, especially Arab and European powers. The first to benefit from the resources of the Gulf were the Arabs who took great advantage of the international trade with West Africa to prosper and act as middlemen between West Africa and the European World. The instrument of this earliest contact was the trans-Saharan trade. Trans-Saharan trade which began in about 1000 B.C. between West and North Africa brought West Africa into the international commerce of the middle Ages (Hopkins, 1977).

The trade was developed by the Carthaginians from about the fifth century B.C. and was given a welcome fillip by the Romans in the eighth century. It experienced a lull in the fourth century A.D. following the collapse of the Roman rule in North Africa but was revived after the Byzantine re-conquest of North Africa in 533 – 35. The trade was given further impetus with the rise of Arab power in the seventh century. On the significance of the trade to the Arabs and Europe within this period, A. J. Hopkins (1977:80) records that:

> The period which corresponds to the Middle Ages in European history was a flourishing time for trade on the Saharan routes, particularly from the Middle of the thirteenth to the end of the sixteenth centuries. This period saw an upswing in demand for West African products in Europe and the Middle East, and at the same time a substantial increase in supply, which was greatly assisted by an era of settled government in North Africa and the Western Sudan.

The Trans-Saharan Trade continued till the nineteenth century. Within this long period, a number of commodities were sent from West Africa to the Arab world and Europe. These included gold, slaves, expensive cloth, spices, especially pepper, ivory, kola nuts, timber, dye-woods, gum, beeswax, leather goods and ostrich feathers. These were, by the standards of the Middle Age, luxury and expensive items. In exchange, West Africa had such goods as cowries, salt, weapons, copper, preserved foodstuffs, glassware, beads and numerous fancy goods.

Of the commodities exported from West Africa, three were very prominent not just because they were luxury goods but also because they facilitated the transformation of Europe and the Arab world from underdeveloped climes into modernity. These were gold, slaves and agricultural produce. The catalytic effects of gold on the Muslim world and Europe between the eleventh and sixteenth centuries are captured graphically by A. G. Hopkins (1977:82) in the following words:

> ... Exports increased during the eleventh century, following the adoption of gold coinage throughout the Muslim world, and they received a further boost after 1252, when gold began to replace silver as Europe's main currency. Between the eleventh and the seventeenth centuries, West Africa was the leading supplier of gold to the international economy, and in the later Middle Ages accounted, according to one estimate, for almost two-thirds of world production. West African gold flowed to Cairo and the Middle East, where it helped to sustain Arab power until the end of the thirteenth century, when the basis of the monetary system changed to silver. African gold contributed to the functioning of the domestic economy in Europe, and also helped to settle international debts. In the later Middle Ages Europe needed bullion to pay for imports from the Far East because most of her exports were too bulky to be worth transporting such a long distance overland. The Italian merchants of Genoa, Florence and Venice had a favourable trade balance with North Africa from the end of the twelfth century, and so were able to import gold. This advantage, together with their geographical situation, enabled them to become the magnificent brokers of international trade. Control over the gold trade also assisted the expansion of Portugal and Spain in the fifteenth and sixteenth centuries, when Seville became, for a while, Europe's 'capital of gold'. Finally, the gold trade was important in Africa itself: it assisted the rise of the ports of North Africa from the end of the twelfth century, and it contributed to the wealth of the great states of the Western Sudan.

Slaves from West Africa were used specifically as soldiers, labourers, servants and concubines. They were especially needed in North Africa and the Middle East. At times slaves were used as currency to buy gold just as agricultural products like kola nuts were equally used to buy slaves. Uya (2005:54) has documented the utility value and experiences of the pre-Atlantic slave trade thus:

> ... as a consequence of the much older Indian Ocean trade, Africans had entered the Middle East, Asia, and even China, before the fifteenth century. Here, they served as workers on the plantations at Basra, Bandar Abbas and Minab; as soldiers in Arabia, Persia and India; as dock workers and dow crews in the Indian Ocean lands; and as domestic servants, concubines, and courtiers.

Trade in slaves started from the earliest times when trans-Saharan trade itself began in about 1000 B.C. and continued well into the twentieth century. Throughout this long period, millions of West Africans were transported to North Africa and Europe especially during the period of the Arab expansion which began in the seventh century. Nobody can tell for sure how many slaves were involved in the trade within the period, but when Mauny's estimate of 2 million per annum is noted, Lewicki's figure of 12 to 15 million slaves that passed through Cairo in the sixteenth century is considered and when Boahen's (1967; Hopkins, 1977) statistics of 10,000 slaves per annum in the nineteenth century are calculated, then it is safe to conclude that a minimum of thirty million slaves were involved.

Of the agricultural products that made much mark in Europe, two were particularly important and these were gum and beeswax. Both products had pharmaceutical and industrial uses. Gum, for example, was used as a raw material in the manufacture of textiles. In point of fact, agricultural goods meant much to the Portuguese as slaves and that is why attempts were made to develop the production of crops such as sugar, cotton and tobacco in the region from the sixteenth century onward.

Contacts through the Trans-Atlantic Slave Trade

The decline of the trans-Saharan trade in the sixteenth century strengthened trade across the Atlantic. The trans-Atlantic trade had effectively begun a century earlier and as stride and Ifeka (1980:171) have recorded: "The Portuguese exploration of the Gulf of Guinea inaugurated a period of growing trade with Europeans at the Coast".

What accounted for the decline in the trans-Saharan trade were a declining interest in gold and a thriving interest in slaves. In fact, the main articles of this new trade were slaves. To be sure, from the beginning of their contact with the West Coast in the fifteenth century, some Africans had been bought and sold by the Portuguese, but it was not until the Middle of the seventeenth century that the world experienced the rapid expansion of the Atlantic trade. And the main victims of this unwholesome trade were West Africans.

The rise of sugar plantations in the West Indies which also revolutionized the economy of the Caribbean was the fundamental reason for high demand in slave labour. Until the mid-seventeenth century, the major export from the West Indies had been tobacco. Explaining how sugar transformed the economy of the West Indies and provoked the triangular commerce between European, Africa and the Caribbean, A. G. Hopkins (1977:90) notes:

> Sugar, however, was pre-eminently a planters' crop, and it required land, capital, and labour on a large scale. The land was there already; the capital came from Europe; and, in the event, the labour came from Africa, not because the continent was overpopulated, but because no other cheaper source of suitable manpower was readily available. The indigenous inhabitants of the Americas had been tried and found wanting, and many of the European pioneers on this particular frontier of the New World chose to cultivate land for themselves elsewhere, especially in Virginia and Carolina, where tobacco was becoming an important export crop. To retain a free labour force where there was abundant land and alternative employment opportunities would have meant paying high wages. Cheap and subservient labour was preferred and was probably essential. Besides being relatively inexpensive and readily available (thanks to the efficiency of the Afro-European delivery system), Negro labourers had a higher survival rate in the West Indies, and therefore had a cost advantage over potential competitors in the labour market. The advantage was a result of their greater immunity from diseases such as yellow fever and malaria, and had nothing to do with the alleged inability of the white man to work in a tropical climate. And so the venturers who had originally sailed to West Africa primarily to trade in gold stayed on to supply labourers for the new sugar plantations of the Caribbean.

Through slave labour, Europe and the Americas benefited economically and Europe in particular used the human resources of the GoG to secure the necessary capital to launch industrial revolution. Like in the case of trans-Saharan trade, the GoG supplied a minimum of thirty million slaves to the New World of America.

In terms of material benefits, the slave economy led to the rise of sea-port towns in Europe. Such towns like Bordeaux, Bristol, Liverpool, Manchester, Marseilles, Nantes and Seville owe their existence to slave trade. The towns also became manufacturing centres which were used to consolidate the gains of industrial revolution. On the African side, there was no equivalent of these port-towns. Besides, in exchange for valuable human resources, most of whom were teenagers; Africans were given rum, gin, trinkets, beads, iron bars, guns, and gun powder. These were worthless conspicuous goods compared with the invaluable ones taken out of the GoG. Guns and ammunitions were used to destabilize states in the Gulf. The crisis that ensued prolonged the colonization of the region by European powers.

The Gulf of Guinea and the Staple Commerce

By the late eighteenth century, leading dedicated reformers in Britain were in the forefront in condemning the Atlantic slave trade and wishing for its termination. These included names like Granville Sharp, Thomas Clarkson and William Wilberforce who were members of the anti-slavery movement. But their humanitarian pressure only yielded fruits when the slave economy acted as brakes to further economic expansion of Britain in particular and other European countries in general. Therefore, the abolition of slave trade responded to new economic demands of the industrial revolution. This new thinking is summarized thus by Stride and Ifeka (1980:224):

> By the second half of the eighteenth century, the industrial revolution in Britain was well under way. What Britain required was not so much easy profits from distributive trades but new and expanding markets for her mass-produced goods. Her factories also needed expanding supplies of raw materials such as palm oil (for soap and lubrication) and cotton. Therefore industrialists felt that it would be economically better for Britain if West Africans remained at home to produce raw materials and provide potential customers for British goods. This feeling had strong theoretical backing from the famous economist, Adam Smith, who argued that a free man always work more productively than a slave.

The result of the abolition of slave trade made Europe to achieve the dual objectives of making the Guinea Coast to become producers of raw materials for European industries and ready markets for the industrial products. This smart Adam-Smithian economics ensured prosperity for Europe and exploitation of the African resources and wealth at the same time. By turning the energies of the Africans into land and agricultural ventures, the GoG became leading exporters of palm oil and produce, groundnut, cotton, coffee, cocoa, timber, gum, and ivory. Gold from the Gold Coast was also exported after the abolition of slave trade.

Most of these agricultural products stimulated industrial growth in Europe. Palm oil, for instance, was used in the production of soap, lubricants and candles. "Soap was required for cleansing the population in the growing urban centres; lubricants were needed to oil the new machinery, especially the railways; and candles were in demand for lighting the expanding towns and factories" (Hopkins, 1977:129). Palm kernel oil which is derivative of oil palm was used in the manufacture of margarine and cattle food.

The palm oil economy led to the emergence of many merchants and industrialists in Europe and also provoked scientific stimulations and innovations and, indeed, Research and Development. A typical example is the case of glycerine, a by-product of the soap industry, which was used to develop explosives. Explosives aided victories in European wars and in peace time, were used in the mining, quarrying and construction companies. Other by-products from the soap industry included cosmetics, shampoos, perfumes, shaving creams, toothpaste and dyes. Groundnuts were used in the manufacture of cooking oil and soap.

From the European side, the imports into the Guinea Coast were as worthless as those of the slave trade era. In the main, they were: textiles, spirits, salt, iron, hardware, tobacco, guns and gunpowder. One thing about these products is that the availability of the foreign ones destroyed the indigenous industries. Long before the birth of Christ, people of the Guinea Coast had developed the manufacture of soap; were famous for the quality of their cloth; were adept at the production of leather goods and were skilful in the mining and utilization of important metals like gold, iron and copper. For example, "people who were noted for their early craftsmanship in iron were the Wolof, the Susu, the Kano Hausa, the Yoruba and the Awka blacksmiths of eastern Nigeria" (Stride & Ifeka, 1980:161). One of the earliest people positively known to have utilized iron was the Nok of Southern Zaria in Nigeria, whose civilization lasted between 900 B.C. and 200 A.D.

Colonial Pillage and Exploitation of Strategic Minerals

For the Guinea Coast, the nineteenth century was critical in many ways. At the beginning of contacts with Europeans in the fifteenth century, the empires, kingdoms, city-states and communities were sovereign and independent and enjoyed undisputed control over their external and internal affairs. The middle of the nineteenth century changed these and brought serious challenges to the sovereignty of these African states. By the turn of the century, their potentates had lost control over their external and internal affairs. These were taken over by the imperial powers which needed these states for geo-strategic reasons ranging from sources of resources to market and extension of their territories overseas. By the beginning of the twentieth century, new nation-states were created out of the various ethnic groups in the region and colonized by these imperial powers. From that stand point, they owned the new territories and exercised sovereignty on them as colonies.

The possession of colonies meant absolute control over the economic resources of the colonies. For the emergent states of the Guinea Coast, the colonizing powers controlled the production and marketing of cash crops, which in any case were sold at pre-determined prices offered by their agents and companies. Same went for the strategic minerals. The GoG is home to a number of critical minerals. The list include gold, salt, lead, zinc, oil and gas, cassiterite, clay, dolomite, marble, tantalite, bentonite, gypsum, kaolin, magnesite, barites, bauxite, limestone, uranium, glass-sand, iron-ore, lignite, phosphate, amethyst, coal, gemstone, manganese, bitumen, feldspar, granite, syenites, tatium, marcasite, aqua marine, asbestos, fluorspar, mica, rock crystal, ruby, sapphire, surpentinite, topaz, tourmaline, copper, pyrochinre, cobalt, chrome and antimony.

In colonial Africa, these minerals were exported to Europe at low prices and they further developed that continent and transformed its industrial setting. They also triggered creation of jobs and a high standard of living of its people. Even after independence, the situation did not change dramatically as the structure of unequal exchange that was first experienced during the slave era continued.

Contemporary Geo-Strategic Calculations

Today, the most important strategic minerals that have made the GoG the darling of the Western World are oil and gas. So far, modern civilization is run and sustained on oil and gas; as long as the trend continues so long would the Guinea Coast be of significant strategic value. For the United States of America which is the biggest user of hydro-carbons, the GoG is of strategic concern the more so as the Persian Gulf slides steadily into anarchy and threats of revolution, religious fundamentalism and terrorism.

Already, the GoG supplies in excess of ten percent of the US demand and it is estimated that it will account for more than twenty-five percent of all US oil demand by 2015. To be sure, the production of oil and natural gas in the GoG has the potential to fulfil the demand for energy in the Western World. Currently, the ***oil triad*** in the GoG made up of Angola, Equatorial Guinea and Nigeria has the capacity to surpass Saudi Arabia, the world's largest oil producer as oil supplier to the US, the world's largest consumer. Besides, new oil reserves are discovered every year in the GoG while other regions are experiencing decline in production. These imply that the GoG promises to be the new headquarters of world oil production within the next generation, thus replacing the Persian Gulf. The region provides a lot of advantages for Western countries. For one, the crude oil from the Gulf is of better quality. Secondly, the region's oil contains little sulphur. Thirdly, oil in the Gulf is mostly extracted from offshore fields, far from the mainland and upland zones that are characterized by domestic disturbances. Finally, the numerous transit chokepoints facing the world oil suppliers add to the comparative advantage of producers in the Guinea Coast, in terms of shipping ease, lower transportation costs and less environmental dangers.

After the 9/11 terrorist attack on the US, most Americans, especially decision and policy-makers, agitated for a shift of oil demand from the Persian Gulf in the Middle East to the GoG in Africa. Already, in terms of cost, the US spends about $50 billion annually on security of oil facilities in the Middle East. Besides, it has involved itself in several conflicts and crises in the Middle East on account of oil. Typical examples include the Iranian revolution of 1979, the First and Second Gulf Wars and the Arab-Israeli conflicts. All in all, today's Western World's strategic engagements in energy cannot be reliable without the GoG in its calculation.

Other strategic profile of the region include enticing ecosystem of high rain and mangrove forests which are critical sources of oxygen for the world. The forests are also sources for global pharmaceutical, building and construction industries. The arrays of flora and fauna in the region are simply amazing. Its rivers and seas contain the much globally-needed sea foods. With abundant water courses running into millions of kilometres, the GoG is a great asset to global trade, waterfront and hospitality industries.

When one travels the length and breath of the region, the eyes cannot fail to behold series of seductive sceneries and surrealistic beauty of the land, including habitats of rare birds and animals. Its beaches and islands, some of which are uninhabited, are inviting and excellent locations for tourist heavens and complexes. What is more, the region is strategically located in a continent that is surrounded by strategic Seas and Oceans-the Mediterranean Sea to the North, the Suez Canal and the Red Sea to the Northeast, the Indian Ocean to the Southeast, and the Atlantic Ocean to the West. The GoG is specifically located in the Atlantic Ocean.

Further Reading

Dorcan, C. F. 1977. *Myth, Oil and Politics: Introduction to the Political Economy of Petroleum.* New York: Free Press.

Licklider, R. 1988. *Political Power and the Oil Weapon: The Experience of Five Industrial Nations.* Berkeley: University of California Press.

Mikdashi, Z. 1972. *The Community of Oil Exporting Countries: Cooperation.* New York: Cornell University Press.

Stoff, M. B. 1980. *Oil, War and American Security: The Search for a National Policy on Foreign Oil, 1941-1947.* New Haven. Pantheon.

SECTION I

The Outline of the Gulf of Guinea

CHAPTER ONE

The Ancient History of the Gulf of Guinea

The Gulf of Guinea (GoG) has a rich history and heritage spanning thousands of years. It is a history full of dependable statescraft, epic battles, resourceful economic endeavours, creative works of arts and crafts, innovative international law and diplomacy and workable religion and cosmology. The GoG was once a location of great empires, kingdoms, city-states and village democracies that were products of geography, felt needs and ingenuity of the people. This chapter attempts to capture the outline of this living history.

Peoples of the Gulf of Guinea

Geographically speaking, there are three life zones in West Africa, namely; the Coastal zone, the Forest zone and the Sudan zone. The concept of life zones concerns the role of environment in shaping the evolution and culture of a people within a given geographical location. Even though there are three life zones in West Africa of which the GoG is a part, the first two zones-Coastal and Forest-really concern the Gulf.

The Coastal zone extends inland for about one hundred kilometres and stretches from Senegal to Angola. It is a low-lying land of plains in Senegambia, of mangrove swamps in Guinea, Sierra Leone and the Niger Delta and of lagoons and creeks from Cote d'Ivoire to the Niger Delta (Stride & Ifeka, 1980). The oldest inhabitants of this zone include the Jola, Pepel and Serer of Senegambia, the Shebro and Bulom of Sierra Leone, the Kru of Liberia, the Akan of Cote d'Ivoire, the Guan of Ghana, the Efik, the Ibibio and Ijaw of the Niger Delta of Nigeria. In the Forest zone, the peoples include the Mende, Temne, Kru, Baule, Asante, Fon, Yoruba, Bini, Ibibio and Ibo. The Forest zone stretches from Sierra Leone to the Cameroons.

Political Organization

From the earliest times, the people of the GoG had engaged themselves in the formation of many states, some of which were empires, kingdoms, city-states and village democracies. Asante and Yoruba people, for instance, established empires; the Bini people established powerful kingdoms and city-states emerged in the Niger Delta, while village democracies were common in many communities of the West Coast.

The Gulf Empires Asante Empire

One of the earliest empires to emerge in the GoG was the Asante Empire which was the most important factor in the political and commercial history of modern Ghana, Togo and Cote d'Ivoire. The empire was founded in the seventeenth century in the region of Kumasi which was also its capital. Kumasi was the cradle of this empire because it was an entrepot of the strategic routes of trans-Saharan trade which attracted Muslim scholars, entrepreneurs from the forest provinces, envoys and diplomats from many places, Dyula traders from Kong and Jenne and Hausa traders from Kano and Katsina in modern Nigeria.

The most important reason for the rise of Asante was the dynamic and military leadership provided by its first three great rulers-Obiri Yeboa, Osei Tutu and Opoku Ware. Obiri Yeboa laid the foundations of the Asante Union and it was left for Osei Tutu and Opoku Ware to consolidate and expand it into an empire. After the death of Obiri Yeboa, he was succeeded by his nephew, Osei Tutu. Osei Tutu is credited as the one who brought stability to the Asante Union. He performed this feat by diplomatic masterstroke where he assembled at Kumasi states friendly to the Asante people and welded them together under Kumasi leadership.

The diplomatic instrument that did the magic was religious and metaphysical performance where his life-long priest and friend, Okomfo Anokye, caused a Golden Stool to descend from the sky in a dark cloud and thunder and announced to the representatives of the states that the stool embodied the soul and unity of the Asante people.

The stool was sacrosanct and under no circumstances was it to be lost, stolen or destroyed and the real masterstroke was that Osei Tutu was to be acknowledged as the divinely ordained head of Asante.

From that period, the Golden Stool became a symbol of the unity of Asante's people. After the Golden Stool exercise, Osei Tutu and Okomfo Anokye drafted a Constitution for the empire and established the office of the Asantehene; that is, the emperor of the Asante people. The Asantehene governed with the advice of Confederacy Council, which was made up of Amanhene, the paramount rulers of states in the Union. All heads of states in the Union had to swear to an oath of allegiance to the Asantehene.

To consolidate and expand the Union, Osei Tutu embarked on wars of conquest. At the end of the day, states like Denkyira, Tafo, Amakom, Ofinso and Akim were incorporated into the Asante Union. As Asante expanded, European traders sent representatives to court Osei Tutu. For instance, in 1701 the Dutch dispatched an ambassador to his court at Kumasi.

After the death of Osei Tutu in the second decade of the eighteenth century, he was succeeded by other able Asantehenes like Opoku Ware, Kusi Obodum, Osei Kwade and Osei Bonsu. During the latter's reign, Asante's experienced civil wars and rebellions from those states that were incorporated into her empire through the use of force. The greatest threat came from the Fante Union which was equally a powerful state like Asante. What particularly aided the Fante campaign against Asante was the alliance that Fante had struck with the British. This unholy alliance was the undoing of the Asante Empire. By the early nineteenth century, Asante was steadily on the path of decline and before too long, it became part of the colonial possession of Britain in the GoG.

Oyo Empire

Another empire in the GoG was the Oyo Empire. It was one of the oldest and greatest states to emerge in the Forest zone. The history of the origin and settlement of this Yoruba Empire is shrouded in mystery and legend, yet the legend itself was a powerful diplomatic instrument of state formation available to the Yoruba people.

It all started at Ile-Ife which the Yoruba hold as the cradle of their civilization. In Yoruba legend, the earth was originally covered with water and on the orders of Olorun, the supreme god, Oduduwa descended from the sky with a chain and armed with a handful of earth, a cockerel and a palm nut. On nearing the water surface, he scattered the earth on the water which turned into land. The cockerel dug a hole in which Oduduwa planted the palm fruit which quickly matured into a mighty tree with sixteen branches, each symbolizing the ruling families of the Yoruba Union. Till today, the Oduduwa chain is preserved in Ile-Ife.

The Yoruba legend is not amenable to rational explanation since it is a transcendental experience. But what is clear from the legend is the use of diplomacy for purposes of state formation. It simply shows a change of dynasty where the pre-Oduduwa groups were conquered and persuaded by the logic of religion to see themselves as one under the Oduduwa suzerainty. In the aftermath of the Oduduwa revolution, the Yoruba people evolved the Oyo Empire that cast its shadows over the areas of today's South-West Nigeria, parts of central Nigeria, the Republic of Benin, Togo, Ghana and Burkina Faso.

The Oyo Empire was founded in the fourteenth century by Yoruba immigrants from Ile-Ife and earned its reputation and prosperity from participation in the trans-Saharan trade. Politically, the Yoruba evolved a monarchical form of government. At the head of the empire was the *Alafin*, who commanded the supreme authority in the land. To prevent political intrigues and secession disputes once **Alafin** was dead, all his personal staff and in some cases, his first-born son, had to die with him.

The duty of selecting a new Alafin was performed by a supreme council of state called the ***Oyo Mesi.*** It was made up of seven members. Before selecting the new head, they had to send the names of the candidates to the *Ifa* oracles for approval by the gods. The one selected was seen as being appointed by the gods. He was then consecrated, initiated into the mysteries of kingship and shown the codes of the sacred cults. Once the rituals had been completed, the Alafin was no longer regarded as an ordinary mortal but the companion of the gods and a semi-divine king whose power was theoretically unlimited by human institutions.

In practice, however, the Alafin did not rule with absolute power. He had to listen to the voices of members of the Oyo Mesi and **Ogboni cult** who had the authority to compel him to commit suicide. Whenever there was a major face-off between the Alafin and members of the Oyo Mesi and Ogboni Cult, the Bashorun who was the Prime Minister of Oyo and the head of the Oyo Mesi and members of the Ogboni would present the Alafin with an empty calabash or a dish of parrot's egg announcing to him: "The gods reject you, the people reject you, the earth reject". This practically means that a vote of no confidence had been passed on his leadership and, therefore, he had to take poison and die; to be replaced by another Alafin.

The Yoruba governmental structure had in-built checks and balances. The Oyo Mesi checked the excesses of the Alafin just as the excesses of the Oyo Mesi were checked by the Ogboni Cult. To be sure, members of the Oyo Mesi were ex-officio members of the Ogboni but, they were not its senior members and being only seven in number, never commanded majority votes.

Another important institution in Oyo politics was the *Eso*, the War Council. It was headed by a strategically-minded General, the Are-Ona-Kakanfo, who was the Supreme Commander of the Army. It was his duty to personally lead all military campaigns where customarily victory was obligatory and defeat carried the weighty punishment of committing suicide. The threat of suicide after failure always energized and challenged the Kakanfo to the limits and to the extent of forcing him to devise strategic plans to secure victory in all battles.

It is not surprising that Oyo Empire expanded steadily to incorporate new territories. But the incorporation of new territories which were non-Yoruba into Oyo and lack of dynamic leadership led to internal tensions. These, combined with constitutional upheavals, dynastic intrigues, military misadventure and British imperialism, led To the collapse of Oyo Empire at the end of the nineteenth century.

Benin Empire

The empire of Benin was yet another state that emerged and thrived in the GoG. The people of this empire called themselves, their capital city and their language *Edo*. They produced one of the remarkable kingdoms and later empires in the fifteenth century. At the time of its splendour and greatest extent in the sixteenth century, Benin Empire extended westward to Lagos and eastward to Bonny while to the North, it included Akure and parts of Ekiti division. Western Ibo land was also a part of this empire. The empire was noted for its artistic achievements such as bronze-casting and splendid works in woods, iron and raffia.

The original traditional socio-political setting of the Edo was more like those of the Ibibio and Ibo than their Yoruba neighbours. The setting was one characterized by village settlements which formed the basic political unit with the male population organized into age-grades representing the fundamental pattern of authority. Additionally, in their kingship and lineage organization, there was a patrilineal bias and emphasis on premoginature. With time, however, this village-centred political system was transformed into the most impressive kingdom and later one of the visible empires with the most long-lived dynasties in the GoG. The dynasty is still in existence today.

Several internal and external factors contributed to the emergence of the Benin Empire. Among the internal factors included culture, custom and political leadership of the people especially as increase in population needed dynamic political responses. Externally, Benin was located at the Southern terminus of the trans-Saharan trade where they exported ivory, pepper, female slaves, dyed cotton, jasper stones, leopard skins and blue coral first to northern markets and later to Europeans at the coast.

These items brought prosperity to the people and required better social organization for sustenance. This was reinforced by the craft industry which became highly organized and specialized, thus demanding credible leadership. Secondly, the impact of the centralized system of government of the Yoruba people who were their neighbours and relations by consanguinity was felt in Benin. Thirdly, outside the Yoruba Empire, other neighbouring states to Benin were weak, which never had the capacity to harbour imperial designs on Benin.

Once Benin had been transformed into an empire, it was governed at three levels. At the top of the political ladder was the Oba who was in most cases, a secluded, semi-divine and sacred figure. The second level consisted of chiefs who were members of the state council. The third tier of government consisted of the tribute units which were in form of chiefdoms headed by overlords. Each overlord was appointed directly by the Oba. The Queen Mother had a role to play in the governance of Edo. She was appointed to head a tribute unit. The Oba's first son and chiefs in the metropolitan city of Benin were similarly appointed to head tribute units. Regardless of this governmental structure, the overriding political power resided with the Oba.

Benin Empire was at its apogee in the sixteenth century. A century earlier, it was the first African state in the GoG to maintain regular diplomatic contact with a European power. But after four hundred years of existence, maladministration, weak leadership, rebellion, economic misfortune and European imperialism led to its decline and ultimate collapse. In 1897, Great Benin became part of the Niger Coast Protectorate in Nigeria.

The City-States of the Gulf of Guinea

The societies that organized themselves as city states were initially structured politically as village democracies but in time they responded to internal and external challenges and transformed into city-states. In the GoG, such societies included Old Calabar and the Ijaw communities of Nembe, Kalabari and Bonny. The Ijaw and Efik of Old Calabar had similar institutions.

The central foundation of the transformation of these communities was the Atlantic slave trade. The trade affected their political institutions, trading pattern and inter-group relations. As a result of the imperatives of competition which slave trade demanded, there was need for a more formal political organization to direct the affairs of the communities. Among the Ijaw people, wealthy citizens with stronger followings than their opponents became kings. But as kings they still needed the support of other wealthy and influential men in the state. To this extent, power resided in household heads, elders and men of influence.

In Old Calabar, the Efik never established a highly centralized monarchy on the Yoruba or Benin model. Rather, they set up a conciliar institution of a federal kind which was the Ekpe Secret Society and it was this institution that constituted the central organ of government. The *Ekpe* institution actually developed in the eighteenth century in response to the need to unite the people and enforce discipline in the society. On its usefulness and character of its operations, Alagoa (1999:257) documents:

> Ekpe exercised wide political, social and economic functions in Calabar society. It made laws, and even the missionaries and British consul enlisted its support to enact laws, such as the law against human sacrifice in 1850. In addition, Ekpe served as a police force to enforce the laws. It collected debts, stopped fights between individuals or groups, disciplined slaves, and generally kept the peace. Ekpe disposed of a range of sanctions as wide as its functions. It could place an offending individual or community on interdiction, boycott or ostracism. Ekpe could impose a fine, detain or arrest an offender, and on occasions, even execute a criminal. **Ekpe**, then, was one institution that brought together all leaders and freemen of wealth and influence; that is, all those in the state with a common interest in peace and prosperity. In this way it helped to prevent in Calabar the type of disruptive political struggles that occurred in the eastern delta states. The weakness of **Ekpe** was that it discriminated against the slave and the poor. It thus created class differences tending to polarize rather than integrate. Ekpe ensured that, unlike in the delta states, the slaves were not integrated into the social and political system. This element of discrimination led to the nearest thing to a slave revolt in Calabar in the rise of the **bloodmen** organization of slaves and the poor.

It is worthy of note to highlight the fact that the discriminatory policy of the Ekpe society led to a slave revolt in Calabar where slaves organized themselves into a pressure group known as the ***order of bloodmen*** to oppose some of the obnoxious policies of the Ekpe society. For instance, they took a blood covenant to defend themselves against the practice of sacrificing slaves at the funerals of kings and house heads (Alagoa, 1999). One of the immediate consequences of the slave revolt was the intervention of the British in the politics of Old Calabar through Consul John Beecroft who in 1850 prevailed on *Ekpe* to enact the law against the ritual sacrifice of slaves.

This was the beginning of the incursion of the British into political governance in Old Calabar. In the last decade of the nineteenth century, the political authority of *Ekpe* and the kings of Calabar were taken over by the British following the declaration of a protectorate in 1885. Calabar was chosen as the colonial headquarters for the administration of southern Nigeria.

Village Democracies

The Ibibio and Ibo people in Nigeria, the Jola and Pepel in Senegal and several other communities in the coastal and forest zones of the GoG operated village democracies as their form of political organization. Politically, the people operated a republican form of government. Because of lack of complex centralized system of government, British and African Anthropologists classify the area as a stateless society, but such reference is wrong. On the surface, it means that the paraphernalia of state system were lacking in these areas. But this was not so. The people designed and practiced simple administrative structure which centred on the village Assembly.

The organization of the society was based on segmentary principles and administration on genealogical lineages. For this, the society was politically organized on the basis of people in various units as families, wards, villages, village group and the clan. In this situation, there was a strict adherence to the principles of primogeniture and power radiated from the elders. It is because of this that the traditional political organization of the Ibibio people, for instance, is at times described as a gerontocracy, but in reality, it was organizational democracy (Akpan, 2003).

In the Ibibio society, agents of powerful and awe-inspiring secret cults like ***Ekpo*** and ***Ekpe*** were employed to execute or enforce laws. In Ibo land, the political organization was equally structured in the village but in the North and West and specifically Onitsha, Nri, Oguta and western Ibo, there existed some form of monarchical institutions even though the king did not have unlimited political power. In the rest of Ibo land, there existed village democracies. Each village was made up of units of lineages, villages and groups of villages. Each lineage was autonomous in its internal affairs. Age groups and title societies equally played prominent roles in the administration of Ibo societies. They were used for police and other security duties.

Arts and Crafts

From the earliest times, the Guinea Coast was part of the moving history of civilization in arts and crafts. The people exhibited superlative dexterity in the use of clay, wood, brass and bronze for art work. The people of Ife and Benin were known for the use of brass and bronze for craft. The ancient Nok culture in central Nigeria produced replicas of human heads and animals of high artistic value in clay. On the general value and quality of arts and craft in the GoG, G. T. Stride and Caroline Ifeka (1980:162) write:

> It would seem that all over West Africa naturalistic art as well as stylized motifs were produced in wood, clay, gold, ivory and, among the Bulom of Sierra Leone, in soapstone; and that high artistic achievement-as a sincere expression of the artistic and religious temperament of the craftsman-is almost as old as the dance. Everyone knows that the rhythms of dancing are inborn in every West African and also what expressiveness the dances convey. At the practical level, these artistic skills are used to produce domestic utensils such as decorated calabashes, spoons made of gourds and a wide and shapely variety of pots and bottles fashioned in earthenware.

To these would be added the observations of F. K. Buah (1967:8) who asserts that:

> Works of art, such as those of the Nok culture in north-central Nigeria, which flourished several centuries before the birth of Christ, the Ife terracotta and other handicrafts in bronze, the superb Benin bronze work, the Asante gold weights and stools produced from hard-wood and the ivory carvings in present day Sierra Leone and the Senegambia, are to this day treasured in the museums of the world.

There is no doubt that even the Europeans were so impressed by the quality of these artwork and the mental dexterity, creativity and ingenuity that attended their practical expression to the extent that there is hardly any museum in Europe without works of arts from the GoG.

Religion and Cosmology

The people of the Guinea Coast had practised their own ancient form of religion prior to the introduction of Islam and Christianity in the region. Their religion is today called African Traditional Religion. The people believed in the existence of one omnipotent God even though they also held in reverence many more earthly deities which could be used to approach the Supreme God. Therefore, the Whiteman never taught the people how to know or worship God. They never taught the people the concept of God either. The concept and particulars of God were indeed part of the African heritage from the very beginning. Uya (1992:21) has much to say about this particular aspect of African religion. Using Nigeria as a case study, he submits:

> Indeed, the traditional Nigerian man was intensely religious, religion being perceived as the basis of reconciliation between man, families, clans, whole nation and the universe. Despite the claims of polytheism ascribed by outsiders to traditional African religions, traditional African religion was essentially monotheistic, each group believing in a Supreme God, the source of all life, the great mover of the universe, so powerful, so distant and yet so near; so great that he had to be approached through the many intermediaries of lesser gods, spirits, ancestors, and so on that are familiar to those conversant with the pantheon of gods that people the religious world of the traditional African. By whatever name he was known (Olorun or Oludamara by the Yoruba, Osenabua by the Edo, Chineke or Chukwu by the Igbo, Abasi by the Efik/Ibibio, and so on), this idea of the Supreme Being was common to all groups. Religion was not an abstraction, a Sunday affair but a factor in every day existence. There was no distinction between morality and law; indeed, the latter derived from the former.

Islam and Christianity are late comers in African religion and cosmology. Even though majority of people in the Guinea Coast are adherents of foreign religions, they still practise mixed religion of the traditional and foreign. Here and now, the people still consult oracles, sorcerers, necromancers, diviners, seers and native priests when the new religions cannot proffer immediate solutions to their problems. It cannot of course be anything else, for the people believes in the existence of witches, wizards, magic, reincarnation, native spirits and mermaids which can thwart or influence a person's destiny. Since these spirits and bodies are environmentally based, only those who know their own ways and understand their needs can intercede on behalf of the afflicted (Akpan, 2003).

While Christianity and Islam have acceptable text or sacred books which are the Holy Bible and the Koran and agreed places of worship which are the Churches and the Mosques, the traditional African religion does not have any. There is no sacred text in African religion but there are sacred codes and the priests are well versed in the religion's oral literature. Similarly, there are no agreed places of worship for any convenient place is enough for the adherents to worship their God.

Unlike the Christians and Muslims who set Sundays and Fridays as special days to worship God, the adherents of African traditional religion set market days as special days to worship their own God. On such days, sacrifices are offered directly to the Supreme Being. Sacrifices act as restitutions to waive or take away curses and to appease the gods or deities. Equally, sacrifices are meant for protection and favours from God. On such occasion, animals such as fowls, goats and sheep are sacrificed and the belief is that the higher the object of sacrifice, the greater the chances of quick and positive results. Before the advent of Christianity, the highest object was man.

International Law and Diplomacy

In pre-colonial period, African states were autonomous, sovereign and independent. As it was necessary to interact among themselves for purposes of trade and exchange and war and peace, they all engaged themselves in the practice of international law and diplomacy. Unwritten customary law prevailed over most of Africa. Teslim Elias, a one-time jurist in the International Court of Justice claimed that customary law "formed part and parcel of law in general" (Elias, 1956: v; Smith, 1989:2).

Though there was a great deal of diversity in the application of the customary law in different parts of Africa, Allot (see Smith 1989) has highlighted those recurring features which distinguish African law to be: the traditional and popular character of the law; basic similarities in judicial procedure, whether in the courts of chiefs or in the arbitral tribunals of villages, clans or households; the role of the supernatural;

patterns of governments which almost always rest ultimately on the consent of the governed; and the role of the community in the interpretation and enforcement of law (see Smith, 1989:3). On account of these features, Allot concludes that African law is, "a unity in diversity" (see Smith, 1989:3).

On his own part, Elias argues that: "in large areas of Africa there ... emerged broadly similar rules of customary law, which makes it possible to speak of the existence of a universal body of principles of African customary law that is not essentially dissimilar to the broad principles of European law" (see Smith, 1989). Therefore, the customary law, "shares with customary international law, the characteristic that its validity does not depend upon any theory of sovereignty (see Smith, 1989:3).

The early European visitors to Africa and the Arabs who had interacted with Africans earlier bore testimony to the effectiveness and indeed efficiency of the African international law. After all, international law is primarily formulated by contractual agreements, which create rules binding upon the parties, and customary rules, which are basically state practices recognized by the community at large as laying down patterns of conduct that have to be complied with.

Just as the Gulf States fashioned out international law to serve their needs, they also practiced highly efficient diplomatic intercourse. In matters of treaties, protocol and procedure, diplomatic privileges and immunities, political asylum and the extradition of criminals, diplomatic correspondence, exchange of ambassadors and appointment of permanent representatives, the Gulf States were not wanting in the period before formal contact with the Europeans.

The tempo of diplomatic intercourse increased after contact with the Europeans, beginning with the Portuguese. For instance, in 1714, the Asante sent a delegation to compose differences between the king of Komenda and the Twifo. Decades later, the Ambassadors of the king of Wassa succeeded in bringing about a league of the coastal states between Cape Apollonia and the Volta so as to prevent the supply of guns to the Asante.

Another alliance against the Asante was designed by Fante diplomacy on the death of the Asantehene Opoku Ware in about 1750

(Smith, 1989:8). In Yoruba land, a typical example of alliance system was the ***Ekitiparapo***, an anti-Ibadan coalition of the 1870s which was engineered by embassies sent by the Ekiti and Ijesha kings to other monarchs in the Yoruba country.

The practice of maintaining resident representatives abroad was part of pre-colonial African diplomacy in the GoG. In the seventeenth century, the king of Denkyra appointed an official named Ampim as his resident trade representative on the coast. In the eighteenth century, Asante had residents in Dagomba to collect tributes and in Accra and Akuapem as trade representatives. Dagomba and Gonja maintained representatives in Kumasi, the capital of Asante. The Alafin of Oyo appointed resident ambassadors in Dahomey to collect tribute and spy on their achievements for policy formulation. Within the same period, the Oba of Benin maintained residents called ***Baelekale*** or ***Abilekale*** in Akure (Smith, 1989).

In terms of the status of diplomatists and envoys, the practice was to send those knowledgeable in royal duties and aspirations. Sometimes, traditional council members, princes, priests, or wives of kings were involved. In the seventeenth century, the kings of Denkyra and Asante sent some of their wives as ambassadors to each other. But this courtesy and goodwill provided a pretext for war as Osei Tutu, the Asantehene, claimed that his Denkyiran brother had behaved undiplomatically towards one of the diplomatists (Smith, 1989).

The practice of immunity was evidenced in pre-colonial African diplomacy. Diplomatists were not harassed, arrested or killed in foreign lands especially when they carried diplomatic credentials. In Ibibio land, ***Nnuk Enin*** (Elephant Tusk) was used to stop feuds or wars between two communities. The tusk did not only stop hostilities, but also provided the chief's envoy with a safe-conduct pass throughout the country and beyond. Any disregard or disrespect of the elephant tusk was tantamount to rebelling against the chief and generally resulted in a serious case against the culprit (Udo, 1980). On the general pattern of practice of immunity in pre-colonial Africa, Robert S. Smith (1989:13) writes:

> Immunity and safe-conduct seem to be rooted in the respect accorded to strangers by nearly communities other than the most primitive. African hospitality and the honour done to strangers were remarked upon by many

of the early European travellers, who themselves received ceremonious and cordial welcomes from the rulers of the countries they visited ...

A study of the theory and practice of diplomacy in pre-colonial Africa, especially in the GoG is a study in ingenuity, dexterity and excellence as well as hospitality in inter-state relations.

The Economy

From the very beginning, the main occupations of the people of Guinea Coast have been farming, hunting and fishing. These provided them with the basic needs of life and with a surplus to exchange for the things they did not produce themselves. Industries grew up to take care of further needs of the people for manufactured goods.

Before long, local trade evolved and then long-distant trade followed. The nature of industries and trade involved several industries-the salt industry, the fishing industry, the soap boiling industry, the cloth industry, the leather industry and distilleries. Other industries which produced finished goods that were needed across the globe include the metal industries utilizing important metals like gold, iron and copper.

From the fifteenth century, slaves and arrays of cash crops were added to the list of economic items that the GoG richly supplied to the world. The impact of these resources on the world economy was phenomenal as Europe and the Americas rode to greatness on the sweats and efforts of people of the Guinea Coast.

By way of summary, it should be acknowledged that the GoG had a rich ancient history that has spanned centuries. There is no aspect of human civilization that its people had not made a major impact. In statescraft, they were able to devise appropriate political systems and institutions to serve their needs. Historical parallels in Europe and Asia show clearly that, Africa was not found wanting and was, indeed, a part of the moving history of mankind. The richness and variety of this history is evidenced in its ancient religion, economy, works of arts and practice of international law and diplomacy.

Further Reading

Asiegbu, J U. 1969. *Slavery and the Politics of Liberation, 1787-1861.* New York.

Bovill, E. W. 1958. *The Golden Trade of the Moors.* Oxford University Press.

Daaku, K. Y. 1970. *Trade and Politics on the Gold Coast: 1600 to 1720.* London, Clarendon Press.

Dike, K O. 1969. *Trade and Politics in the Niger Delta.* London, Clarendon Press.

Griffiths, I. LI. 1995. *The African Inheritance.* London: Routledge.

Illiffe, J. 1995. *Africans: The History of a Continent.* Cambridge: Cambridge University Press.

McEvedy, C. 1995. *The Penguin Atlas of African History.* London: Penguin.

Noah, M. E. 1980. *Old Calabar: The City States and the Europeans, 1800-1885.* Uyo Scholars Press.

Noah, M. E. 2002. Ibibio Pioneers in Modern Nigerian History. Calabar: Scholars Press (Nig.) Ltd.

Northrup, D. 1978. *Trade without Rulers: Pre-colonial Economic Development in South-Eastern Nigeria.* Oxford: Clarendon Press.

Northrup, D. 2008. *Crosscurrents in the Black Atlantic, 1770-1965: A Brief History with Documents.* Boston: Bedford/Martins.

Porter, D. H. 1970. *The Abolition of the Slave Trade in England, 1784-1807.* Hampden Connecticut.

Priestley, M. 1969. *West African Trade and Coast Society.* Oxford University Press.

Rodney, W. 1989. *How Europe Underdeveloped Africa.* Nairobi: East African Educational Publishers.

Udo, E. A. 1980. *Who Are the Ibibio?* Onitsha, Africana Fep Publishers Limited.

Uya, O. E. 1971. *Black Brotherhood: Afro-Americans and Africa.* D.C Heath and Company.

Uya, O. E. 1984. *A History of Oron People of the Lower Cross River Basin.* Manson Publishing Company, Oron.

Uya, O. E. 2005. *African Diaspora and the Black Experience in New World Slavery.* Calabar, Clear Lines Publication

CHAPTER TWO

The Modern History of the Gulf of Guinea

The states of the modern Gulf of Guinea are the creations of the European powers. They were all created in the nineteenth century. This means that by the twentieth century they had taken their forms and shapes. In specific terms, the modern states of the Gulf were once colonies of four European countries, namely: Britain, France, Spain and Portugal.

Even though Germany initially had two states, Cameroun and Togo, they were taken away from her, after she lost the First World War, and handed over to Britain and France to administer as Trusteeship territories. Needless to add here that they were never returned to Germany. Of all these European countries, Portugal was the first to have direct contact with the Guinea Coast and there is no modern state of the GoG today that did not have Portuguese influence.

Indeed, Portugal created a Portuguese empire in the Gulf for about two-hundred years, beginning from the fifteenth century. She only lost this empire to other European powers as a result of the logic of change domestically in Portugal and externally in Europe and in the GoG. Even at that, the Portuguese heritage which still abounds in the Gulf includes Portuguese names of cities and nations in the region.

Such names include Lagos in Nigeria which means lagoon and which was contracted from ***Logo de Curamo*** (Smith, 1978); ***El Mina*** in Ghana which means "The Mine", ***Serra Lyoa*** meaning "mountain" and "lion", which eventually became the name of Sierra Leone and Rio dos Cameroes (River of Prawns) from where Cameroun derives its name. In the case of Ghana, the coastal region from where the Portuguese mined gold was named ***Da Costa da El Mina***, from which name was derived: "The Gold Coast", the name by which Ghana was known up to 1957 when it had independence. Indeed, for centuries in the Guinea Coast, Portuguese language was the commercial ***lingua franca.***

Portuguese Influence on the Guinea Coast

Portuguese influence on the Guinea Coast was a direct result of navigation and exploration which took place in the fifteenth century. In 1443, Diniz Diaz rounded Cape Verde and two decades later, the Cape Verde islands were reached. Between 1445 and 1448, Nuno Tristam and Zarco were at the borders of modern Sierra Leone and in 1460, Portuguese sailors were at the Shebro Island. In 1445, they sailed about 400 kilometres up the Gambia River and penetrated the Senegambia region (Rodney, 1970:71).

In 1471, they were in Elmina in modern Ghana and two years later they reached the eastern end of the GoG where Fernao do Po discovered the island of Fernando Po (Equatorial Guinea) and Ruy de Sequira reached São Tomé Island. Fernando Po was named after Ferna do Po, the Portuguese navigator. From these two islands in the Niger Delta region, Portuguese explorers had contact with the Benin Empire in 1874. In 1482, the Portuguese reached the mouth of the Congo and even penetrated the hinterland. By the end of the fifteenth century, they had completely traced the coastal line of the Guinea Coast up to Angola and had in fact sailed round the southern tip of the continent, reaching India in the East.

In the Upper Guinea, the headquarters of Portuguese activities was the Cape Verde Islands which served mainly as supply centres for slaves, but from 1484, Santiago became the most important centre. The economic activities in the area centred on cotton-growing and cattle-breeding. Slaves taken to Santiago were re-exported to Europe and the New World of the Americas.

Additionally, items for export included hides and skins, rice, dyes, cloth, ivory and livestock. The third centre of Portuguese trade in Upper Guinea was the Sierra Leone Bay where slaves and ivory made the bulk of export goods. In Lower Guinea, the main centre of Portuguese activities was Elmina in the Gold Coast. Though the Elmina settlement was not as large as the one on the Cape Verde Islands in Upper Guinea, it was quite important and strategic for Portugal's national interest. It was a port of call for all Portuguese sailors en route to their Niger Delta trading ports, Angola, Mozambique and the Far East. At Elmina, slaves mainly from the

Niger Delta and off-shore islands who, in any case, came from the Niger Delta were re-sold and exported to Europe and the Americas.

In the off-shore islands of São Tomé and Fernando Po, the Portuguese established permanent settlements. In these colonies, they set up large-scale plantations for sugar cane. Other agricultural crops and even fruits introduced to the islands included guava, pawpaw, orange, tangerine, lemon, maize, sweet potato, pineapple, melon, banana, plantain, avocado pears, cassava, cocoyam and coconut.

From these islands, the crops and fruits were introduced to the entire tropical Africa. As F. K. Buah has rightly argued, the introduction of a variety of these tropical crops from all over the world was perhaps the greatest legacy of the Portuguese in the Guinea Coast (Buah, 1967).

The Rise and fall of the Portuguese Empire in the Gulf of Guinea

For about two hundred years, the Portuguese bestrode the Guinea Coast like a colossus and created an empire in Africa, but by the seventeenth century they were overthrown by other European states. Several factors accounted for the rise and fall of their empire in the Guinea Coast.

The Portuguese Empire in Africa

To locate the foundation of the Portuguese empire in Africa, one must trace the underlying factors for Portuguese exploration. The most strategic reason for their exploration of the West Coast of Africa was economic. Having obtained information on the economic gains of the trans-Saharan trade between Western Sudan and the Arab world, Portugal, which is located in Southern Europe and close to Arabs in North Africa, wanted to share in the trade in order to prosper, but they were confronted with the hurdle of the Muslims in North Africa who did not allow them to use the Saharan routes. A way out of this was to find alternative routes through the Atlantic Ocean which they equally shared with Africa. With royal patronage and encouragement they began the schemes of exploration.

By the time Gil Eannes sailed past Cape Nun in 1434, which until now was a point of no-return for any sailor and for which the African Atlantic waters was called the Green Sea of Darkness by the Arabs, the prospect for Portuguese empire in Africa was bright. That same year Eannes reached Cape Bajador further down the West coast of Africa. The successful attempts of Eannes encouraged other Portuguese explorers who reached the entire Guinea Coast within three decades.

Politically, Portugal enjoyed national unity and stability whereas other European countries were troubled by internal strife and external wars. For instance, within the period Britain and France were locked up in the Hundred Years' War which lasted for a century; the people of the Netherlands were fighting their wars of independence against Spain and Spain was busy fighting against the Muslims. All these point to the fact that the energies of other European countries were absorbed in domestic and external engagements which did not permit adventurism on the scale of Portugal.

Geographically, Portugal was a maritime state and its fishermen were familiar with the waters of the Atlantic Ocean and the North African ports of Ceuta and Tangier. According to F. K. Buah: "their deep-sea fishing enterprises had given them some knowledge of the hazards that awaited long distance sea-faring and the skills required to face them" (Buah, 1967:15). These skills were taught and perfected at an observatory on a Promontory in Sagres in Portugal built in 1419 by King Henry (also known as Prince Henry, the Navigator) and at the Portuguese Nautical College which attracted all over the world the best astronomers, geographers, cartographers and navigators. The college was equipped with the best navigational instruments, maps and charts for would-be sailors.

As the commercial successes of the Portuguese on the Western coast of Africa became known, other European nations became interested in navigation and exploration. Spain was particularly interested in the venture and that is why in the late fifteenth century, it started to send voyagers westward. The spate of reaching new areas unknown to Europeans led to rivalry between Portugal and Spain as the two nations made claims and counter-claims against one another (Ikpe, 2000).

In order to keep peace and maintain friendship between the two, the Pope, Alexander VI, intervened and arranged a settlement where Portugal and Spain signed the ***Treaty of Tordesillas*** in 1494. As a result of the Treaty, Spain's sphere of influence was limited to 370 leagues west of the Cape Verde Islands. Portugal thus had monopoly of all lands to the east of this dividing line. This line of demarcation effectively locked out other European nations from exploration and the so-called schemes of discoveries of new lands. Writing on the rivalry between Portugal and Spain and on the impact of the intervention of the Pope, W. D. Hussey (1977:52) notes:

> The problem arose of how Portugal and Spain were to get recognition from all other states of their exclusive right to the new lands and oceans they had discovered. Resort was made to the Pope, who as head of the Catholic or Universal Church was traditionally regarded as having the power to dispose of new lands. The Pope's decisions were sent in a document or 'Bull' which to a greater or lesser extent was accepted by other rulers as binding on them. Thus the Portuguese had in 1431, 1455 and 1456 obtained Papal Bulls which recognized their sole right to the lands discovered by the sea-captains of Prince Henry. The Bull of 1456 had granted to the Portuguese all lands 'as far as to the Indies'... in 1493 four Bulls were issued by the Pope; the most by the Pope; the most famous of them, 'Inter Caetera' of May 1493, set up a dividing line between the Spaniards and Portuguese; Castile was granted all islands and lands found west of a line running from north to south and fixed at 100 leagues west of the Cape Verde Islands. In the following year (1494) the Treaty of Tordesillas between Spain and Portugal confirmed this arrangement, but fixed the line at 370 leagues to the west of the Cape Verde Islands. This change was greatly to the advantage of the Portuguese, who thereby not only kept the Spaniards well away from their sea route to the east but were also, a few years later (1500), able to claim Brazil as falling on their side of the line. Pope Julius II by a Bull of 1506 confirmed this treaty.

The implication of the Pope's intervention was that Portugal and Spain divided the world into two and monopolized between them the resources and lands in their respective spheres of influence; Portugal having the eastern hemisphere and Spain the western.

The Decline and Collapse of the Portuguese Empire in the Gulf of Guinea

In spite of the Papal Bull of Demarcation which favoured only two European countries, Portugal and Spain, the monopoly of Portugal in the Guinea Coast was seriously challenged by other European countries in the sixteenth century. The King of France, Francis I, 1525-1547, was said to have cynically but seriously claimed that he would like to see the clause in Adam's Will which excluded his nation from a share in the treasures of the world. In his words, he said: "I should like to see the clause in Adam's will that excludes me from my share of the world" (Hussey, 1977:56).

There is no doubt that the immense wealth that the Guinea Coast gave to Portugal, especially in gold, inspired other European nations to repudiate the Treaty of Tordesillas. Having consigned it to the dustbin of history, The Netherlands, France, England, Belgium, Denmark and Switzerland rushed to overthrow the Portuguese and participate in the spoils of the GoG.

The French challenge to the Portuguese monopoly started in the late fifteenth century when their sailors became active in the waters of the GoG, harassing Portuguese ships. In 1492, French pirates attacked and seized Portuguese ships on the Gulf laden with gold and pepper bound for Portugal. In 1542, a French ship visited Cape Three Points in Ghana and returned home with a cargo of 28 kilograms of gold. In 1659, St Louis was made the first permanent French settlement on the mouth of the Senegal River.

The British were late comers in the rush to pillage the Guinea Coast. They were attracted in the sixteenth century by the wealth of Portugal, Spain and France which they got from the West Coast of Africa. Until now, Britain was interested in finding a new route to the riches of the Far East. She did this to avoid the spheres of influence established by Spain and Portugal (Buah, 1969). But when efforts to find a north-east passage round Canada and a north-west passage round Russia failed, she jumped at the opportunity presented by the Guinea Coast.

In 1553, her explorers led by Thomas Whydham reached Ghana and the Niger Delta where they returned home with valuable items like gold, silver and pepper. Another English explorer John Hawkins visited the Guinea Coast in 1562, 1564 and 1567 where he bought slaves. On that same visit, he challenged and seized a number of Portuguese vessels. The British established bases on the Gambia River zone, Gold Coast and the Niger Delta within the period.

After slave trade was abolished in all British possessions following the Lord Mansfield's judgement in 1772, the British established a settlement in Sierra Leone for freed slaves and thereafter Sierra Leone became the headquarters of British administration in the Guinea Coast. Meanwhile, the value of gold obtained from the Gold Coast was so much that the British mint struck the first *guineas* which was worth £1.1 shilling. The currency unit was so named to honour the Guinea Coast, the source of the resources of the money.

The Dutch presented the greatest challenge to the Portuguese monopoly in the Guinea Coast. Within half a century of their active participation in the exploration of the region, in 1593 they had crippled the Portuguese commercial interest in many areas. In 1637, the Dutch ousted the Portuguese from Elmina. Within the same period, they allied with the British and sent the Portuguese away from the Niger Delta, Southern Nigeria, southern Ghana and Sierra Leone.

In Upper Guinea, the Dutch threatened the Portuguese interest in Goree and the Cape Verde Islands. From 1596, they mounted pressure on the Portuguese Island of Fernando Po and paved the way for Spain to take possession of it. By the mid seventeenth century, the Dutch had taken over possession of critical ports like Arguin and Goree in Upper Guinea, São Tomé in the Niger Delta and Elmina, Shama and Axim on the Gold Coast from the Portuguese. Before then the Dutch had commanded the volume of trade that was greater than any other European power. After about fifteen years on the Guinea Coast, about twenty ships loaded with assorted commercial goods sailed yearly to West Africa.

Generally speaking, by the end of the seventeenth century, the Portuguese had lost to fellow European powers all their possessions in the GoG except Guinea-Bissau, the Cape Verde Islands and Angola.

Outside the competition from other European nations which led to the collapse of the Portuguese influence in West Africa, Portugal was a very small country with a small population which lacked the capacity to manage and defend such vast empire they created in the Guinea Coast. Additionally, Portugal's administration of her settlements, which in any case were mainly located on the coast, was harsh and oppressive to the extent that her rulership was resented by both the indigenous people and Portuguese settlers. It is not surprising that these settlers in Fernando Po and Cape Verde Islands wished for independence from Lisbon. The end of the Portuguese era was followed by formal colonization of the GoG by other European nations.

Colonization and Colonial Rule

For the empires, kingdoms, city-states and village democracies that flourished in the GoG, the nineteenth century was very critical in several ways. At the beginning of African-European relations in the fifteenth century, they enjoyed absolute control over their external and internal affairs. But, the middle of the nineteenth changed these patterns of relationship altogether. Where, until the nineteenth century, European possessions were limited to the coast, from the mid-nineteenth century, the Europeans had penetrated the hinterland and had begun to possess territories there. Territories were got through the instrumentalities of tricks, intrigues and treaties. But as many European nations were interested in territories, it sparked competition which resulted in the scramble for, and partition of, Africa.

Many reasons have been adduced for the ***Scramble for Africa.*** But the main ones are economic factors, political forces and religious zeal. Economically, as industriali-zation in Europe created new problems which demanded sources of raw materials and new markets, European nations were interested in formally owning colonies to ensure uninterrupted supplies and predictable markets. Even in cases where some countries like Britain were initially not interested in colonial possession, members of their commercial class manoeuvred them into it.

Politically, colonies were status symbols for the European nations, some of which had small sizes and population. Therefore, geo-strategically, possession of colonies was a necessity for European nations. Religious reasons also supplied the fuel for colonization.

Africa was perceived as a region zoned for hell-fire, for the simple reason that Christianity had not found a foothold there. In the process of evangelizing the people, the missionaries were challenged and at times killed by the indigenous population. While attempting to protect the missionaries, their home governments were interested in outright colonization of African territories.

The unregulated struggle for territories in West Africa almost led to political instability and war in Europe. In order to prevent these, the Berlin West African Conference was convened in Germany by the German Chancellor, Otto Von Bismark, between February 1884 and February 1885. During the Conference, important decisions were reached on acquisition of colonies in Africa. One critical decision concerned claims to territories where an interested party was to inform others of such claims. Another decision concerned the principles of effective occupation where any nation claiming a territory was required to maintain an effective occupation in the area by installing administrative machineries. The Conference declared River Niger and the Congo River as international waters to be used by all sovereign states. Additionally, the Congo Free State was recognized as a personal possession of Leopold II, King of the Belgians. In line with its free status, it was decided that all European powers had the right to trade freely in the state. One critical outcome of the Berlin Conference was that it increased the tempo of the scramble for territories in Africa and laid the foundation for colonial rule.

Colonial Rule

The colonial powers in the GoG adopted different methods to govern their possessions. The administrative styles were determined by conditions in Africa and the overall national interests of the European nations. Regardless of the different methods, the focus was the same: peace as a foundation for economic exploitation.

The British adopted a policy of ***Indirect Rule*** to administer their territories in the second decade of the twentieth century. The policy meant that the British should use the traditional institutions of the people to govern through the supervision of British personnel. The policy itself was necessary because of lack of funds, lack of enough

British personnel, fear of revolts, unhealthy interior for the whites and an attempt to save cost. Nigeria was the first place where Indirect Rule was applied. It succeeded in the Northern part of the country; it achieved partial success in the Western part and in the Eastern zone it was a fiasco.

The North had political structures that suited the application of Indirect Rule. In this region, the Emirs ruled with absolute authority and there was a native treasury to pay taxes and levies into. In the West, the Oba, though monarchical never had absolute authority as there were the Oyo Mesi and Ogboni cult that shared power with him. In the East, the operations of village democracy meant that authority did not revolve around a single individual, yet a major requirement of the success of indirect rule was the availability of a chief to direct the affairs of his people directly.

Despite the problems associated with the Indirect Rule method of governance in Nigeria, it was introduced in other British possessions in West Africa. It was introduced in the Gambia in 1933, Sierra Leone in 1937 and the Gold Coast in 1944. All in all, the Indirect Rule mechanism created more problems for the British. It was opposed by the educated elite who felt that the British empowered illiterate chiefs to rule over them. The pattern of opposition by the elite created the opportunity for direct participation by the educated elements, especially after the Second World War and placed the British territories on the road to independence.

Whereas for the British, peace was seemingly attained through the policy of Indirect Rule, for the French, peace was attained through the policy of Assimilation. Indeed, up to the beginning of the scramble for colonies in Africa, French administration was based entirely on the theory of Assimilation and later Association (Akpan, 2005). Some books refer to the policy as that of identity (Assimilation) and that of paternalism (Association) (Crowder, 1976:179). The theory grew out of the practice of French Revolution which accepted all men as equal (Ayandele, *et al*, 1971). Following from this, the French made a declaration which conferred the right of French citizenship on every inhabitant of a French colony. The declaration became imminent because France believed that her culture and civilization were the best in the world and that it was her mission to admit her colonies into this rich heritage (Ayandele, *et al*, 1971). To this extent, France further believed that it could accomplish this task by teaching the colonial peoples the French language, by subjecting them to French law and by giving them French civil and political rights. Under this system, the Africans were made identical with the French citizens.

It is interesting to note that, this theory worked for some time when France had few colonies in Africa. It worked essentially in the communes of Senegal where they were given outright French status. As early as 1848, the Senegalese had elected Africans to the French Chambers of Deputies. But by the beginning of the twentieth century, the policy was abandoned for an entirely new doctrine.

Political and economic reasons accounted for the shift in policy. Politically, by 1880, many Frenchmen had begun to criticize the policy which dared to equate Frenchmen with Africans. Additionally, as a result of the scramble for, and partition of, Africa, France had acquired large territories with large population. This implied that in the French Deputies, Africans would elect more candidates given their control of many territories and this means that there would be more black faces in the legislative chambers than white faces. A direct consequence of that was the obvious fact that Africans would be making laws for France (Akpan, 2005). The prospect of this simple truth becoming a reality did not go down well with Frenchmen.

Economically, the argument was that once Africans were given equal status with French citizens, they would not be exploited. Indeed, it was because of this, that, the policy of Assimilation was transformed to that of Association or paternalism. In this process, the Africans, although potentially equal to human beings were not to be regarded as complete human beings. This being the case, they had to be tutored and civilized for some years before they could become equals to Frenchmen regardless of the level of idiocy of some Frenchmen (Akpan, 2003). As it turned out, this policy became the main organ of French administration throughout the twentieth century.

The policy of Association allowed the French to exploit the labour of Africans and to maximize the exploitation of Franco-phone Africa. One peculiar outcome of the new doctrine was that French colonial policy now respected the culture of her dependent people and allowed each group in its own way, rather than force all to adopt French civilization and culture. To attain this goal, France governed each group through its traditional political institutions similar to the British policy of Indirect Rule.

The German, Portuguese and Belgian rules were similar in all respect. They were harsh and inhuman. In the GoG, Germany controlled Togoland and the Cameroons. German colonial administration was harsh, rigid and highly regimented. Administration of these territories was centralized. Though laws were made in the German parliament for colonies, colonial officials were given the freedom to devise their own administration. The use of martial law and forced labour turned Africans in these territories into outright slaves.

Like France, Portugal regarded her colonial possessions in Africa as provinces of Portugal. Therefore, as an integral part of Portugal, laws for colonies were made in Lisbon, the capital of Portugal. In the implementation of these laws, the minority Portuguese settlers in these territories were accorded full Portuguese citizenship whereas the vast majority of the indigenes were denied such right. They were designated as ***indigena***. For an ***indegena*** to acquire Portuguese citizenship he had to fulfil certain requirements among which were:

1. He must speak Portuguese fluently
2. He must be a Christian
3. He must be over 18 years of age
4. He must not be polygamous
5. He must be engaged in a craft, trade or occupation from which he derived enough income to support himself and his family, or, have adequate resources for this purpose
6. He must be of good conduct, and should have attained the level of education and acquired the habits which were conditions for the unrestricted application for the public and private law pertaining to Portuguese citizens and
7. He must not have refused to perform military duties or have deserted.

Those few Africans who met these requirements were accorded Portuguese citizenship. Such an African was referred to as a ***civilizado***, meaning a civilized African.

In Leopold's *Congo Free State*, the African lost his right to his land; his trade was declared illegal and destroyed and he was ultimately turned into a slave in his land (Chinweizu, 1980). As in the case of Portugal, Belgium was of the view that Congo was an integral part of Belgium and everything in the colony belonged to King Leopold II, including the indigenes who were regarded as subjects and not citizens.

Decolonization and Independence

Portugal was the first European nation to come into contact with the GoG and was the last imperial power to leave the region. Its imperial control came to an end in 1975 when its colonies of Cape Verde Islands and Islands of São Tomé, Angola and Principe declared independence.

By 1900, colonialism was firmly established in the West Coast of Africa and even before then, Africans had begun to challenge it. This came through the instrumentality of African nationalism. Nationalism itself is a theme in Africa that has evoked a lot of controversy. Historians and Social scientists do not agree on what African nationalism means. On the issue, there are two schools of thought.

The first school is the traditionalist school led by James Coleman. Coleman is of the view that all resistant movements which preceded colonial rule cannot be regarded as nationalist movements. According to him, these movements were negative in disposition because they were looking back to the period before colonial rule instead of asking for a forward-looking policy with regards to independence. He argues that, since the pre-colonial experiences they were yearning for were actually working against the emergence of a large, multi-national polity, they were not nationalist movements. Almost on a note of finality, he argues that since such movements were never embraced by the educated elite, they were merely tribal associations (Coleman, 1954).

For Coleman, therefore, African nationalism is a by-product of colonial use. This is because it was colonialism that supplied the necessary stimulus to nationalist movements through its economic, political and educational policies. These in turn led to the emergence of nationalist movements. Coleman concludes that to talk of nationalist movement in terms of uprisings is a misnomer and very negative. He is of the view that colonialism contradicted itself by producing elite thereby digging its own grave. In other words, before the emergence and participation of elite in Nigerian politics, for instance, Nigeria only experienced ethnic nationalism like the Yoruba nationalism, Ibo nationalism and Ibibio nationalism. To him, these movements were merely defending their immediate environments and clans and generally their selfish interests.

Coleman is, however, taken to task by the members of the Dar es Salaam School. A representative view is that of T. O. Ranger who says that African resistance movements to colonial rule before 1940 were nationalist movements; that all the activities of the Africans from the time they resisted the European to the achievement of independence could be called nationalism (Ranger, 1972). According to Ranger, the primary resistance movement (against colonial rule) determined the nature of colonial rule and in effect created an environment in which modern nationalist movements sprang up. In other words, there are connections between the primary movements and the nationalist movements which sprang up in the 1940s.

He argues that, the two were almost going on at the same time because after the conquest of the natives, there were some resistance and in some African countries, the leadership of primary and secondary movements of the 1940s were the same. Besides, most African nationalists recognized that the primary movements ought to be given due recognition. Primary movements were a spontaneous reaction to colonial penetration where the native saw the old world as better than the new world that they could not comprehend.

Both schools are correct and the degree of their correctness lies in what each school sees as nationalism. In Africa, Thomas Hodgkins is of the opinion that, any movement which stood in opposition to colonial rule, no matter its institutional form and objectives, was a nationalist movement.

Be that as it may, a number of factors in the twentieth century facilitated the end of colonial rule in Africa. These included western education which produced educated elite to challenge the colonialists; the impact of the two World Wars; the reverberations of the Great

Depression of the 1930s; the American and Soviet pressure; pressure from the United Nations; the formation of African independent movements and fear (on the path of European nations) of losing colonial possessions. These factors led to constitutional development, dialogue and negotiations and general colonial reforms especially in the Anglophone and Francophone Africa. In the Lusophone and Hispanophone states, lethal dialogue in form of arms struggle was the main instrument of decolonization.

Ghana was the first country in the GoG to achieve independence. That was in 1957. Three years later, majority of states in the Gulf had independence. While other European nations had the foresight to grant independence to their colonies by 1960, Portugal and Spain sought to maintain colonial principles in the region. But ten years of guerrilla wars, beginning from 1962, created strains which precipitated a military coup in Portugal. It was the military government in Lisbon that abandoned the colonial principle and in the aftermath, independence was quickly granted to Guinea-Bissau in 1974 and for the Cape Verde Islands, Angola and São Tomé and Principe in 1975. For Spain, it had granted independence to Equatorial Guinea in 1968 even though it never prepared the citizens for it.

Further Reading

Ajayi, J.F.A and I. Espie. 1969. eds. *A Thousand Years of West African History.* London: Nelson & Ibadan University Press.

Boahen, A. A. 1964. *Britain, the Sahara, and the* Sudan. Clarendon Press.

Davidson, B. 1964. *Old Africa Rediscovered.* London: Oxford University Press.

Duffy, J. 1959. *Portuguese Africa.* Harvard University Press.

Fage, J. D. 1963. *An Atlas of African History.* Arnold.

Greenberg, J. H. 1963. *Languages of Africa.* London: Indiana University Press.

Lugard, F. D. 1923. *The Dual Mandate in British Tropical Africa.* London: Blackwood.

Mathieson, W. L. 1926. *British Slavery and Its Abolition, 1823-38.* London: Longmans.

Murdoc G. P. 1959. *Africa: Its Peoples and their Culture History.* New York, McGraw-Hill.

Nadel, S. F. 1942. *A Black Byzantium.* London: Oxford University Press.

Oliver, R. and A. Atmore. *Africa Since 1800.* London: Oxford.

Simmons, J. 1955. *Livingstone and Africa.* London: Oxford University Press.

CHAPTER THREE

The Political Economy of the Gulf of Guinea

The political economy of the GoG is as chequered as its history and politics. Attempts to merge economic analysis with practical politics are not new as much of classical economics was nothing other than political economy. Therefore, to view economic activity in its political context is not only appropriate but also germane to the discussions of the problems and challenges of development in the GoG.

As elsewhere, political and economic issues are deeply interwoven. A healthy political system is a function of economic development and rising economic expectations. Fundamentally, political economy is increasingly recognized as necessary for any realistic examination of development challenges. Without doubt, economics plays a critical and even dominant role in determining politics and vice versa. Whether one looks at the political economy of the GoG through the lens of economic nationalism, economic internationalism or economic structuralism, it would be discovered that the region has for centuries been confronted with lots of political and economic challenges that are externally and internally directed.

Technically and relatively speaking, Africa is poor and it is the poorest of the continents of the world. This state of poverty presents any researcher on African studies with a puzzle, paradox and indeed a satire: Africa is poor because it is rich. It is one continent that has arrays of natural resources in superfluous quantity and quality. In terms of power generation, Africa houses 40 percent of the world's hydroelectric potential. It also has over 12 percent of the world's natural gas reserves, and 8 percent of global oil extraction. Similarly, the continent produces 70 percent of the world's cocoa beans and 60 percent of its coffee (Thompson, 2010). With fertile soils for agricultural production and its earth rich in strategic minerals, Africa cannot ordinarily afford to be poor; but the reality of the situation is that it is poor.

With particular reference to the GoG, which also reflects the continent's challenges, a number of reasons can be adduced for the proverbial state of poverty. These include slave trade, the challenges of artificial boundaries and cultures, colonial legacy, debt crisis, false paradigm, crisis of accumulation and governance, conflicts, crisis, political instability, rentier economies, resource curse and low state capacity.

Slave Trade as the Prologue of African Crises

Slave trade is beyond doubt the beginning of series of crises in Africa. Slavery and slave trade were not practices that were peculiar to Africa. In fact, the institutions of slavery and slave trade were agents of human dispersal and old globalization in world history. The ancient records of the Assyrians, the Egyptians, the Phoenicians, the Hebrews, the Persians, Indians and Chinese make references to slaves and how the institutions were organized (Anene, 1966).

The Greeks and the Romans raised the bar in the practise of slavery and slave trade. Their economies depended on slave labour. About ninety percent of the population of Greece consisted of slaves and in the Roman Empire; there were more slaves than freemen. The slaves in Greece and the Roman Empire came from Europe, Asia and Africa. Even after the collapse of the Roman Empire, Arabs and Africans traded in slaves for centuries, but the Atlantic slave trade of the Euro-American World crippled Africa and prologued the crisis of development in the region.

The Atlantic slave trade lasted for four hundred years, and, overall, more than 30 million Africans were traded across the Atlantic to the New World of the Americas. It is important to note that; the Atlantic slave trade ranks as the greatest migration in world history. As a result of the trade, the most vibrant segment of the African society that would otherwise have engaged in production was uprooted to the New World. On the loss, Walter Rodney (1986:105) remarks:

> The massive loss to the African labour force was made more critical because it was composed of able-bodied young men and young women. Slave buyers preferred their victims between the ages of 15 and 35, and preferably in the early twenties; the sex ratio being about two men to one woman. Europeans often accepted younger African children, but rarely any older person. They shipped the most healthy wherever possible, taking the trouble to get those who had already survived an attack of smallpox, and

who were therefore immune from further attacks of that disease, which was then one of the world's great killer diseases.

It should be noted that during this period, human labour was the most critical form of energy known to man and for the most productive group to be absent in any society that society could only bleed socio-economically. Therefore, with the Atlantic slave trade, Africa bled profusely and its economic endeavours were retarded. The unequal exchange that characterized the trade led to the collapse of the continent finally. For instance, while human energy was given to the Euro-American World, worthless items like mirrors, beads and handkerchiefs were given to the Africans. To worsen matters, guns and gun powders that were introduced as instruments of slave raids turned out to institute human tragedy and political instability in the continent. In addition, they laid the ground for imperialism and colonialism to thrive.

The Challenges of Artificial Boundaries and Cultures

All states in Africa are artificial creations by the imperial powers who ignored existing pre-colonial political, social and economic divisions. State formation in pre-colonial Africa did not acknowledge permanent, precisely delineated boundaries. Series of conquests and expansion by political groups never resulted in any hegemony and, in any case, the new polity that was founded as a result of these exercises was in most cases temporary-shifting in accordance with the astuteness or lack of it on the part of statesmen. For example, at a time, Zaria conquered the adjourning territories and expanded to incorporate the whole of Northern Nigeria and Southern Niger Republic; at another epoch, her greatness declined and the same environment that Zaria had dominated fell into the hands of Kano.

The same was true of the states of the Niger Delta and empires of Yoruba (Akpan, 2003). The Western Sudan also experienced the same fluidity in the diplomacy of state formation. The environment of the ancient empire of Ghana was the same environment where the old empire of Mali and Songhai existed and flourished. New empires were erected on the ashes of the old ones. Additionally, new states emerged in distant areas to escape political hegemony of already established states. Therefore, not wanting to submit to a certain political authority, a group would simply migrate to land further away to find new settlements and states. "As a result there has been a long tradition of population flow in Africa, with groups of people creating new polities, moving their community, or choosing to join other states" (Thompson, 2010:11).

With colonialism, newly created states in Africa became hegemonic and constricted the free movement of people. What is more, the boundaries of these states were arbitrarily drawn to reflect: "the short-term strategic and economic interests of the imperial powers and not the interests of the Africans they housed" (Thompson, 2004:13). Most boundaries in Africa are ruler-straight, following geographical lines of latitude and longitude. This should not surprise anyone. A lot of decisions on the boundary question in Africa were taken by those who never set their feet on the continent. Lord Salisbury, the British Prime Minister, said these about the boundary exercise during the Anglo-French Conference of 1890:

> We have been engaged in drawing lines upon maps where no white man's foot ever trod; we have been giving away mountains and rivers and lakes to each other, only hindered by the small impediment that we knew exactly where the mountains and rivers and lakes were (Wilson, 1977:95).

A curious dimension to the episodes of the scramble for, and partition of, Africa was the notion that Africa was not owned by anyone and to that extent most of its regions qualified as objects to be seized by any interested European power. This policy of ***terra nullius*** strengthened the scramble and partition games in the continent and made any power a stakeholder in any region. For this reason, Queen Victoria seized Mount Kilimanjaro and donated it as a birthday gift to her cousin, Willie, the German Emperor (Touval, 1984). Willie immediately seized the opportunity and made the area the German colony of Tankanyika.

Nevertheless, as the historic demarcation of boundaries ignored natural lines of division between different peoples, political lines were often not congruent with ethnographic regions. In many places, one "people" straddles a border between two countries (Jones, 1985).

Typical examples abound: Burundi and Rwanda are two countries in Central Africa with same peoples. The population of Burundi is primarily composed of three ethnic groups-the Hutu, the Tutsi and the Twa. The Hutu constitutes about 90 percent of the population. Rwanda equally has the same ethnic composition-the Hutu, the Tutsi and the Twa with the Hutu constituting about 90 percent of the population. The case of Somalia is unique. The people were divided into five states, namely: British Somaliland, Italian Somaliland, French Somaliland, Ethiopia and Kenya. There are other numerous cases such as Yoruba in Nigeria and Benin Republic; Hausa in Nigeria and Niger Republic and Ewe in Togo and Ghana. This state of affairs provokes nationalism, separatism and irredentism-particularly Irredentism.

Irredentism is the struggle of a people for reunification and the irredenta is a territory where a portion of the ethnic nation resides that is regarded as either stolen or lost. The irredentist territorial claim normally evokes resistance from the state whose territory is claimed since its aggregate size would be reduced in the event of a successful claim (Jones, 1985). Irredentism is the cause of some of the violent conflicts and perennial wars in Africa, especially in the Great Lakes region and the Horn of Africa.

The case of Cabinda is intriguing. The oil-rich territory is part of Angola and yet it is separated from it by the DR Congo. This situation occurred because the King of Belgium, Leopold II, insisted that his African Kingdom should adjourn the Atlantic Ocean. Today, Cabinda is a hot-bed of secession. There is also the case of Caprivi Strip in the north-east of Namibia. This strip which gives Namibia a rather odd shape sandwiches four countries; Angola, Botswana, Zambia and Zimbabwe.

The strip and the odd shape of Namibia owe their origins to the fancy of Count Von Caprivi, the German Foreign Minister, who for strategic reasons wanted Germany in South West Africa to have access to the Zambesi River so as to deploy a gunboat. There are also the intriguing cases of the Gambia and Lesotho. Lesotho is a sovereign state which is completely engulfed by South Africa and the Gambia is the smallest state in the GoG that is almost engulfed by Senegal.

Additionally, many states in Africa, about 14 in all, are land-locked as a result of imperially imposed borders while others do not have enough resources, including land, minerals and rivers to build their nations and economies. Landlocked states, for instance, have to depend on their neighbours that have access to the sea for sustenance. When there are frictions between these states and their benefactors, they are readily exposed to the diplomacy of blackmail. Therefore, arbitrary boundaries are at the root of major crises of post-coloniality in Africa. To add to these is the issue of foreign cultures which has served to drive a wedge between peoples in the continent. In the main, these are Anglophone, Arabic, Francophone, Hispanophone and Lusophone cultures.

The Colonial Heritage and Burdens of the International Economy

The entire GoG was once the Portuguese empire in Africa and later became protectorates and colonies of the various European states. From the very beginning, almost all European states were involved in the plunder of resources of the region but ultimately a handful of them had colonies in the region. These were Belgium, Britain, France, Portugal and Spain. Even though many European merchants had had contacts with African states since the fifteenth century, it was only in 1900, the beginning of the twentieth century that it can meaningfully be said that colonial rule started in Africa.

For over six decades, imperial powers used their colonies to supply themselves with food, fibre and other resources. As in the case of the Middle East, one direct consequence of their colonial policies was to thwart transition in the GoG from producer to industrial and service economies and because the imperial power supplied law and order and other basic services, they delayed the process of nation building in the region (Serenson, 2008). Additionally, as local economic elite could not compete effectively with foreign capital, they were left to engage in unproductive enterprises.

Further examination of the colonial economy shows that it was characterized by what Claude Ake calls ***disarticulation*** or ***incoherence*** (Ake, 2002). As he aptly emphasizes: "a disarticulated economy is one whose parts or sectors are not complementary" (Ake, 2002:43). On the other hand, a coherent economy benefits from regional and or sectoral complementarity and reciprocity (Ake, 2002).

The principles of complementarity and reciprocity will ensure that an economy benefits from forward and backward linkages in production. But in Africa, colonial capitalism was a one-way traffic; it was interested only in the most profitable primary commodities. On its operations and outcomes, Claude Ake (2002:45) documents:

> To obtain an adequate supply of the most preferred commodities it was sometimes necessary to discourage the production of some other commodities. When this necessity arose it was accepted without too much thought being wasted on the implications of encouraging or discouraging the production of particular commodities. It was assumed that what was good for international capital was good for the colony. More often than not colonial capitalism used persuasion or forces to compel a concentration of effort on the production of particular export crops.

Alex Thompson (2010:191) has brilliantly extended the discussion by arguing that:

> During the colonial years, limited development based on the continent's primary sector had been undertaken (in agriculture and mining), and a basic infrastructure was built to support this. Yet, the actual level of economic growth enjoyed in Africa was scant reward for this activity. Profits, on the whole, were exported to the West, rather than being invested locally. This left independent Africa with highly specialized export economies, a minute manufacturing base, a lack of access to technology, and populations where few were trained in the ways of modern business, social services or public administration.

The question of colonial capitalism and how it has underdeveloped Africa is the central theme in Walter Rodney's classic, ***How Europe Underdeveloped Africa***. With regards to lack of manufacturing base, Rodney (1986:239) summarizes the point neatly by asserting forcefully that: "the vast majority of Africans went into colonialism with a hoe and came out with a hoe". In details, Rodney (239) writes:

> Industrialization does not only mean factories. Agriculture itself has been industrialized in capitalist and socialist countries by the intensive application of scientific principles to irrigation, fertilizers, tools, crop selection, stock breeding etc. The most decisive failure of colonialism in Africa was its failure to change the technology of agricultural production. The most convincing evidence as to the superficiality of the talk about

colonialism having 'modernized' Africa is the fact that the vast majority of Africans went into colonialism with a hoe and came out with a hoe. Some capitalist plantations introduced agricultural machinery, and the odd tractor found its way into the hands of African farmers; but the hoe remained the overwhelmingly dominant agricultural implement. Capitalism could revolutionize agriculture in Europe but it could not do the same for Africa.

For Claude Ake (2002:46):

The colonial government did not do very much to encourage the development of manufacturing. Their interest in a colony lay primarily in the fact that it was a source of raw materials as well as a market for selling metropolitan manufactured goods.

Table 3.1 shows the range of problems created by the colonial inheritance in Africa.

Table 3.1: Potential Problems created by the Colonial Inheritance

Arbitrary boundaries	**Potential Problems**
	* Illogical territorial units * Divided communities * Irredentist movement * Internal ethnic competition * Inappropriate economic units (landlocked, under-resourced)
Non-hegemonic states	**Potential Problems**
	* Inability to project state power into Hinterland * State power concentrated only on strategic and profitable region
Weak links begween state and society	**Potential Problems**
	* A shared political culture between * State and society * A deficit of legitimacy * Unaccountable states * Distant civil societies * Society disengaging from the state
Formation of a state elite	**Potential Problems**

| | * Strong association between political
* Office and personal wealth
* Social mobility dominated by access to the sate
* Corruption
* An exploitative 'bureaucratic Bourgeoisie' |
|---|---|
| **The economic inheritance** | **Potential Problems** |
| | * Disadvantage in the international Economy
* Underdevelopment of human Resources
* Lack of public services
* Economies over-reliant on primary Sector
* Over-reliance on exports
* Bias towards European, not local or regional markets |
| **Weak political institution** | **Potential Problems** |
| | * Fragile liberal democratic institutions without historical moorings
* Return to colonial style authoritarian and bureaucratic state |

Source: *Alex Thompson: 2010, Introduction to African Politics. London: Routledge: 22*

Even after independence, Africa did not have the capacity to change the direction of unfavourable relations of production because of the ubiquitous hands of neo-colonialism which Kwame Nkrumah, the first President of Ghana, called the last stage of imperialism. Explaining a typical state of neo-colonialism, Nkrumah (1965: ix) argued that: "the essence of neo-colonialism is that the state which is subject to it is, in theory, independent and has all the trappings of international sovereignty. In reality its economic system and thus its political system is directed from outside". On its general character, Nkrumah (1965: xi) further emphasized:

Neo-colonialism is also the worst form of imperialism. For those who practice it, it means power without responsibility and for those who suffer it, it means exploitation without redress. In the days of old-fashioned colonialism, the imperial power had at least to explain and justify at home the actions it was taking abroad. In the colony those who served the ruling imperial power could at least look to its protection against any violent move by their opponents. With neo-colonialism, neither is the case.

Neo-colonialism has had the mortal effect of sustaining and consolidating the principles of unequal exchange that started during the slave trade era. At independence, African states still had highly specialized "monocrop" economies-usually producing one, two or three crops for export (Thompson, 2010). There was no strategic alternative or substitute to lean on to mitigate the effects of a slump in the commodity market or against a bad harvest. The worse part of it is that: "given that there was little local demand for merchandise such as tea and coffee on the continent, all this produce had to be exported. Africa, as a result, was totally dependent on the West to buy its products" (Thompson, 2010:192). It was a typical case of Africa producing what it did not eat and at the end of the day, eating what it never produced.

Be that as it may, the principles of unequal exchange put Africa at a disadvantage. The West operates "close-markets" where the prices of these commodities are determined by them and since Africans never produced the commodities to use as show-pieces, they had to sell at ridiculous prices offered by the Western buyers. According to Alex Thompson (2010:193):

> This structural inequity meant that the continent had to buy expensive Western-manufactured goods with the income generated by the export of these cheaper primary products. In effect, Africans had to buy back their own raw materials, in a manufactured form, at inflated rate. A United Nations report estimated that 85 percent of the value of manufactured goods was kept in the West. Only 15 percent of this capital found its way back to the country that had provided the raw materials. What is more, over time, prices paid for primary commodities, fell while the price of manufactured imports increased. Consequently, the West's terms of trade improved, while those of the developing world declined.

Nigeria provides a typical case of the unequal exchange with its petroleum products. The country's crude oil is sold at the international market at the prevailing market price, but the country imports the end products at higher prices. Nigeria is the largest producer of oil in Africa. All over the continent, whether one looks at commodities like diamonds, cocoa, cotton, coffee and rubber, a greater portion of raw materials are sold with no added value only for the countries to purchase goods manufactured from these resources by the West at exorbitant prices. Therefore, for the continent to develop and progress, it has to diversify its economies and manufacture products with its own raw materials and rather sell the finished products to the West.

Debt Crisis

Since independence, Africa in general and the GoG in particular have been groaning under the welter of debt crisis, or what Percy S. Mistry (1991), calls *debt cancer*. African states took the decisions to borrow in order to grow their economies because development requires investment capital which they lacked in the aftermath of independence. Unfortunately, this approach to development did not work. Rather it became a typical Shakespearean case of he who goes a-borrowing goes a-sorrowing. By the end of the twentieth century, these debts had crippled the continent.

In the mid-1990s, sub-Saharan Africa's total indebtedness had increased from the equivalent of 15 percent to 90 percent of its Gross National Product (GNP). The amount set aside to service these loans further damaged the African economy. The service on the $221 billion debt cost the continent the equivalent of 21 percent of its annual export income (Thompson, 2010). With so much capital taken from Africa, the case for its development is simply not possible.

A combination of internal and external factors accounts for the sorry state of the debt crisis in Africa. Internally, the causes include corruption, reckless management of loans, the crisis of accumulation and the crisis of governance or state legitimacy. Externally, the causes included the continent's declining terms of trade; the oil shocks of the 1970s and a rise in interest rates in the early 1980s. Internally, some states in Africa spent the loans on useless and worthless ventures that were counter-productive. Worse still, as Aniekan Ekpe and O. Okereke (2002:151) have documented, "in some instances, corrupt

African leaders were helped by the very banks that lent them money to transfer it as private funds back to Europe and the United States. Given the fact that the loans were not used for productive ventures, debt crisis was a logical consequence". Even where the loans would have been put in the most productive sectors like agriculture, industry or infrastructure, the fact that the continent has a deformed socio-economic matrix in education and health sectors meant that the loans would not have been quite profitable for Africa. In some countries, natural disasters like droughts and floods had disastrous effects on their economies and threw out of gear their projections for loan-servicing and pay back schedules.

Externally, the deformed structure of African economies at independence is to blame for a gargantuan appetite for loans in order to overcome backwardness and guarantee sustainable development (Ekpe & Okereke, 2002), but the falling price of cash crops made it almost impossible for the governments to repay their loans. The two oil shocks that hit the world in 1973 and 1979 dramatically worsened the situation for most countries. As the West sank into recession, Africa bled profusely. The amount required by the non-oil states to buy fuel jumped through the roof and consequently the continent's terms of trade worsened.

In the first oil shock, the oil-producing states had invested large amounts of their wealth in the banking system of the West. These surpluses in form of petrodollars were offered to African countries as cheap loans but the second oil shock of 1979, triggered high interest rates which knocked off the economies of most African states and imposed on them heavy debt burdens. It was not until the formulation of a Multilateral Debt Relief Initiative (MDRI) in 2005 that most African economies began to be released from this debt trap. At the Gleneagles Summit, G8 members pledged to cancel the external debts of 17 of the world's most ***Heavily Indebted Poor Countries*** (HIPCs). By the time the pledges were fulfilled the beneficiaries had reduced their debt service payment by half. Even at that, the crippling effects of debt crisis in Africa are still there for everybody to see. They include poverty, malnutrition, unemployment, high infant mortality rate, low life expectancy and political instability. It is probably on account of these weighty indices of underdevelopment that Susan

George (1993:68) exclaims that: "one can almost hear the sound of Africa sliding off the map".

False Paradigm and Impact of Structural Adjustment Programmes

The false-paradigm model is an international-dependence approach to development. It attributes underdevelopment to faulty, inappropriate advice provided by well-meaning but often uninformed, biased, ethnocentric and perhaps race-conscious international *experts* from advanced-country assistance agencies and multilateral donor organizations (Todaro & Smith, 2004).

In many instances: "these experts offer sophisticated concepts, elegant theoretical structures, and complex econometric models of development that often lead to inappropriate or incorrect policies" (Todaro & Smith, 2004:125). An extension of this logic is that leading intellectuals, civil servants and policy-makers in the Developing Countries imbibe alien concepts and elegant but inappropriate theoretical models and use same to attempt to solve their countries' problems but at the end find that they only try to further the existing system of elitists' policies and institutional structures.

The Structural Adjustment Programmes (SAPs) are examples of such false paradigm models cooked and served Africans by the West. When it failed as it did, hardship became the lot of the people of the continent. Essentially, SAPs were introduced by the International Financial Institutions (IFIs), when the governments of African states were not able to raise new loans to service their previous borrowing and the IMF and the World Bank were now the only sources of credit.

By their designs, SAPs were structured on conditional lending where the beneficiary states were to liberalize their economies in return for loans. In other words, their economies were to be open to international and domestic private capital. The role of the state in economic governance was to be reduced drastically through commercialization and privatization programmes. With no other sources, African states had to comply with these conditions in order to raise the loans. SAPs had three universal pillars. According to Alex Thompson (2010:197), "lending was conditional on: first, that development strategies should favour agricultural production; second, that governments operate more "realistic" trade and exchange-rate policies; and third, that the public sector should be made more efficient".

As it turned out, SAPs were a complete fiasco in the continent. Alex Thompson (2010:199) has captured a part of this tragedy thus:

> ...The Berge Report clearly suggested that Africa should concentrate its efforts on increasing income from the export of primary produce. As the World Bank's 1995 report confirmed, SAPs are about "putting exporters first". Yet the problem with pushing export-led growth is that this simply reproduces the disadvantages of unequal exchange experienced before. Also, where African countries have succeeded in increasing output, this was often offset by other SAP countries doing likewise. IFIs, after all, were encouraging a multitude of SAP countries worldwide to expand primary production. Since all these states have devalued their currencies and increased production, there was little relative advantage to be gained. International markets have reacted to the increased availability of primary goods by lowering commodity prices. Consequently, increased production did not realise greater income. Africa was running in order to stand still, still plagued by falling commodity prices and unequal exchange.

It is not surprising that Percy Mistry of the World Bank remarked that: "to the extent that (Africa) continues to rely on primary commodities to generate further export earnings, it is cutting its own throat" (see Thompson, 2004:186).

The suicidal nature of SAPs could be seen in the fact that far from attracting capital in form of foreign investment, the opposite was the case; aridity of capital. This is so because the "Transnational Corporations (TNCs) will not invest in fragile economies, whose governments, partly due to the impact of SAPs, cannot guarantee a stable currency, the immediate maintenance of infrastructure, public order or administrative continuity" (Thompson, 2010:200). This explains why the TNCs have left Africa in droves to Asia and Latin America.

The social and political impacts of SAPs were as insidious as the economic effects. For one, the public sector reforms resulted not only in cuts in public services but also massive loss of jobs. Additionally, since government spending had to be curtailed and subsidies removed as requirements of the SAPs regime, hardship and poverty became the partners of the citizens of most African states. These social impacts affected the political development of Africa tremendously and ultimately eclipsed the prospects of institutionalizing the Western-valued mantra of democracy. Politically, SAPs led to endless protests, trade union disputes, ethnic tensions, food riots, emergence of militia groups, military regimes and civil wars. However one looks at the situation, SAPs are the harbinger of political instability in Africa; in fact, agent provocateur.

The major problem with SAPs is that the designers ignored in Africa the role of the ***residual*** which was discovered by economists in the 1950s. The residual is the term assigned to that part of growth apparently not accounted for by the conventional factors (Landes, 1991). That part of growth is essentially the human factor and the human factor hinges on attitudinal and cultural elements, educational and professional training. SAPs were implemented in the environment that lacked the basic ingredients to ginger growth and development in the first place.

Secondly, the designers of SAPs suffered the problems of over-generalization, -simplification and -universali-zation of models. Yet, these models were not products of time-tested ideals. In a critique of such models based on the pure theory of international trade, J. Bhagwati (1964:45) writes:

> In contrast to the general richness and synthesized character of pure theory in its comparative statics, dynamic propositions in international trade are comparatively few and bear no trace of any uniform design, each having been developed in virtual isolation. Dynamic trade theory, where it exists, has grown in an essentially **ad hoc** fashion and has witnessed none of the interaction of analysis which usually accompanies the development of an area of knowledge and produces a common design, a unifying frame.

Africa has to design home-grown strategies of development based on the requirements of its environment and the starting point should be the human security.

The Crises of Accumulation and Governance

A major crisis of post-coloniality in Africa is the crisis of accumulation. This in turn has resulted in the crisis of governance. In order to fast-track the development of the continent, a number of economic strategies were adopted but mostly based on the false paradigm models already discussed. Two of such strategies revolved around Import Substitution Industrialization (ISI) and the need to over-expand the institutions of the state. Alex Thompson (2004:202) has rightly asserted that ISI "became the centrepiece of most African development plans". ISI was not only a *sine qua non* of African development strategy but also a *disseratum* because of the imperative of diversifying economies away from existing secondary manufacturing sector. The immediate goals were to reduce Africa's dependence on foreign goods and to embark on self-reliance. As it turned out, most of the projects of ISI were largely inefficient and since they depended on the state for protection and survival, they constituted conduit pipes for capital flight. Providing further reasons for their unproductive nature, Alex Thompson (2010:218) writes:

> Large, prestigious production units often became "white elephants", not sustainable given the underdeveloped nature of their host economies. State-of-the-art assembly plants, for example, were of little use when Africans could not afford to buy the goods they produced. Indeed, ironically, most of the technology and materials needed to run these operations had to be imported from the West, given that the local manufacturing base was unable to supply these needs. With little demand locally, and their goods uncompetitive in international markets, many of these import substitution industries became a burden on African economies rather than their saviours. Political leaders needed to be much more selective in the type and scale of the industries they sought to stimulate. Instead, sectors where genuine competitive advantage could have been built were swarmed by projects based more on ambition and prestige. The capital invested in import substitution would have been more profitably invested in the agricultural sector. This, after all, was where most Africans earned their living. Diversifying farms away from export crops into the production of goods demanded locally (such as food) may have generated more wealth for a greater number of people.

Today, moribund cars and truck assembly plants in Lagos (Volkswagen), Kaduna (Peugeot), Bauchi (Styre) and Awka (Anamco), the iron and steel industry in Ajaokuta and the Machine Tools Factory at Osogbo, all in Nigeria, are typical examples of the wasteful nature of the ISI. These are, indeed, graveyards and museums of false paradigm models. If the capital invested in ISI was invested in the agricultural sector, Nigeria would have attained the status of a developed economy by the turn of the century.

Another aspect of the crisis of accumulation has been the steady expansion of the public sector. Until recently when the IFIs forced African states to privatize their economies and down-size their workforce, they had *overdeveloped* public sector. In most states, the salaries of civil service alone accounted for more than 50 percent of state expenditure. Across the continent, "bureaucracies simply became too large to be supported by their own economies" (Thompson, 2004:203). These bureaucracies absorbed colossal amounts of public finance that could have been actively invested in self-generating sectors of the economy. Everywhere state-owned enterprises (SOEs) were established mostly for political reasons as against sound economic necessities. Essentially, patronage and rent-seeking were the foremost motives in their establishment. On their operations and impact, Alex Thompson (2010:219) writes:

> Thus, with political considerations overriding administrative or economic needs in these neo-patrimonial institutions, efficiency inevitably suffered. Public servants were often employed because of their loyalty, or faction or ethnic links, not for their skills, experience or ability to do the job. Indeed, the need to provide patronage often left these institutions considerably over staffed. In this respect, African bureaucracies were far removed from the legal-rational institutions of Western civil services. Over-developed bureaucracies may have represented a good **political** investment for ruling elites. Yet, in **economic** terms, the investment of scarce resources in this manner was clearly unproductive. These bureaucracies accounted for considerable sums of public finance, yet generated few profits. No capital was accumulated, and no surplus was available for re-investment. Instead, throughout Africa, bloated bureaucracies became burdens on fragile economies.

The Political Economy of the Gulf of Guinea

Corruption is also an issue that is the bane of development in Africa. In the public life, it is a critical aspect of the client-patron network. Services are not rendered on the basis of need but as a result of kick-backs, bribery and payment of service fees whereby individual government workers and even those in the private sector demand fees for their services. These become personal fees as they are not paid into the government treasuries.

Corruption in Africa is a response to the continent's state of underdevelopment and absence of human security. Therefore, the few that had the opportunity to be employed use their positions to provide welfare services to themselves; services that they are denied by their governments. In aggregate terms, it is the continent that suffers as monies used to service corruption could have been used as capital for investment.

Side by side with the crisis of accumulation is the crisis of governance. The burdens associated with the crisis of accumulation weigh so heavily on the African states that they precipitate crisis of governance and perpetual state of underdevelopment. Some of the issues involved in this crisis include insecurity, political instability, weak state syndrome and state collapse. Most citizens in Africa are highly unsecured and the state themselves are on the verge of collapsing. To avert the impending doom, Africa has to look in-wards to discover itself and then march on to the future with honour, glory and prestige.

Resource Blessings, Resource Curse and Rentier Economies

The GoG is undoubtedly one of the richest regions in the world. There is hardly any natural resource of note that is not found in the region. In the chapters on individual countries in the Gulf (see Chapters 5 to 23), these minerals and their sources are catalogued. Ordinarily, these resources should bring blessings to the region and facilitate the process of economic development because of the compelling factor that there is hardly any country in the international system that does not need a combination of these resources for industrialization and development.

Two of such critical resources are oil and gas. To be sure, the GoG does not have as much volume of oil and gas as the Middle East which boasts of 75 percent of the world's proven petroleum reserves and 33 percent of the world's total supply of natural gas; but certainly it has in excess of 5 percent of the world's value of the two resources.

With good governance and management, the production value of these resources should act as catalysts for development, security and peace but these do not take place. Instead, they constitute 'resource curse'. This is the greatest paradox of the GoG and it is of ancient origin. Since the beginning of contacts with the outside world in the period of the BCE-Before the Common Era-with the Arabs down to the Portuguese era in the fifteenth century, the political economy of the GoG has always been characterized by the uncanny paradox of poverty in the midst of wealth. Indeed, since the BCE, resources in the region ought to have constituted gentle and abundant blessings but sadly they have always constituted the reverse: resource curse. In the era of colonialism, the imperial powers could be blamed for this sad state of affairs but with independence, the leadership of the region does not have excuses for the continuous state of de-development of the region.

The main factor that accounts for 'resource curse' in the GoG is over-dependence on natural resources because these resources, regardless of their quantity and quality, are extremely detrimental to state capacity (de Soysa and Neumayer, 2007). This is the situation that Biodun Alao calls the tragedy of endowment (Alao, 2007). This situation prevails because all states in the region operate rentier economies. Rentier economies depend considerably on foreign revenues for a greater part of their income, with the rent accruing to governments (Sorenson, 2008).

To this extent, only a few people are involved in the production of rentier wealth. The oil industry, for instance, employs only a fraction of the population and in this era of robotics even fewer people are needed in the industry. The implication is that in countries with rentier economies, majority of the citizens are lazy and un-industrious. Besides, they do not pay taxes on account of the false notion that their governments already have wealth through sales of mineral resources. In most cases, governments use these rent resources to buy peace through subsidies, to placate political opponents by controlling wealth distribution, and to dispense patronage.

In addition, many SOEs and parastatals are run by rentier regimes to further placate their cronies for support. Of course, it can not be anything else. Since the citizens do not pay taxes, they do not have the moral obligations to hold their rentier regimes accountable for corruption, abuse of office and violation of human rights.

One odd outcome of a rentier economy is that political reforms necessary to drive development and security cannot be embarked upon successfully and this explains why none of the GoG states is fully democratic. At best selective aspects of democracy are flaunted while the main essence of democracy which is competition is largely jettisoned. Besides, in most of these states, voters are coerced to vote in a particular manner. It is a typical case of those who pay the piper dictating the tune. And the tiny few who challenge this seeming state of anomie are driven into exile, jailed after trumped-up charges or are simply assassinated. This is the sad state of the GoG.

Conflicts, Proliferation of Small Arms and Light Weapons and Civil Wars

Conflicts occur as a result of incompatibility of interests between parties. They are, indeed, inevitable and inexorable in the affairs of men. Therefore, wherever there are human beings there is bound to be conflicts and they occur in the course of their interactions. As conflicts cannot be wished away, the society has the sole option to put in place mechanisms to resolve conflicts before they are transformed into crisis and violence. That is why Kenneth Boulding emphasizes that what is important about conflict "is not occurrence as such but how the parties attempt to deal with it" (1977:84). Even so, conflict should be seen as the motor of transformation and is either positive or negative. It can be creatively transformed to ensure justice, equity and harmony; or destructively transformed to engender injustice, inequality and acute insecurity (ECOWAS Commission, 2008).

In the GoG, as elsewhere in most developing countries, conflicts are always located in the negative conflict zones as against positive conflict zones which should trigger development, peace, and security. Therefore, human insecurity in the region is driven by the negative transformation of structural factors through the exacerbation of conflict accelerators while the degeneration of conflict into open violence is often sparked by triggers (ECOWAS Commission, 2008). According to the Commission (2008:10) structural factors refer to:

> Systemic variable conditioned by decades and centuries of interactions with regard to external, regional and internal power relations (global and local governance); fault-lines in the architecture of the post-colonial African states; and the vulnerability of the continent in the vagaries of global processes and nature, such as the region's disadvantaged position in the world market and environmental degradation. The root causes of violent conflict, such as poverty, exclusion, gender and political/economic inequalities are traceable to these global and local fault lines. They have always constituted a time bomb under governance processes in West Africa, being the primary source of latent, indirect violence

For the Commission (2008:11), accelerators refer to:

> Feedback events and processes that progressively worsen the impacts of structural factors, such as collapsed educational systems, repressive security apparatuses and curtailment of freedoms, corruption, religious/ethnic discrimi-na-tion, and worsening cost of living (while) triggers refer to sudden events with catalytic effects on accelerators that spark a crisis, which could in turn lead to violent conflict, such as the sudden increase in the price of a staple, which could culminate in civil strife or a coup d'état.

On the relationship between structural factors, accelerators, triggers and human tragedy, the Commission (2008:11) submits that:

> Structural factors mask latent (indirect) violence, that is, harm perpetrated against the individual or group and which are embedded in the structure of our societies, such as the sources of illiteracy and innumeracy, unemployment and environmental degradation. Their possible degeneration into direct violence is a function of how, and in what direction, people interact with each other and with nature to transform them. For instance, a repressive regime may create a security racket to protect itself, crack down on the labour movement, muzzle the press, imprison opposition figures, and fill a voters' register with double entries and ghost names, all in the attempts to cling on to power. All these practices accelerate the negative transformation of structural factors and nudge society towards direct violence. A step too far, such as the assassination of a popular opposition figure or the cancellation of unfavourable election results by the dictator, may just provide the trigger that tips the scales in favour of violence. Such

> violence causes immediate physical or psychological pain, which could be consequence of armed insurgency, torture, ethnic cleansing, police brutality, banditry, robbery or domestic conflicts.

Clearly, the observations of the ECOWAS Commission in West Africa could be applied to the entire continent of Africa without committing ecological fallacy; that is, erroneous inference (Robinson, 1950). The observations constitute the black box of conflicts, crises and wars in Africa. But what worsens the conflict situation in the GoG in particular is the proliferation of Small Arms and Light Weapons (SALWs).

In UN parlance, small arms refer to pistols, rifles and carbines, sub-machine guns, assault rifles and light machine-guns; while light weapons (a separate category) refers to heavy machine-guns, grenade launchers, portable anti-aircraft guns, portable anti-tank guns, portable missile launchers, mortars of less than 100mm; and "ammunition and explosives" including cartridges for small arms, shells and missiles for light weapons, hand grenades, landmines, and explosives (see the UN General Assembly Report of the Panel of Governmental Experts on Small Arms: 11-12).

The world has in excess of 1 trillion SALWs and Africa has in excess of 100 million of these weapons. According to the UN, only 3 percent of these arms are used by governments, military or paramilitary forces (Naim, 2003); the rest are in illegal hands especially in conflict-prone areas. Outside outright sales and military programmes, SALWs are spread through covert and "gray market" channels especially in Africa (Akpan, 2007). Their low cost nature, portability, ease of maintenance and operations make them perfect instruments for use by insurgents, criminal bands, separatist groups and other sub-and non-state actors (Jayantha, 2005). In fact, the increasing sophistication and lethality of some of these weapons have given these social actors a firepower that often exceed that of any nation's security operatives.

With such weapons capable of firing up to 300 rounds a minute, one individual can threaten a society in no small measures. Besides, the simple nature of SALWs can be demonstrated with the use of AK 47. The assault rifle has about 30 moving parts and is so simple that it can be used and maintained by teenagers. Most of these weapons require few hours of training for users to be highly skilled in using them. The phenomenon of child soldiers in the GoG is structured on SALWs.

Conflicts and SALWs have turned the Gulf of Guinea into one risky region. The risk index for the inhabitants, visitors, governments and investors is extremely high especially in the natural resources endowed areas. For the TNCs that extract minerals, the prospects of jumbo profits have made them to endure the risk. Even so, most of them have engaged the services of Private Military Companies (PMCs) to provide them with security thus constituting themselves into governments within governments in the region. For the governments, repression is the name of their game.

This situation takes place because in almost all states, the regimes are neither fully democratic nor excessively authoritarian. As mixed regimes, they do not have the capacities to contain warlordism, secessionists and other social actors challenging them. If they were fully democratic, channels of accommodation would have been created for the oppositionists to flower, thus asphyxiating the prospects of tension and instability in the society. On the other hand, if they were extremely draconian, they would have coerced people to toe the line. But possessing neither excellent credentials of democracy nor authoritarianism, the result is the weak state syndrome and limited sovereignty. Ordinarily, as sovereign states, they should have absolute monopoly of violence but because of the weak state capacity, this glory is shared with other actors and the citizens are caught in the web of violence. In most cases, lethal dialogue (force) is called upon to resolve conflicts and the effects are disorder and anarchy.

Natural resources also play some roles in long-term conflicts and civil wars in the GoG. Most scholars in conflict studies argue that, natural resource wealth is a major cause of civil war (Berdal & Malone, 2000; Klare, 2001; Ballentine & Sherman, 2003; Collier *et al*, 2003; Fearon & Laitin, 2003; Ross, 2003; Ross, 2004; Fearon, 2005; Soysa & Neumayer, 2007). Two models are often used to explain why natural resource is a major determinant of civil war.

First, is the "looting rebels" model and the second is the "state capacity model" (Soysa & Neumayer, 2007). The looting rebels model concerns a situation where resource wealth provides finance and motive for rebels to fight governments whereas the state capacity model argues that, the political Dutch disease weakens state capacity and makes government's easy prey for social actors. According to Indra de Soysa and Eric Neumayer (2007:202):

> Natural-resource-dependent countries have a lower level of bureaucratic capacity than their level of per capita income would suggest and, in extreme cases, suffer from socioeconomic and political breakdown. This could be either because dependence on natural resources weakens states or because natural resource abundance allows states to become rentier economies, with few incentives for the ruling elites to develop the broader economy as would rulers of natural-resource-poor economies that are forced to provide broad public goods in order to raise productivity. Natural resource abundance might induce leaders to foster corruption, patronage and rent-seeking behaviour rather than effectiveness, efficiency, and competence.

Natural resources are triggers for secessionist rebellions for at least three reasons:

a) They are not found in all regions of a country, but in a particular region of it
b) The question of ownership arises as to who owns it-the whole nation or the lucky region and
c) If it is managed by the central government, are the proceeds evenly distributed with special consideration to the lucky region?

On account of these reasons, the World Bank Policy Research Report (2003:60) argues that: "statistically, secessionist rebellions are considerably more likely if the country has valuable natural resources, with oil being particularly potent". Typical examples include Cabinda in Angola, Katanga in the DR Congo, Aceh and West Papua in Indonesia, Scotland in Great Britain and the Niger Delta in Nigeria.

Outside secessionist rebellions, a number of countries in the GoG have experienced outright civil wars as a result of rivalry with warlords over possession of natural resources like oil and diamonds. These countries include the DR Congo, Nigeria, Liberia, Sierra Leone, and Angola. Angola had one of the longest civil wars in Africa, lasting for about a quarter of a century; same with the DR Congo.

In fact, in the DR Congo, the sensational Second Congo War which started in 1998 involved about seven foreign armies and that is why it is always known as the *African World War*. This was the world's deadliest civil war which killed about six million people and turned millions of citizens into refugees across the Great Lakes Region. The first Congo War started in 1960 in the Katanga province over natural resources. Katanga was the wealthiest of the Congo's provinces and the secessionist rebellion was aided by Belgian mining interest represented by Belgian officers and civilians in the DR Congo.

To overcome both the challenges of the looting rebels and the political Dutch disease, the Gulf States should restructure their societies and key into time-tested mechanisms of conflict resolutions like federalism, democracy and diversification of the economy – away from natural resources.

The Burdens of Low Income, Trade and Investment

The GoG is a region that is characterized by the extremes of poverty. This development could be gleaned from the value of the GDP of the states in the region. Typical examples for 2008 are as follows:

Table 3.2: GDP of Selected States in the Gulf of Guinea

Country	Population	GDP ($)
Benin	8,000,000	640
Cameroon	16,000,000	6,770
Cape Verde	500,000	1,909
Cote d'Ivoire	19,000,000	2,350
DR Congo	70,000,000	1,082
Guinea	10,000,000	1,260
Guinea Bissau	1,500,000	826
Liberia	4,000,000	876
Nigeria	150,000,000	2,400
Republic of Congo	4,000,000	1,170
São Tomé and Principe	167,000	191
Senegal	12,000,000	1,260
Sierra Leone	5,000,000	2,000
Togo	6,000,000	2,770

The Political Economy of the Gulf of Guinea

Compare the statistics from selected GoG states with the states in the high income and upper middle income groups. By comparison, the GDP per capita for the US is $45,000 and $29,000 for Israel (population; 7 million) whereas for a majority of the GoG states, the GDP per capita lies between $191 and $6770. These figures represent extremes of poverty and low economy.

The current classification of economies of countries by the World Bank is reflected in table 3.3.

Table 3.3: Country Economic Classification

Category	Income Range Per Capita GNP ($)	Numbeof Countries	% of World Popu-lation	Average Per Capita GNP ($)	Average per Capita GNP/PPP ($)
High Income	≥10,066	42	16	32,112	31,009
Upper Middle Income	0,065-3,256	38	9	4,769	10,186
Lower Mid-dle Income	3,255-826	53	38	1,686	5,829
Low Income	825	59	37	587	2,258

Source: World Bank

From the classification, all states of the GoG are in the category of the low income while OECD countries and others located in the northern hemisphere are in the high income group as table 3.4 reveals.

Table 3.4: Classification of Economies by Region and Income

Gulf of Guinea Low Income	**OECD High Income**	**Other High Income**
Angola Benin Cameroon Cape Verde Cote d'Ivoire DR Congo Equatorial Guinea	Australia Austria Belgium Canada Denmark Finland France	Andorra Aruba Bahamas, the Barbados Bermuda Brunei Cayman Islands

Gabon	Germany	Channel Islands
Gambia	Greece	Cyprus
Ghana	Iceland	Faeroe Island
Guinea	Ireland	French Polynesia
Guinea Bissau	Italy	Greenland
Liberia	Japan	Guam
Nigeria	Luxembourg	Hong Kong, China
Republic of Congo	Netherland	Israel
São Tomé and Principe	New Zealand	Kuwait
	Norway	Liechtenstein
Senegal	Portugal	Macao, China
Sierra Leone	Spain	Malta
Togo	Sweden	Monaco
	Switzerland	Netherlands Antilles
	United Kingdom	New Caledonia
	United States	Northern Mariana Islands
		Qatar
		San Marino
		Singapore
		Slovenia
		Taiwan, China
		United Arab Emirates
		Virgin Islands (US)

Source: Michael P. Todaro & Stephen C. Smith 2004. *Economic Development.* Singapore: Pearson Education: 36

The facts behind the statistics show that the world is generally divided into two spheres, the **economic halves**, in the high-income group and **have nots** made up of the low and middle income countries. The lowest of the lowest are located in the GoG.

Many reasons account for the poor indicators for the states of the GoG. Like average LDCs, the Gulf States take in considerably less capital through such methods as exports and inflow of investment money, both of which are major sources of income for the rich nations. As a matter of fact, trade differences leave the advanced economies relatively advantaged. In 2005, for instance, they exported 77 percent of all goods and services. That left less than a quarter of all exports for the less developed countries. While China accounted for 33 percent of all LDC exports, sub-Saharan Africa managed to ship only 1.5 percent of world exports (Rourke, 2008). What products a country exports also makes a difference. A diverse range of manufactured goods and services exports, account for more than 90 percent of what the advanced economies sell abroad.

By contrast, manufactured goods and services make up only 69 percent of middle-income country exports and only 50 percent of low-income country exports. These LDCs rely more than do advanced economies on the export of primary products, such as food, fibres, fuels, and minerals. This disadvantages the LDCs because the price of primary products is often unstable and also generally has not risen as fast as the price of manufactured goods.

Additionally, investment differences also favour the advanced economies. First, they have the flow of most investment capital. Capital investment is critical to economic progress. Every day, international investors move billions to markets around the world, lured by the promise of high returns (Sorenson, 2008). Foreign investment is critical to the GoG, but investors are not heading towards that destination. For example, in 1998, the US invested $149 billion in Europe, $48 billion in Latin America, $47 billion in Asia and the Pacific, $2.3 billion in the Middle East, with $2.1 going to Israel. The sub-Saharan Africa was largely by-passed. Therefore, capital investment flows to the regions of advanced economies rather than to the less developed economies like those of the GoG where the need is greatest. The suffocating socio political and geo economics environments in the GoG are the major causes of low income, trade and investment.

Further Reading

Ayittey, G. B. N. 1993. *Africa Betrayed.* New York: St. Martin's Press.
Cheru, F. 1989. *The Silent Revolution in Africa: Debt, Development and Democracy.* Harare: Anvil.
Collier, P. 2007. *The Bottom Billion: Why the Poorest Countries Are Failing and What Can Be Done About It.* New York: Oxford University press.

Davidson, B. 1964. *Old Africa Rediscovered.* London: Oxford University Press.
Duffy, J. 1959. *Portuguese Africa.* Harvard University Press.
Fage, J. D. 1963. *An Atlas of African History*. Arnold.
George, S. 1993. *Uses and Abuses of African Debt.* In: Adedeji, A. ed. *Africa Within the World: Beyond Dispossession and Dependence.* London: Zed.
Greenberg, J. H. 1963. *Languages of Africa.* London: Indiana University Press.
Gutkind, C. W. and I. Wallerstein. 1976. *The Political Economy of Contemporary Africa.* Beverly Hills: Sage.
Homer-Dixon, T. F. 1999. *Environment, Scarcity and Violence.* New Jersey: Princeton University Press.
Landes, D. S. 1999. *The Wealth and Poverty of Nations.* New York: Norton.
Murdoc G. P. 1959. *Africa: Its Peoples and their Culture History.* New York, McGraw-Hill.
Sandbrook, R. 1993. *The Politics of Africa's Economic Recovery.* Cambridge: Cambridge University Press.

CHAPTER FOUR

Politics in the Gulf of Guinea

Almost all states in the GoG were bequeathed the instruments and traditions of democracy, but within a decade of independence they had all turned into despotic, autocratic or authoritarian regimes. All started with multi-party system but as soon as the President or Prime Minister was elected and sworn into power, the new leader made sure that he was the only cock to crow in the political landscape.

Political parties other than theirs were banned and the opposition elements were thrown into jails, killed or forced into exile. In countries where civilian dictatorship was not experienced, military despotism was the order of the day. There is hardly any state of the Gulf that has not had a military junta at the helm of affairs. Where the military did not gain access to state power, they had attempted to overthrow civilian rule at least once as table 4.1 shows. What may be wrong with the political set up in the GoG?

Table 4.1: Military Coups in the Gulf of Guinea since Independence

State	Date of Independence	1950-1960	1970-1980	1980-1990	2000S	REMARKS
Angola	1975					0
Benin	1960	1963 1965 1967 1969	1972			5
Cameroon	1960		1984			1
Cape Verde	1975					0
Cote d'Ivoire	1960			1999	2001	2
DR Congo	1960	1960 1965				3
Equatorial Guinea	1968		1979			1
Gabon	1960		1964			1

Country	Independence					Total
The Gambia	1965			1994		1
Ghana	1957	1966	1972	1980		6
		1969	1979	1981		
Guinea	1958		1984		2008	2
Guinea-Bissau	1974		1980			
Guinea	1958		1984		2008	2
Guinea-Bissau	1974		1980	1993	2003	5
			1983	1999		
			1985			
Liberia	1847		1980			1
Nigeria	1960	1966	1975	1991		12
		1966	1976	1993		
			1983	1996		
			1985			
			1986			
Total						53

Background to Authoritarian Regimes in the Gulf of Guinea Colonial Heritage

Perhaps the greatest political challenge of the crisis of post-coloniality in the GoG, as elsewhere in Africa, concerns weak political institutions. Weak political institutions were part of the enduring but negative legacies of the imperial powers. The character of imperialism was exploitative-socially, economically and politically-and to that extent sufficient attention was not paid to the development of credible and strong political institutions including the civil society that would have been the guardians of the state from the outset.

Of course, it was not necessary to develop the institutions since the imperial powers never contemplated political independence and sovereignty for their subjects until the changing international circumstances occasioned by the emergence of the Union of Soviet

Socialist Republics (USSR), the de-isolation of American international relations and the two World Wars forced them to hand over power, at least symbolically to the African nationalists.

Fundamentally speaking, as the imperial powers achieved pyrrhic victories in the two wars but lay in ruins and as agitations for self-government by the nationalists had reached a crescendo, they hurriedly negotiated power with the latter for crises to be avoided and exploitation to continue. Therefore, in most colonial territories, negotiation was the key to political independence. Such countries included Nigeria, Ghana, Sierra Leone and the Gambia. Indeed, the Anglophone states achieved independence on a platter of gold through negotiation. The Francophone states never really wanted independence since they were guaranteed membership of the French Community and indeed many individuals were granted French citizenship. It was in this spirit that Leopold Sedar Senghor repudiated the quest for independence while speaking in France in 1950. He said, ***inter alia:*** \

> ...to speak of independence is to reason with the head on the ground and feet in the air, it is not to reason at all, it is to advance a false problem (Chinweizu, 1980:97).

For the Lusophone states which achieved independence through armed struggle, it should be noted that by the 1970s the groundswell of international opinion was against continuous colonization; in any case, independent African states and liberal-minded states in the international system provided the diplomatic platform for them to succeed. Be that as it may, in all African states the imperial powers hurriedly transferred power to the educated elements who lacked experience on their newfound assignments and whose states lacked capacity on account of availability of weak state institutions. Commenting on the weak links between state and civil society at independence in Africa, Alex Thompson (2010:16) writes:

> A natural consequence of this lack of state penetration was that independent Africa also inherited weak links between state and society. Colonial political authority had been gained on the continent through conquest, and political institutions imposed. Coercion acted as a substitute for legitimacy. The state, in this sense, never rested on a social contract between government and people. Indeed, colonial administrators were not even

accounted to the Africans they ruled. Instead, they obeyed orders emanating from their superiors back in the capitals of Europe. Government was therefore about maintaining order, balancing budgets and overseeing the extraction of raw materials for export. It was never about the provision of public services for citizens... By comparison, stronger links between state and society developed more organically within the modern European state. Here, the state had both grown out of, and been shaped by, its own society. Over centuries, elements of civil society had competed with monarchs and emperors, resulting in first the middle class, and then the working class, gaining empowerment. Each group eventually succeeded in shaping state institutions to reflect their demands. Today, notions of democracy underpin this relationship between state and society, and a complex provision of public services has resulted. This contrasts strongly with Africa, where the modern state arrived almost overnight, and its nature owed little to existing indigenous civil society. Africans were simply left out of any representative relationship between government and people. Consequently, trust and shared political values never developed between the rulers and the ruled. State institutions never sought or gained the respect of the people. This was a situation that did not bode well for a successful interaction between the state and society in post-colonial Africa.

Essentially, since colonialism was about control and expropriation, bureaucracy and authoritarianism and absence of legal-rational institutions, its creation in form of independent Africa had to be a replica of itself.

Centralization of Political Structure

As soon as independence was achieved, those who inherited the colonial political system began to subvert the will of the people by the over-centralization of the state organs, thereby ruling through fear and coercion. Many had no legitimate basis to continue to be in office. Legitimacy in governance is based on trust, respect, the rule of law and social contract. It was indeed legitimacy based on legal-rational government that was supposed to be the driving force of political development. This means that the focus of governance ought to be the citizen and his welfare needs. In this structure, political officers should officiate impersonally, putting the state's interest above their own.

According to Alex Thompson (2004:108), "a bureaucratic culture of public service overrules any ideas officials may harbour about using state institutions for their own private gain". In exchange for this rational system of administration, the citizens obey state laws and pay taxes. But as it turned out to be in Africa after independence, these time-tested principles were asphyxiated from the very beginning and the continent gyrated steadily towards personal rule and political hegemony. In these circumstances, political institutions like the legislature, bureaucracy, judiciary and political parties exist only in name but are functionless thereby denying, the state the platform of checks and balances required for a healthy democratic set up. Where the political parties, for instance, are not allowed to exist on the pages of newspaper, they are out rightly outlawed. The character of such regimes is captured pointedly by David S. Sorenson (2008:97) who in his analysis of the Middle East writes:

> Authoritarian regimes still exist worldwide despite the global trend toward democratization. Their characteristics include rule by a single leader with almost unbridled power, often within a single political party... authoritarian regimes are systems with total rule by a single individual or small group, with only symbolic opposition. They may have parliaments, but the ruling party appoints the legislators; they have a court system, but their function is to uphold the dictates of the ruler rather than to dispense objective justice; there may be a news media, but the ruling party owns it. Opposition is illegal in autocracies, so political opposition is usually underground or out of the country. Open public discourse is strictly limited, and criticism against the regime or its policies can bring swift retribution by security forces...Constitutions may exist, but there is no means of enforcing their provisions.

In the GoG, Ghana under Kwame Nkrumah, Cote d'Ivoire under Houphouet-Boigny, Liberia under William Tolbert and Guinea under Sekou Toure all exemplify countries where only the parties of the rulers were tolerated. In Ghana, the Preventative Detention Act was passed by the Parliament in 1958 to muzzle the opposition and the Press. They were accused of subvertion and quite a number of the citizens were clamped into detention. In Cote d'Ivoire and Guinea, oppositionists were driven into exile.

In countries that experienced the political nightmare of personal rule and centralization of the state through single-party structures, the usual justification hinged on; national security. The argument by leaders in these countries was that multi-party activities were socially divisive; they engendered separatist tendencies and at times irredentism and secession. In other words, as Africa is composed of ethnically divided societies, attempts at unity and nation building required unanimity of purpose and consensus as against competition in the sense of the Western World. Houphouet-Boigny of Cote d'Ivoire went the extra mile of declaring that opposition did not exist in his country (Thompson, 2010).

The effects of personal rule and political hegemony constitute the major challenge of the crisis of post-coloniality in Africa. These include absence of the rule of law, inefficiency, ostentation, corruption, lack of legitimacy, factionalism, schisms, purges, coups and the weak-state syndrome. Typical examples included the personal decision of Houphouet-Boigny to move the capital of Cote d'Ivoire from Abidjan to his home village of Yamoussoukro; the movement of political leaders in private jets, motorcades, expensive vehicles and the use of palatial residences and offices and refusal to be bound by formal rules regardless of the fact that these rules were made by them (Thompson, 2004).

With regards to the rule of law, Aristotle once opined that whoever refuses to obey the law was either a god or a beast; the person was either above the state or below it (Asirvatham & Misra, 2006). In most African states, the leaders constitute themselves into gods and their political contractors into beasts. The end results come into the form of state terrorism and weak state syndrome. Commenting on elite security strategies in weak states and their consequences, Richard Jackson writes:

> Weak state elites typically employ a mix of internal and external strategies aimed at regime survival. Internally, elites employ a mix of carrot and stick approaches to challengers. First, lacking both infrastructural capacity and wider social legitimacy, weak state elites are often forced to rely on coercive power and state intimidation to secure continued rule. This entails creating or expanding the security forces, spending large sums of the national income on military supplies and using violence and intimidation against real and perceived opponents of the regime. This is perhaps the most common survival strategy of weak state elites, and it is reflected in the appalling human rights record seen in a great many developing countries. Typically, regimes try to suppress opposition through the widespread use of

torture and imprisonment, assassination and extra-judicial killings, disappearances, the violent suppression of political expression, forced removals, destruction of food supplies and in extreme cases, genocide, mass rape and ethnic cleansing. A key dilemma for elites is that the instruments of coercion-the armed forces-can themselves develop into a threat against the regime. For this reason, elites sometimes deliberately weaken the armed forces by creating divisions, establishing elite units such as presidential guards and fomenting rivalry between different services. Such divide and rule strategies are also used against other potential sources of opposition, such as state bureaucracies, religious groups, traditional authorities and opposition politicians. From this perspective, the deliberate undermining or hollowing out of state institutions can be a rational and effective means of preventing the rise of potential centres of opposition to the regime. On the other side of the ledger, elites sometimes find it easier to try and create positive inducements for supporting the regime. Typically, this entails the establishment of elaborate patronage systems, whereby the state elites and various social groups are joined in complex networks of mutual exchange. In this way, corruption acts as a form of redistribution and a means of integrating the state in an informal power structure...

This picture of **regime security**, as against **national security** painted by Jackson, typifies politics in almost all the states of the Gulf of Guinea.

Triggers of Military Coups d'état

Since independence, military coups and violent overthrow of governments have been the recurring decimal in the GoG. In some countries, the military had once threatened to seize power while in others there had been series of successful coups and counter coups. While Cape Verde and Equatorial Guinea recorded just one coup, Nigeria and Ghana had more than a dozen coup attempts, successful coups and countercoups. In the Nigerian political history, there have been twelve cases.

The frequency of coups in Africa forces George Ball, a US diplomat to pen down cynical remarks in his memoirs, thus: "During the years I was in the State Department, I was awakened once or twice in a month by a telephone call in the middle of the night announcing a coup d'état in some distant capital with a name like a typographical error" (Thompson, 2004:131). Notwithstanding, the hyperbole that underlines the remarks; the GoG experienced military regimes in the twentieth century than civilian governments.

Some of the names like typographical errors in the memoir of Ball include Lome; Togo (Gnassingbe Eyadema), Lagos; Nigeria (Kaduna Nzeogwu), Accra; Ghana (Akwasi Amankwaa Afrifa), Kampala; Uganda (Idi Amin Dada) and Monrovia; Liberia (Samuel Kakan Doe). In most cases, these characters, many of whom were mixtures of middle-ranking, junior and non-commissioned officers, "would seize government buildings and communication centres, and then detain the President and the cabinet or force them to flee. Once these symbols of the state had been captured,- the coup plotters would then use the radio to broadcast to the nation" (Thompson, 2010:135). Ruth First adds that the coup template in Africa was as simple as: "Get the keys to the armoury; turn out the barracks; take the radio station, the post office and the airport; (and) arrest the person of the President" (First, 1970:4). In some cases, the person of the President or Head of State was either killed in, or assassinated before, the coup exercise.

A number of reasons and theories have been put forward as possible causes of coups in Africa. The reasons range from corruption to ineptitude and nepotism (Ademoyega, 1981). These complaints had indeed become familiar refrain and coup anthem in Africa. On the theories of military intervention in the continent, at least two schools of thought are dominant.

The first group of scholars, who are mainly environmentalists like Samuel Huntington and S. E. Finer, places emphasis on the state's socio-economic environment (Finer, 1962; Huntington, 1968). According to them there is the likelihood that coups would occur in states that lack institutionalized political cultures and also experience at the same time development challenges and deep social division (Thompson, 2010). Kwame Nkrumah's government was toppled in 1966 as a result of the falling cocoa price than any other reason. Similarly, the Shehu Shagari regime in Nigeria was brought down in 1983 by the plummeting price of crude oil.

The economic misfortunes in these two countries fuelled other latent forces and prepared the environment for the coups.

The second school of thought, represented by scholars like Morris Janowitz, dwells so much on the organizational ability and character of the military institution (Janowitz, 1974:77). Pointing to the patriotism, discipline, professionalism and cohesion found in the military service, Janowitz argues that, these factors inspire the military to sack civilian governments which are seen as inept, corrupt and sensuous. The positions of these two schools, though theoretically sound are not empirically anchored on facts; for in the final analysis the absence of legal-rational institutions since colonial days account for the weak capacity of states in Africa, state of underdevelopment and political instability. By not creating and strengthening such institutions in the continent, the African political actors unwittingly allow the military to become the sole guardian of the state and any crisis of confidence in the system easily results in coup d'états instead of negotiation, dialogue and trade-offs. Nigeria, DR Congo and Ghana are cases in point.

Cold War Diplomacy and Sustenance of Despotism in the Gulf of Guinea

The Cold War diplomacy affected politics in the GoG significantly. The war raged between 1945 and 1991. Almost all states in Africa achieved independence between 1955 and 1975 which was the significant period of the Cold War. As global politics were dominated by the Cold War there was no where that Africa, though relatively new in international affairs, could have isolated itself or be insulated from the Cold War diplomacy.

This explains why, having been locked in a nuclear stalemate in Europe, the superpowers, the US and the USSR, advanced elsewhere to gain strategic advantage. Therefore, on account of the pursuit of the goals of geo-politics, Cold War rivalries were extended to Africa, Latin America, Asia, Australia and indeed all parts of the world. For African politics and international relations, the consequences were quite dramatic and disastrous.

For Washington and Moscow, Cold War was a strategic game which was symbolized by series of moves and countermoves on the diplomatic chessboard aimed at undermining the opposite number. The US worked with her allies to undermine the USSR and the USSR equally worked with her allies to affect the value of the US in the international system. Though the two never fought directly as they only engaged in Cold War, hot and proxy wars were fought across the continents for strategic gains.

In Africa, the Cold War era marked the second scramble for, and partition of, the continent. The disintegration of the state system in the Horn of Africa and the Great Lake regions-particularly in the Democratic Republic of Congo-is the sad aftermath of the Cold War diplomacy in Africa. In the GoG in particular, the USSR forged fraternal links with the radical states of Ghana, Guinea and Mali and later the Marxist-Leninist state of Angola (Karnet, 1974; Albright, 1980; Thompson, 2004; 2010). With time, it gained access to a network of airfields and seaports across Africa. On the immediate gains, Alex Thompson (2010:159) writes:

> This advanced the Soviet Union's Cold War capabilities considerably. Flights out of Conakry in West Africa, for example, enabled Moscow to monitor Western shipping in the Atlantic, while defence facilities in Somalia, and then in Ethiopia, enhanced Soviet naval operations in the Indian Ocean.

The US also selected a number of African states as allies. These included the Democratic Republic of Congo, Morocco, Ethiopia, Somalia and Kenya. In the GoG, Congo was of particular interest to the US.

The impact of the Cold War diplomacy on African politics was quite negative especially in the sensitive areas of nation-building and political development. The USSR paid rent in the facilities it possessed in the continent through supply of arms. The value of arms supply to Africa rose from US$150 million in the 1960s to US$2.5 billion in the 1970s and US$2.7 billion in 1980. By 1980, the US had contributed $1.6 billion worth of weapons to Africa. Weapons are instruments of conflicts, crimes, conflict resolution and foreign policy.

In Africa, weapons were used in the Cold War era to create new conflicts and to strengthen the old ones. Even efforts to use weapons for purposes of conflict resolution had the effect of expanding the scale of original conflicts and creating more crises in the process especially as the interests of patrons had to be accommodated as well.

Politically, weapons were used to subvert the will of the people by creating and sustaining despots through coup d'état and regime-change. In 1960 in the DR Congo, the US directed its might against Prime Minister Patrice Lumumba who was labelled a communist by the American Central Intelligence Agency (CIA). The US activity in the Congo crisis led to the assassination of Lumumba and the emergence of Mobutu Sese Seko. Throughout his thirty years' rule, Mobutu monopolized politics of his country and violated the rights of his countrymen. But he was not alone in such evil practices. All countries in the GoG and indeed Africa during the Cold War era had despots as either civilian or military heads Heads of States who were supported by the NATO and the Warsaw Pact.

Post-Cold War Democratic Transformation and Hiccups

The Cold War politics ended in 1991, when the political reforms of the Soviet President, Mikhail Gobachev, made him the first target of being a President without a country. The Soviet Union disintegrated and split into separate sovereign states and its grip on the socialist states of Eastern Europe was naturally abandoned.

This marked the commencement of a New World Order; a global atmosphere devoid of proxy wars and intolerant of authoritarian regimes. In Africa, the various despotic regimes lost the privilege of diplomatic and military support. Jeffery Lefebrvre has captured graphically the import of the New World Order for Africa thus: "The days of right-wing and left-wing dictatorial regimes being lavished with aid and excused for their internal excesses were over" (see Thompson, 2010:166).

The New World Order laid the foundation for democratic transformation in Africa. In 1990, a year before the collapse of the Soviet empire, Western powers and International Institutions had started to agitate for democratic transformation in Africa. In June of that year, the British Foreign Minister, Douglas Hurd commented on the need for good governance in Africa. International institutions like the International Monetary Fund (IMF) and the World Bank made democratic reforms as conditions for loans and financial assistance.

In a similar vein, François Mitterrand, French President warned that French aid would not go to, "regimes that have an authoritarian approach without accepting an evolution towards democracy" (Olsen, 1997:306). To show its seriousness, France suspended development aid to the Congo in 1991 and Togo in 1993 because they refused to embark on the process of democratic reforms. Therefore, as Africa depends largely on foreign aid and diplomatic support from democratic countries, it had to succumb to the seemingly diplomatic blackmail to democratize.

But the democratic transformation in the post-cold war Africa is a reincarnation of the democratic practices of the immediate post-independence era; if not worse than it. It is largely cosmetic; indeed a façade. It is typified by the careful manipulation of democratic political process by the elite for private gains. Commenting on the new strategy which is a character of the weak state syndrome, Richard Jackson (2007:154) writes:

> Due to the external vulnerability, a great many weak states have been forced by international donors-developed states and international financial institutions (IFIs) such as the IMF and World Bank-to begin the process of democratic reform. A great many weak state rulers have successfully managed the transition of multiparty democracy and retained control of the state, primarily through careful manipulation of internal opponents and external perceptions. Typically, this involved monopolizing and controlling the media, the cooption of opponents, setting up fake parties to split the vote, gerrymandering, ballot-rigging, candidate and elector disqualification and manipulating the electoral rules. Constructing the outward appearance of democracy without any substantial concessions can actually function to bolster regime security by giving it a degree of international legitimacy.

From Nigeria, the most populous of the Gulf States to Cape Verde, the least populous, the trend is the same: manipulation of democratic political processes. This makes the states of the GoG to be semi or quasi-democratic.

Foreign Relations

The states of the GoG maintain cordial relations among themselves at the diplomatic and multilateral levels. Almost all of them have established diplomatic relations with each other in order to strengthen their unity, at least symbolically. Additionally, they have created for themselves a number of inter-state organizations to further their socio-political, economic and diplomatic interests. The motives for the creation of these institutions and organizations are multifarious and divergent. Speaking generally, five of such motives are:

1. Belief in Pan Africanism and African unity;
2. The imperatives of maintaining and consolidating previous historical ties;
3. Diplomatic reasons and security needs;
4. Constraints of smallness of size, and
5. The necessity of securing foreign aid.

On the basis of historical ties, for instance, the strength of the Mano River Union (MRU) derives partly from the similarities in the history of the founding of Liberia and Sierra Leone and, more importantly, from the traditional ties and substantive movements of people in the area now broken into Liberia, Guinea and Cote d'Ivoire (Akpan, 1986).

Outside the GoG and the African continent, the Gulf States equally maintain strong ties with their former colonial masters. Therefore, France, Britain, Portugal and the Western World generally have close relationship with the states of the GoG and are also their trading partners. Generally, table 4.2 shows the characteristics of Africa's external relations since independence.

Table 4.2: Africa's External Relations since Independence

COLD WAR PERIOD	
The Soviet Union	* Limited strategic interests on the continent * Sympathetic to national liberation and socialist ideologies * Seeking military bases on the continent * Provides limited amount of aid * Sells/provides large numbers of weapons to allies

	* Large commitment of weaponry to several hot-spots (e.g. Angola, Ethiopia) * Assistance to 'national liberation' movements in southern Africa (e.g. ANC, SWAPO, ZANU) * However, no large-scale or long-term involvement on the continent
United States of America	* Limited strategic interests on the continent * Seeking allies on continent who would help to contain communism * Willing to overlook authoritarian behaviours of anti-communist allies (e.g. Zaire and South Africa) * Provision of aid to allies * Some assistance to 'client' rebel groups
United Kingdom	* Relations largely confined to consolidating and expanding economic interests
COLD WAR PERIOD	
France	* Continued very close contacts with ruling elites * Underpins monetary system in ex-colonies * Intervenes militarily to defend allies * Large aid donations * Strong economic links * Expands influence in former non-French colonial countries
Ramifications of the 'New World Order'	* End of proxy wars * Africa strategically downgraded * Decrease in aid donations * Political conditions attached to aid * Cold War clients lose support * United States attempts humanitarian intervention, but hesitant after Somalia debacle * France continues to seek to expand influence on the continent * Britain undertakes small-scale humanitarian intervention in Sierra

	Leone * China builds strong diplomatic relations to secure economic resources * Africa's international affairs become more 'Africanized'

Source: Alex Thompson. 2010. *An Introduction to African Politics*. London: Routledge: 176

During the Cold War period, Ghana, Guinea and Angola maintained special relations with the socialist countries while other states in the Gulf were extremely pro-West in their foreign policies. After the Cold War, ideological considerations took the back seat in the choice of friends; national interest took the front seat. For these reasons, the Gulf states, like other states in Africa, befriend China and allow her access to their resources. These resources include oil and gas, solid minerals and forest products.

China is the major partner in oil exploration and production in the GoG. The countries they operate in include Angola, Nigeria, Gabon, Congo-Brazzaville, Equatorial Guinea, Gabon and Cameroon. The country is also involved in extracting timber from Cameroon and the Congo basin and iron ore from Gabon. Angola became China's single largest supplier of petroleum products since 2006. Continentally, Beijing is now Africa's most strategic commercial partner; Africa is a destination for its manufactured goods.

In 2006, the continent imported goods to the value of US $26 billion from China, thus constituting the largest volume of trade from one country. China has about 1000 companies operating in Africa. But there are several disadvantages that Africa has with respect to its relations with China. For one, China has the worst records in safety, health and environmental matters in its industrial operations and these have been taken to the countries where they operate in Africa. Secondly, their products are of low quality; though cheap. Thirdly, since African manufacturers cannot compete with the flood of these cheap Chinese goods, they have to fold up. The Nigerian textile industry is a case in point where more than 300,000 jobs are lost as a result of cheap textile goods from China.

The direct consequence of these exports is closure of the Nigerian factories. Fourthly, as China is busy propping up despotic regimes in Africa with cheap loans, democratic reforms are delayed while continuous violations of human rights go unabated. Lastly, China's long term strategic interest is to shift its excess human load to Africa through emigration policy linked to its economic deals with Africa. For instance, in most transactions, 70 percent of the work force must be Chinese while Africans constitute the dregs of 30 percent. Even at that, the plum jobs are the prerogative of the Chinese while the Africans make do with menial leftover. This is the worst form of human exploitation and communist imperialism in the continent.

Beyond state actors outside Africa, States of the GoG relate well with the non-state actors in the international system. These include the UN, the Commonwealth of Nations, the World Bank, the International Monetary Fund (IMF) and the Federation of International Football Association (FIFA).

Further Reading

Akpan, O. E. 1989. *Militarization and Regional Security: A Case Study of the Horn of Africa.* MSc. Dissertation, University of Jos.

Albright, D. E. 1980. *Africa and International Communism.* London: Macmillan Press.

Bratton, M. and N van de Walle. *Democratic Experiment in Africa: Regime Transitions in Comparative Perspective.* Cambridge: Cambridge University Press.

Bayart, J. F. 1993. *The State in Africa: The Politics of the Belly.* London: Longmans Ltd.

Clapham, C. 1985. *Third World Politics: An Introduction.* London: Routledge.

Davidson, B. 1964. *Old Africa Rediscovered.* London: Oxford University Press.

Duffy, J. 1959. *Portuguese Africa.* Harvard University Press.

Decalo, S. 1976. *Coups and Army Rule in Africa: Studies in Military Style.* London: Yale University Press.

Fage, J. D. 1963. *An Atlas of African History.* Arnold.

Foltz, W. J. and H. S. Bienen. eds. 1985. Arms and the African: Military Influences on Africa's International Relations. New Haven: Yale University Press.

Glickman, H. 1995. Ethnic Conflict and Democratization in Africa. Atlanta: African Studies Association.

Goran, H. and M. Bratton. eds. 1992. *Governance and Politics in Africa.* Boulder: Lynne Reinner.

Greenberg, J. H. 1963. *Languages of Africa.* London: Indiana University Press.

Huntington, S. P. and J. M. Nelson. 1976. *No Easy Choice: Political Participation in Developing Countries.* Cambridge: Harvard University Press.

Huntington, S. P. 1991. *The Third Wave: Democratization in the Late Twentieth Century.* Norman: University of Oklahoma Press.

Jackson, R. and C. G. Rosberg. 1982. *Personal Rule in Black Africa: Prince, Autocrat, Prophet, Tyrant.* Berkeley: University of California Press.

Kanet, R. E. 1974. *The Soviet Union and the Developing Nations.* Baltimore: The John Hopkins University Press.

Murdoc G. P. 1959. *Africa: Its Peoples and their Culture History.* New York, McGraw-Hill.

Ottaway, M. 1982. *Soviet and American Influence in the Horn of Africa.* New York: Praeger Books.

Rothchild, D. and N. Chazan. eds. 1998. *The Precarious Balance: State and Society in Africa.* Boulder: Westview.

Stockwell, J. 1978. *In Search of Enemies: A CIA Story.* London: Andre Deusch.

Section II

The Countries of the Gulf of Guinea in the Central African Sub-Region

Cameroon, DR Congo, Equatorial Guinea, Gabon, Republic of Congo and São Tomé and Principe

CHAPTER FIVE

Cameroon

The Republic of Cameroon (République du Cameroun) is a Central African nation in the GoG bordered by Nigeria, Chad, the Central African Republic, the Republic of Congo, Equatorial Guinea and Gabon. It covers an area of about 475, 000 square kilometres and has a population of about 16 million people. It is ethnically diverse and its population is among the most urban in Central Africa. Its largest city which is also its economic nerve centre is Doula while Yaoundé is the capital. The important towns in Cameroon include Nkongsamba, Bafoussam, Bamenda, Maroua and Kumba.

The country's name is derived from Rio dos Cameróes, meaning the River of Prawns. This was the name given to the Wouri River estuary by Portuguese explorers of the fifteenth and sixteenth centuries. Cameróes was also used to designate the river's neighbouring mountains. Until the late nineteenth century, English usage confined the term the Cameroons to the mountains, and the estuary was called the Cameroon's River or, locally, the Bay (Encyclopaedia Britannica, 1999). In 1884, the Germans extended the word Kamerun to their entire protectorate. The particulars of Cameroon in English and French languages are ***Cameroon*** and ***Cameroun*** respectively.

Most of the coastline in Cameroon is low, with swamps, creeks and lagoons, but near the Cameroun Mountain,

Fig. 5.1: Political Map of Cameroon

which is an active volcano of over 4,000 metres high, there are steep cliffs. Inland from the coastal plain, most of the country is a plateau between 400 and 900 metres high, but the valleys of the main rivers, such as the Voum and the Sanaga, are lower. In the north-west are the volcanic Adamawa Highlands, which are over 2,000 metres high. The valley of the Upper Benue River and the extreme north near Lake Chad are low-lying areas, which are swampy in the rainy season.

In the coastal areas the range of monthly temperatures during the year is small, and there is an average rainfall of about 4000 millimetres a year, with no long dry season. The vegetation is thick rain-forest, which becomes open woodland and then grassland as the land rises. In the north, average rainfall decreases to below 1000 millimetres a year, with a long dry season, a greater range of temperatures, and an open savanna vegetation. The high plateaux of Adamawa are cool, and covered with grassland without trees. Mount Cameroon which is 4069 metres high, near the coast is the highest elevation in the country. The main rivers are the Benue, Nyong and Sanaga.

The People

Cameroon has about two hundred ethnic groups. There are, however, three main, linguistic groups: the Bantu-speaking people of the South, the Sudanic-speaking people of the north, and the semi-Bantu speaking people of the west.

The earliest inhabitants of Cameroon were the Pygmies, locally known as the Baguielli, Bakas and Babinga. They lived and still inhabit the forests of the south and eastern provinces. They have been hunters and gatherers for thousands of years. The Bantu came to the Cameroons from Equatorial Africa. They originated in the Cameroonian highlands. The first group that invaded the country were the Maka, Ndjem and Duala. In the nineteenth century, they were followed by the Fang and Beti peoples. The Sudanic-speaking people include the Sao of the Adamawa Plateau; the Fulani and the Kanuri. In the late eighteenth and early nineteenth centuries, the Fulani, pastoral Islamists from the western Sahel, conquered most of today's northern Cameroon through evangelization and force. The third ethnic group was the small group of people other than the Bantu-related Bamileke who lived around the lower slopes of the Adamawa Plateau and Mount Cameroon. There are other semi-Bantu-speaking groups like the Tikar who live in the Bamenda region and in the western high plateau.

About forty percent of the population are adherents of the African traditional religion; forty percent are Christians, mainly Roman Catholic while twenty percent are Muslims. Cameroon has a literacy rate of sixty four percent of adult population and life expectancy of 56 (women) and 54 (men). Infant mortality rate is currently 71 per 1000 live births.

History

From the earliest times, Cameroon had established kingdoms and states. The most important of these states was the Sao (So) which emerged in the Lake Chad region in the fifth century. It was established by the Kanuri people, a race formed from inter-marriage between nomadic desert people and the cultivators of the savanna belt (Stride & Ifeka, 1980). The Sao kingdom reached its height in the tenth century after which arose the Kanem-Borno Empire, which destroyed it completely. Kanem-Borno extended over large portions of northern Cameroon and Nigeria.

Islam was a powerful force in the northern and central parts of the Cameroons through conquest, immigration and commerce. Islam was naturally the religion of the Trans-Saharan trade between North and West Africa and this explains why it was a force in northern Cameroon and Nigeria. By the eighteenth century, Islam in northern Cameroon was championed by the Fulani and in the nineteenth century by Usmanu dan Fodio, a Fulani cleric based in Sokoto in Nigeria. The Fulani expansion reached its southernmost point with the conquest of Bamoun, a kingdom in the grassland areas of Cameroon but its influence was ephemeral.

Islam as a powerful external force entered Cameroon through the north while Europeans as another set of influential force entered through the south. Although Hanno, a Carthaginian sailor, had sailed through the Cameroon coast more than 2000 years ago, Fernao do Po, a Portuguese navigator was the first European to set foot on Cameroon in 1472. In the aftermath of Po's visit, many Portuguese came to Cameroon to trade in slaves. Important slave ports included Bimdia and Akwa (Doula).

By the time slave trade was abolished in the nineteenth century, the people turned to staple trade in rubber, palm oil and other cash crops. Within the same period, Portuguese and Dutch influences in the country were replaced by the British and Germans. Side by side with

European influences were the activities of religious missions pioneered by the Presbyterians, Baptists and Roman Catholics.

From 1869, the Germans competed for trade in the coast against the British. German explorers and agents penetrated the interior to establish political and commercial influence. In 1884, Germany declared a protectorate over the Cameroon area which was later extended to Lake Chad. In 1911, it was enlarged by the addition of French Equatorial Africa. After the defeat of Germany in the First World War, Cameroon was divided into British Cameroon (in the West) and French Cameroon (the larger part, in the east) by international agreement. The British Cameroon was administered from, and as part of, Nigeria.

After the Second World War the tempo of African nationalism increased. In 1948, the first nationalist party, the Cameroon Peoples' Union (UPC) was formed to work for the unification of the two parts of the country and for political independence. Despite internal differences among the nationalists, in 1957 Cameroon achieved internal self-government in the East and full independence in 1960.

In British Cameroons, the most critical question was whether to remain in Nigeria or to rejoin Cameroun. In a plebiscite initiated and supervised by the United Nations in 1961, the northern side voted to become a part of Nigeria while the southern area joined the Republic of Cameroon. The two parts, East and West, formed a Federal Republic, with a capital in the East, (Yaounde, which is also the Federal Capital) and another capital in the West (Buea). But in 1972, the old administrative divisions of the two parts were abolished for one unitary state with one capital at Yaounde.

Cameroon is a bilingual state on account of the fact that French had been the main language of the East and English was spoken in the West.

Politics and Structure of Governance

At independence in 1960, Cameroon was ruled by Ahmadou Ahidjo who was in power till 1982. Like all dictators, he centralized power in himself and in the capital city, Yaounde. During his reign, Cameroon became an authoritarian, one-party state without civil rights. As a result of major health problems, Ahidjo resigned in 1982 and handed over power to Paul Biya who until that year was the country's Prime Minister. Ahidjo later regretted handing over power to Biya because the new President refused to see him as his political godfather and the father of modern Cameroon. In the minor struggle for the soul of the only political party, Paul Biya and his coalition won. At the instigation of Ahidjo, coup was attempted on April 6, 1984 but it was never successful. Since then Biya consolidated power and his rulership in Cameroon became excessively draconian. Even when Biya makes pretence to democracy and multi-party system, he remains the soul and brain of the contemporary political system in the country. He won single-candidate elections in 1984 and 1988 and highly flawed multiparty elections in 1992, 1997, 2002 and 2007.

The powers of political officers in Cameroon are derived from the Constitution. By the Constitution of 1961, the country was a federation of states of West Cameroon and East Cameroon. The Constitution of 1972 created the United Republic of Cameroon and a centralized government thereby replacing the federation. The 1984 Constitution changed the name of the country to the Republic of Cameroon.

The Republic of Cameroon has a unicameral National Assembly with 180 members directly elected for a five-year term. Legislative decisions are taken on a simple-majority basis.

Cameroon is divided into 10 provinces which are administered by governors. Each province is further divided into departments.

From 1966, the Republic of Cameroon was officially run as a one-party state. Politics was dominated by the Cameroon National Union as the only political party. In 1985, the party was reformed and renamed the Cameroon Peoples' Democratic Movement. In the 1990 Constitutional amendment, a multi-party system was established and the 1993 Constitutional reforms decentralized administration in the country.

The legal system of Cameroon consists of the Supreme Court as the highest court and other courts such as the Court of Appeal, High Courts and Circuit Courts. In the events of a dispute between the President and the Legislature, it is the duty of the Supreme Court to decide whether such a bill is receivable by the National Assembly. The

Court also gives judgement on appeals in respect of actions of the government and decisions of the Court of Appeal. There is also the Court of Impeachment which passes judgement on the President in case of high treason and on matters of felony on government officials. A Higher Judicial Council of Cameroon guarantees the independence of the judiciary and also acts as a disciplinary body. The body equally advises the President on the nomination of magistrates and judges.

Economy

The pillars of the economy of Cameroon revolve around mining and oil and gas. Until these sectors played prominent roles, the structure of the economy was basically agrarian. Therefore, in the nineteenth and early twentieth centuries, agriculture, forestry and fishing contributed significantly to the GDP. Primary agricultural and forest products provided about thirty percent of total export earnings, with cocoa and coffee being the leading exports. Cocoa is grown mainly in the south: Cameroon ranks as the world's fifth largest producer.

Robusta coffee accounts for eighty-five percent of the coffee crop and is grown in the southern warm and humid parts of the country and in the western high plateau, where Arabica coffee is also grown. Other cash crops include cotton, palm oil, rubber and sugar. The main subsistence crops include yams, coco yams, beans, plantains, bananas, corn, cassava and oil palm in the south and cassava, millet, guinea corn and groundnuts in the north. The country is self-sufficient in food production. Domestic consumption of meat is quite high and livestock is exported to the neighbouring countries such as Nigeria, Equatorial Guinea and the Congo. Hides and skins are equally exported to Nigeria and Equatorial Guinea. About half of the country is forested even though only one-third of the hardwood forest resources are exploited for domestic consumption and export. Commercial fishing accounts for one-third of the total marine catch.

Cameroon is endowed with a lot of mineral resources. These include bauxite and aluminium silicate at Minim-Martap and Ngaoundere at the Adamawa Plateau, iron ore at Kribi, cassiterite at the Darle River valley, limestone at Garoua, gold in East Cameroon and oil and gas located at Rio-del-Ray, including the disputed Bakassi

Peninsula. Most of these natural resources have been exploited. Since 1980, oil has been the mainstay of the economy and the main source of revenue.

Tourism is fast becoming a source of revenue in Cameroon. The country is developing its forest resources for that purpose. Its dense forest and waters are inhabited by different species of lions, elephants, rhinos, buffalos, baboons, antelopes, leopard, red and green monkeys, chimpanzees, mandrills, crocodiles, rodents, bats and uncountable birds ranging from tiny sun-bird to giant hawks and eagles. Cameroon has six national parks. ***Le Parc de Korup*** is the oldest rainforest in Africa and has numerous gorillas, chimpanzees, elephants and leopards. The Waza national park was established for the protection of giraffes and antelopes.

The major developmental challenges in Cameroon revolve around lack of capital for development, foreign debt and the direct participation of government in the running of the industrial sector. However, great efforts have been made to respond to these challenges.

Foreign Relations

The foreign policy of Cameroon, like most African states, is conditioned by its colonial history, its environment and aspirations for economic development. In foreign relations, Cameroon is pro-West and especially pro-French. France has a defence pact with Cameroon and French oil company, ELF, is the major oil company in the country. Most insurance and service companies are French-owned. Although most trade is carried out with the European Union (EU), France is the largest individual trading partner. It supplies about one-third of the country's imports and receives more than one-fourth of the exports.

Cameroon is linked together with many West African countries in a monetary union with a common currency, the CFA (Communatè Fianciere Africaine). The CFA franc is convertible into any currency, but France must approve direct investment by citizens within the franc zone in countries outside of it. France has representatives on the board of directors of the Central Bank of Cameroon.

On account of its bilingual nature and relations with Anglophone Nigeria, Cameroon recently became a member of the Commonwealth of Nations, an international organization made up of Britain and her former colonies.

In its African relations, Cameroon exhibits Pan-Africanist tendencies. It supported the position of the Organization of African Unity (OAU) with respect to apartheid in South Africa, decolonization and African Unity. During the Nigerian Civil War, Cameroon supported Nigeria firmly and refused to toe the line of the French policy for the disintegration of Nigeria (Ede, 1985). Of course, the position of Cameroon on the civil war in Nigeria was understandable. The people of South West Cameroon suddenly woke up to the need to liberate themselves from the grip of the French-speaking north and wanted secession. The success of secession in Nigeria would have strengthened the cause of the people of South West Cameroon.

Further Reading

African Encyclopaedia. 1974. London: Oxford University Press.
Davidson, B. 1964. *Old Africa Rediscovered.* London: Oxford University Press.
Duffy, J. 1959. *Portuguese Africa.* Harvard University Press.
Fage, J. D. 1963. *An Atlas of African History.* Arnold.
Greenberg, J. H. 1963. *Languages of Africa.* London: Indiana University Press.
International Encyclopaedia of the Social Sciences. London: Macmillan.
Murdoc G. P. 1959. *Africa: Its Peoples and their Culture History.* New York, McGraw-Hill.

CHAPTER SIX

Democratic Republic of the Congo

The Democratic Republic of the Congo (Republique Democratique du Congo) which was formerly called Zaire is the largest state in Central Africa, the GoG and indeed sub-Saharan Africa. It has an area of 2.3 million square kilometres. This makes it the second largest nation in Africa after Algeria and the eleventh largest in the world. The country is bigger than the Republics of France, Germany, Norway, Spain and Sweden put together. The DR Congo, as the country is commonly referred to, is the fourth most populous state in Africa after Nigeria, Egypt and Ethiopia. It has a population of about 70 million people. The country borders the Central African Republic and Sudan to the north; Uganda, Rwanda and Burundi in the east; Zambia and Angola to the South and the Atlantic Ocean to the West. It is separated from Tanzania by Lake Tanganyika in the east. The republic has a short 40-kilometre coastline on the Atlantic Ocean at Muanda and the nine-kilometre-wide mouth of the Congo River which opens into the GoG.

DR Congo covers the basins of the Congo River and the rivers that flow into it. It is principally thick forest and wet swamp land, about 400 metres high. The Congo rain forest is the world's second largest rain forest after the Amazon in Brazil. The Congo River is on the whole more than 4000 kilometres long. Its main tributaries are the Ubangi,

Democratic Republic of the Congo

Fig. 6.1: Political Map of the Domocratic Republic of the Congo

Sangha, Aruwimi, Lulonga and the Kasai.

Round the central lowland the ground rises to plateaus between 500 and 1000 metres high in the north, east, and south. The Mitumba Mountains in the south-east rise to above 1500 metres and the Volcanic Virunga Mountains north of Lake Kivu rise above 3000 metres. The country's highest point of 5119 metres high is in the Ruwenzori Mountains. The large lakes in the mountainous country of the east are part of the Rift Valley of East Africa. The republic lies on the Equator, with one-third of the country to the north and two-thirds to the south.

Kinshasa, which is located on the Congo River, is the capital of the DR Congo. Other major cities include Bandundu, Bukavu, Goma,

Kindu, Kisangani and Lumumbashi. The DR Congo has historically been known by different names such as the Congo Free State, Belgian Congo, Congo-Leopoldville, Congo Kinshasa and Zaire.

The country at independence in 1960 was named the Democratic Republic of Congo. In 1971 Mobutu Sese Seko changed it to the Republic of Zaire and in 1997, Laurent-Desire Kabila reverted the name of the country to its official name at independence. The republic derives its name from the Congo River.

The People

DR Congo has about seven hundred languages and dialects but three main linguistic categories and about 250 ethnic groups. The three categories are Pygmy, Bantu and Nilo-Saharan. The Bantu people occupy more than two-third of the country and constitute majority of the population. Before the European presence in the fifteenth century, the Bantu peoples had established kingdoms such as Kongo, Teke, Luba, Pende, Tetela, Songe, Kuba, Lunda and Yaka. Today, the major groups are the Mongo in the centre, Kongo in the West, Luba in south central, Lunda in the south, Bemba in the south east and the Kwango and Kasai in the south west. The Bantu ethnic groups in the north and north east are the Babwa, Bira, Budja, Kumu, Ngala and Rega.

The non-Bantu African groups of Sudanese extraction are found in the north of the country and they include the Abarambo, Azande, Bana and Mangbetu. The Nilotic people live in the north east and they are the Alur, Bari, Kakwa, Logo and Lugbara. The Tutsi who live in the Kivu region are part of the Hamitic peoples from North Africa and Rwanda.

The earliest inhabitants of the forests of Central Africa were the Pygmy people who settled the area since the late Paleolithic period. About one million of these aboriginal populations live in the forests of Kibali and Huri and the regions of Lakes Kivu and Tanganyika and the Luabala, Tshuapa, Sankuru and Ubangi rivers.

French is the official language in DR Congo but there are four national languages to accommodate the interests of the three linguistic categories-Bantu, Nilo-Saharan and Pygmy. The four languages are Kongo, Lingala, Swahili and Tshiluba.

About 70 percent of the population are Christians; 10 percent are Kimbanguists (members of the Church of Christ on Earth by the Prophet Simon Kimbangu); 10 percent are Muslims and the rest are adherents of other sects and beliefs. Life expectancy in DR Congo is 51 years and infant mortality rate is 92 per 1,000 live births.

History

The earliest inhabitants of the area known as DR Congo were the Pygmies. Between the seventh and eighth centuries A.D. Bantu peoples from the present day Nigeria settled and populated the area. The Bantu people of the north, such as the Bangi, Ngala and Bira entered the DR Congo from Cameroon in about 500 AD. Bantu Africa extends from south east Nigeria, especially in the Ibibio-Efik corridor, to the tip of southern Africa in the Republic of South Africa.

With the knowledge of metal working and of relatively advanced agricultural methods, peoples of the Bantu language group had established many kingdoms which lasted for centuries. One of such kingdoms was Kongo which traded with the Portuguese in the fifteenth century. Kongo gave its name to the Congo River from which the country derives its name. At the time it reached its apogee in the sixteenth century, it had expanded to cover the northern part of today's Angola. The Luba kingdom was established on the River Lualaba in the sixteenth century; it later controlled the area between the Kasai and Lake Tankanyika. In the seventeenth century, the kingdom was established by the Kuba people on the Kasai River and became very powerful in the eighteenth century. In what is now Shaba, there was the Lunda Kingdom which survived up till the nineteenth century. All these states traded with themselves and with the Portuguese and Arab merchants. The articles of trade were copper, ivory and slaves.

The first European to visit the Congo was Diego Cao, a Portuguese mariner, who came to the area in 1482. Cao stumbled on the Congo Estuary while searching for a passage linking the Atlantic to the Indian Ocean. Even though the Portuguese were the first Europeans to visit and trade with the people of the area that became the DR Congo, the Belgians ultimately gained the possession of the territory through the personal ambition of their king, Leopold II (1865-1909).

The Belgian king wanted a colony in Central Africa for his country, Belgium, but when his aspirations did not gain the support of his government and people, he still went ahead with his colonial project through private initiatives. Therefore, in his private capacity, he financed the establishment of his own state in Central Africa that was called the Congo Free State. He was able to achieve this feat through the efforts of a British Journalist, Henry Morton Stanley, whom he paid to make treaties with African potentates. In 1885, the state was officially colonized as a personal possession of Leopold II. He had hoped to use the colony for trade in rubber and ivory. In achieving these commercial goals, he was excessively brutal with the inhabitants of the area. After much mis-governance which attracted international protests, the Belgian government in 1908 took over the administration of the state. Katanga (now Shaba) was in 1933 added to the colony.

The Belgian system of colonial rule was very oppressive and inhuman. It was based on the dual policies of centralization and paternalism. The affairs of the colony were directed from Brussels. Until 1957, there were no elections in the country. However, that year elections were held into municipal positions. In 1958, the following year, many political parties sprang up and demanded political independence for the country. After series of riots in January 1959, the Belgian government speedily set up machinery to grant independence to the Congo. Indeed, at the round-table Conference held with Congolese representatives in January and February 1960 in Brussels, the Belgian government fixed the independence of the Congo for June 30, 1960.

Politics and Structure of Governance

DR Congo did not have political stability for up to a week after independence when crisis erupted. The first act of destabilization occurred in July, 1960, when the Force Publique, made up of the army and gendarmerie, mutinied. Closely on the heels of this crisis, the governor of the Katanga province attempted secession; politics became largely ethnicized and deadly; the UN was forced to intervene; Prime Minister Patrice Lumumba, a symbol of African nationalism in the Congo, was murdered in mysterious circumstances and as a consequence of the Cold War politics of the East-West rivalry and to cap it all the country experienced military intervention when Colonel Joseph Desire Mobutu seized power.

But curiously, when Mobutu seized power in September 1960, he ceded the government to Kasavubu who became the President (Kasavubu was the President at independence and Lumumba, the Prime Minister).Cyrille Adoula was made the Prime Minister. The government ruled for three years. In 1964, rebellion started in the Kwilu region and the eastern and north-eastern parts of the country. In another curious move, Moise Tsombe, the governor of the Katanga province and the architect of the Katanga secession was appointed the Prime Minister of the country.

But in 1965, Mobutu, who had become a Lieutenant General, seized power from Tshombe and declared himself President for five years. In 1970, when he had ruled for five years, Mobutu refused to relinquish power to democratically elected government. In yet another curious move that was experienced in the country, he centralized power in himself and got elected unopposed. From that period DR Congo became a one-party state and with Mobutu in power, the country slided steadily into an abyss of despair and uncertainty.

With the end of the Cold War politics coupled with internal protests and external pressures for political reforms, the Mobutu regime in April 1990, accepted the principles of multi-party system and constitutional democracy for the Congo. After about two years of delay, the country in 1992 convened a Sovereign National Conference to determine its future. About 2000 representatives of political parties were involved. The Conference went a step further to give itself a legislative mandate whereby Archbishop Laurent Monsengwo was elected as Chairman and Etienne Tshisekedi as Prime Minister.

Mobutu rejected the exercise and instead created a rival government with its own Prime Minister. This resulted in a political stalemate which was never resolved properly for the next two years. In 1994, DR Congo was affected by the genocide in the neighbouring Rwanda where fleeing rebels used the country as their bases. In October 1996, Laurent-Desire Kabila's armed coalition, the ***Alliance des Forces Democratiques pour la Liberation du Congo-Zaire***

(AFDL), in league with Rwandan and Ugandan armies embarked on a military campaign to oust Mobutu from power. After the breakdown of talks between Mobutu and Kabila in May 1997, Mobutu went into exile. On May 17, 1997, Kabila marched into Kinshasa and declared himself the President of DR Congo.

The Kabila years in power were not markedly different from the Mobutu years in terms of repression, violation of human rights and incidents of political instability. In fact, under him DR Congo was divided into three sections-one controlled by himself; others by Rwanda and Uganda. Rwanda assisted him to get to power and Uganda has over the years been backing a rebel group in the northern axis of the country. The Lusaka Accord of 1999 which sued for ceasefire did not work. On January 16, 2001, Laurent Kabila was assassinated and was succeeded by his son, Joseph Kabila.

The structure of governance in the DR Congo is as chequered as its political system. At independence, the President was the Head of State and Prime Minister the head of government. The President was elected through universal suffrage. During the Mobutu years, a centralized presidential form of government was instituted where the sole party in the country-the Movement Populaire de la Republique, MDR-would present only Mobutu for the electorate to vote for.

Under Laurent Kabila no attempts were made to introduce constitutional reforms, but under his son, Joseph, the country has experimented with some curious constitutional developments. In 2003, a transitional Constitution was instituted with a political system composed of a bicameral legislature; Senate and a National Assembly. The Senate was given the mandate to draft a new Constitution. The executive branch of a 60 - member council was headed by a pentarchy made up of a President and four Vice Presidents. The contraption, which was derisively called *The 1 plus 4 Presidency*, made the President the Commander-in-Chief of the Armed Forces. The transition Constitution also created a judiciary, headed by a Supreme Court.

The Constitution of the Third Republic came into effect in February, 2006. Under the 2006 Constitution, the President is the Head of State and the Prime Minister the head of government. The Prime Minister is to be appointed from the party with the majority at the National Assembly. The legislature is bicameral. The Constitution also creates provincial parliaments with oversight functions over the governors who are elected. The Constitution equally whittles down the power of the Supreme Court by vesting the prerogative of the interpretation of the Constitution on the Constitutional Court. On the basis of the 2006 Constitution, DR Congo had its first multi-party elections since its independence in 1960. In the elections held on July 30, 2006, Joseph Kabila had 45 percent of the votes while his opponent, Jean-Pierre Bemba, Vice President, ex-warlord and son of Congolese billionaire Bemba Saolona, had 20 percent.

The results of the election were disputed and were greeted with street violence. Bemba called for its cancellation which the government responded to by fixing a new date for a new election. Thus on October 26, 2006, a new election was conducted in which Kabila won with 70 percent of the votes. On December 6, 2006, Joseph Kabila was sworn in as the President and on that date the Transition Government came to an end. DR Congo has eleven provinces, each headed by a governor.

Economy

The economic profile of the DR Congo is both impressive and unimpressive. It is impressive in the sense that on account of its resources, mostly natural resources, it is easily the richest country in the world and it is unimpressive in the fact that because of years of conflicts which so far have killed more than six million people and instituted warlordism, the country is the poorest state in the world.

The value of the mineral resources of the DR Congo is worth about $30 trillion which is in excess of the GDP of the American continent. Minerals which are available in the country in superfluous quality and quantity include cadmium, copper, cobalt, industrial and gem-quality diamonds, gold, silver, zinc, tin, manganese, radium, uranium, coal, bauxite, iron ore, cassiterite, platinum, germanium (a brittle element used as a semi conductor) and palladium (a metallic element used as a catalyst and in alloys). They are found in the south-eastern region of Katanga.

It is instructive to note that mineral resources in the DR Congo are found in almost all regions. In the Kivu region there are columbotantalite (a natural oxide), wolframite (a source of tungsten), cassiterite, beryl (a mineral containing beryllium and aluminium), gold and monazite (a phosphate of the cerium metals and thorium). Around Lake Kisu the minerals include carbonic, nitrogen, natural gases and a vast reserve of methane. In the Kasai regions (Kasai-Oriental and Kasai-Occidental) there are industrial diamonds, jewellery diamonds and iron ore. The Bas-Congo region has gold, bauxite and petroleum resources while the Haut-Congo region has coal, iron ore and gold. The Equator region contains gold, monazite and diamonds while the Bandundu region has diamond deposits. The limestone deposits occur throughout the DR Congo and they are adjudged to be of the best quality in Africa.

Most of these minerals are strategic and critical to the industrial economies. Take cobalt for example. It has both industrial and military uses. Used as superalloys, cobalt is very critical in the making of jet engine parts. It is also used in magnetic alloys and in cutting and wear-resistant materials such as cemented carbides. In the chemical industry, cobalt is used as catalysts for petroleum and chemical processing, drying agents for paints and inks, ground coat for porcelain enamels, decolorizers for glass and ceramics and pigments for ceramics, paints and plastics. Cobalt therefore is critical to the establishment of many industries and creation of millions of jobs. DR Congo has over 80 percent of the world's reserves of cobalt. The country also has 70 percent of the world's coltan and about 50 percent of the world's diamond reserves. Coltan is a mineral used in the manufacture of mobile phones. DR Congo is the world's second largest producer of colobine-tantalite which is a key raw material in the manufacture of satellite and telecommunications products.

Sadly, these minerals, as typical lootable wealth, are largely looted by warlords. Since independence, they have been providing powerful incentives for conflicts, irredentism and secessions. These local problems have always been fuelled by industrial nations and neighbouring states; each aspiring for a share in the Kinshasha scramble. These states are the US, Russia, Britain, Japan, India, Brazil, China, France, Rwanda, Uganda and South Africa. Regardless of the unfortunate state of the country's mining business, it still accounts for 70 percent of the national budget and about 80 percent of total exports.

By the time that the DR Congo achieved independence in 1960, it was obviously the second most industrialized economy in Africa after South Africa. It had a productive mining sector and a growing agricultural sector but conflicts and crises have consigned it to the lowest rank in the continent. Its second position has been taken over by Nigeria. In the agricultural sector, the DR Congo has a lot of export crops. They include coffee, rubber, cotton, cocoa, sugar, tea, palm oil, plantain and groundnuts. DR Congo is the fourth largest producer of rubber in the world. Food crops include corn, cassava, legumes, plantain and groundnuts.

There are forest products that are of economic value in the DR Congo. They include timber of various shapes, sizes and quality. The country's forest reserves cover about 60 percent of the DR Congo and constitute the largest in Africa.

Additionally, the river system in the DR Congo is the backbone of the country's economy and transportation. The river basin, which is really the Congo and its tributaries, occupies almost the whole country and an area of nearly 1,000,000 square kilometres. Besides, the river system has the capacity to provide hydroelectric power to the continent of Africa. This is because the country's hydroelectric resources are valued at 15 percent of the world's capacity and over 50 percent of Africa's potential capacity. There are many rapids along the rivers of the Congo system to make these capacities possible. Already the country exports electricity to the neighbouring states like Angola, Burundi and the Republic of the Congo.

Foreign Relations

The DR Congo maintains cordial relations with many states in the international system beginning with its neighbours. These states include the Central African Republic, Congo, Sudan, Uganda, Rwanda, Burundi, Zambia and Angola. Angola is of strategic importance to the DR Congo because all Congo-bound ships must use the Angolan territorial waters of the Congo River. Outside Zambia, the other states surrounding the DR Congo are highly unstable and to that extent the DR Congo cannot be immune to cross-border sparks of political instability and insecurity. This explains why security issues are of priority concern to the DR Congo in its dealing with its neighbours. These security issues have produced series of bilateral and multi-lateral treaties between the DR Congo and its neighbours. For example, in 2004, the country established a Tripartite Commission with Uganda and Burundi to address security matters in the Great Lakes region. When Burundi joined the Commission in 2005, it became known as the Tripartite Plus.

Even though the DR Congo is located in Central Africa, aspirations for enhanced security and rapid development made it to join the Southern Africa sub-regional economic group, the Southern African Development Community (SADC). This membership paid off strategically in August, 1998, when the Angolan, Namibian and Zimbabwean troops intervened on behalf of the Laurent-Kabila government to drive away the Rwandan army that was bent on marching on Kinshasa to oust Kabila. The logic of the intervention of the three states was that it did so to assist a member nation from external attack.

Additionally, the size, strategic location in the centre of the continent of Africa and possession of critical mineral resources have made many state-and non-state actors to be interested in the DR Congo. For these reasons, many states and corporations in the US and Europe have made their presence felt in the country by establishing diplomatic missions and subsidiaries. For instance, the Katanga Mining Corporation, a London-based company owns and operates the Luilu Metallurgical plant, which has a capacity of 175,000 tonnes of copper and 8000 tonnes of cobalt annually, thus making it the world's largest cobalt refinery. Other countries with business interests in the DR Congo include China, France, Japan, Britain, Brazil, Israel, the US, Russia and India.

The DR Congo is a member of the UN, IMF, World Bank and many international institutions. In Africa, it is a member of the AU and NEPAD.

Further Reading

African Encyclopaedia. 1974. London: Oxford University Press.
Chabal, P. and J. P. Daloz. *Africa Works: Disorder as Political Instrument.* Oxford: James Currey.
Davidson, B. 1964. *Old Africa Rediscovered.* London: Oxford University Press.
Duffy, J. 1959. *Portuguese Africa.* Harvard University Press.
Fage, J. D. 1963. *An Atlas of African History.* Arnold.
Greenberg, J. H. 1963. *Languages of Africa.* London: Indiana University Press.
International Encyclopaedia of the Social Sciences. London: Macmillan.
MacGaffey, J. ed. 1991. *The Real Economy of Zaire: The Contribution of Smuggling and other Unofficial Activities to National Wealth.* London: James Currey.
Murdoc G. P. 1959. *Africa: Its Peoples and their Culture History.* New York, McGraw-Hill.
Reno, W. 1998. *Warlord Politics and African States.* Boulder: Lynne Reinner.
Sandbrook, R. 1985. *The Politics of Africa's Economic Stagnation.* Cambridge: Cambridge University Press.
Young, C. and T. Turner. 1985. *The Rise and Decline of the Zairian State.* Madison: University of Wisconsin Press.
Zartman, I. W. 1995. *Collapsed State: The Disintegration and Restoration of Legitimate Authority.* Boulder: Lynne Reinner.

CHAPTER SEVEN

The Republic of the Congo

The Republic of the Congo (Republique du Congo) which has been variously known as the Congo-Brazzaville, the People's Republic of the Congo and the Congo lies astride the Equator in West Central Africa; that is, half of the country lies above the Equator and the other half lies below the Equator. It is bordered to the east and south by the DR Congo, to the west by Gabon, to the north by the Central African Republic and to the northwest by Cameroon. To the southwest, the country shares a common border with the Angolan enclave of Cabinda.

The Congo has a coastline of 160 kilometres long on the Atlantic Ocean. Its total area is 342,000 square kilometres and it has a population of four million. The country's population is concentrated in the south-western part, while the rest of the country is sparsely inhabited. The bulk of the population, more than 70 percent, live in Brazzaville, Pointe-Noire and Dolisie. Congo is about the most urbanized country in Africa. The national capital is Brazzaville which is located on the Congo River. There is a low plain behind the lagoons of the coast, and further inlands there are hills and plateaus rising to a height of above 500 metres. The north of the Congo lies in the valleys of the River Congo and its northerly tributaries. French is the official language in the country while Lingala and Munukutuba are national languages. About 50 percent of the population are adherents of African Traditional Religion. The Christian community is made up of about two-thirds Roman Catholics and one-third Protestants including the Kimbanguists and the Evangelical Church of the Congo. The Muslim population is about 2 percent made up mostly of aliens in Brazzaville and Pointe-Noire. Life expectancy in the Congo is 54 years and infant mortality rate is 80 per 1,000 live births.

The Republic of the Congo

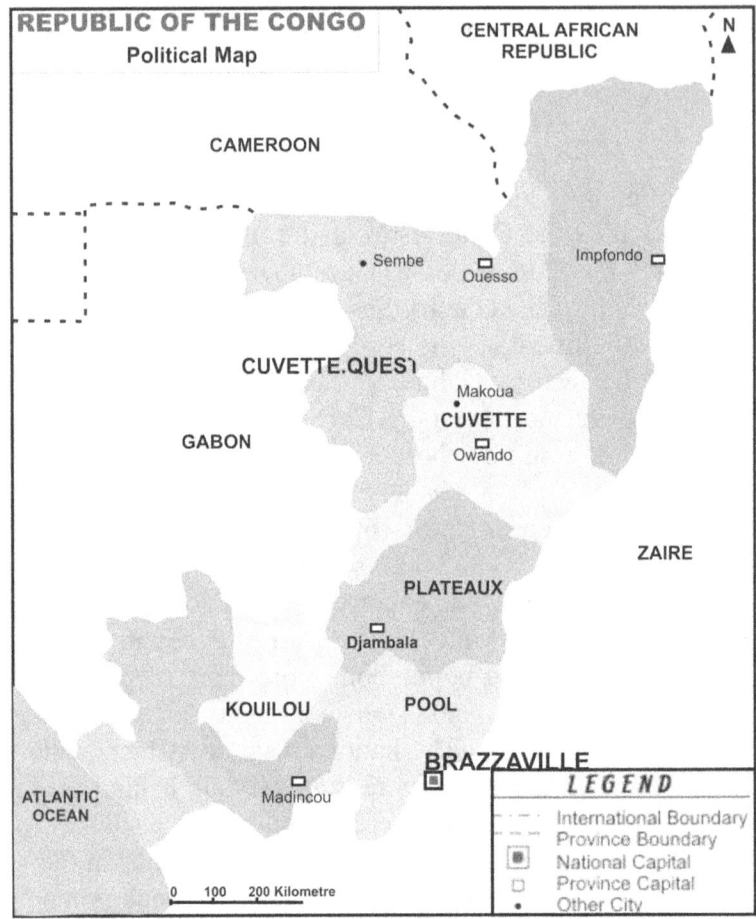

Fig. 7.1: Political Map of Republic of the Congo

The People

The earliest inhabitants of the Congo were the Pygmies. With time they were replaced by more advanced Bantu-speaking peoples such as the Kongo who today constitute half of the people of the Congo. The main Kongo groups are the Bembe, Dondo, Kamba, Kongo, Kougni, Lali, Vili and Yombe. The Ubangi people include the Bonga, Kougou, Likouala, Mboshi and Ngala. The Binga Pygmies live in small groups. All the groups mentioned above, except the Pygmies, speak Bantu languages. However, to facilitate interactions and commerce, two languages, Lingala spoken in the north of the capital and Munukutuba spoken between the capital and the coast, were developed and declared as national languages.

History

The Pygmies who were the early inhabitants of the Congo came from the region of the Ubangi River. The Kongo people who displaced them came from the Kwango in about the fifteenth century. These Bantu peoples lived in agricultural settlements and later established kingdoms. These were the kingdoms of Loango and Bakongo which were vassal states of the Kingdom of the Kongo in today's DR Congo.

In 1482, the Portuguese adventurer, Diego Cao, sighted the mouth of the Congo River and since then Portuguese influence spread throughout the immediate region of the river. Trade in slaves and ivory was carried on through the ports of Cabinda, Loango and Mayumba. Slave trade and the introduction of guns caused wars among the kingdoms and its suppression in the nineteenth century led to their collapse and subsequent replacement with colonial rule.

Though the Portuguese were the first Europeans to transact business in the Congo River, the French gained more and ultimately colonized the region of the river. Between 1877 and 1878, there was competition for the control of the Congo River Basin between Henry Morton Stanley, the agent of the Belgian King, Leopold II, and Pierre Savorgnon de Brazza, a French adventurer and empire dreamer. de Brazza outsmarted Stanley and secured treaties between 1882 and 1891, with the potentates on the right bank of the river who placed their territories under French protection.

These treaties formed the basis of the colonization of the Congo because by agreement with other imperial powers in Africa, France was left to extend its power over the northern side of the Congo. Meanwhile, Stanley concentrated his energy on the other side of the river for King Leopold II. In 1891, the colony of the French Congo was created and in 1910, Brazzaville was made the capital of French Equatorial Africa comprising the Middle Congo (as the modern Congo was called), Gabon, Chad and Central African Republic.

Until 1946, there was not much political agitation for independence. However, when the Congo became an overseas territory of France in 1946, with representatives in the French National Assembly and an elected territorial assembly, the Congolese took a leading part in the political development of the country. Political agitations for independence continued until the *cadre law* (framework law) of 1956 gave it an elected government. In November 1956, the Congo became a republic within the French Community with Fulbert Youlou, a Catholic Priest as the Prime Minister. That same year, the other territories of the French Equatorial Africa also became autonomous members of the French Community and the Middle Congo was now renamed the Congo Republic. On August 15, 1960, the Congo achieved formal independence with Youlou as the first President.

Politics and Structure of Governance

The political parties that agitated for independence in the Congo in the 1950s were ethnicaly-based and ideologically-driven. The two main ones were the *Movement Socialist Africain* (MSA) led by Jacques Opangault and the *Union Democtatique de Defense des Interests Africains* (UDDIA) led by Fulbert Youlou. While the former had socialist orientations, the latter had Christian-democratic traditions and while the former drew strength from the Mbochi people in the north, the later had supporters from the Kongo people in the south. Therefore, from the very onset a north-south dichotomy existed in the political system of the country and this dichotomy was to haunt the country in the years to come.

When Fulbert Youlou was narrowly elected to form a government in 1958, by the National Assembly, accusations of vote-switch and sabotage were alleged. These resulted in rioting and inter-ethnic crises in Brazzaville and Pointe Noire. Though, Youlou became the President of the country at independence in 1960, he was forced to resign in 1963, by a coalition of opposition forces and labour unions. The military reigned briefly and handed over power to a civilian regime headed by Alphonse Massamba-Debat. The Debat presidency drove the country into the Marxist orbit and to give expression to this desire, just one party with Marxist flavour was formed. This was the ***Movement National de la Revolution*** (MNR). This political manoeuvre did not stop his regime from being toppled by Captain Marien Ngouabi in August 1968. Curiously Ngouabi took steps to advance the country more towards socialism and he underlined this importance by renaming it in 1969 the People's Republic of the Congo.

On March 18 1977, Ngouabi was assassinated and Colonel Joachim Yhomi-Opang was made the new President. He formed a new ruling party for the country, the ***Parti Congolais du Travail*** (PCT) to replace the MNR. On February 5 1979, the PCT accused Yhomi-Opango of corruption and high-handedness and on the strength of these removed him from office. He was promptly replaced with Colonel Denis Sassou-Nguesso, the Vice President and Defence Minister. Meanwhile, Yhomi-Opango was placed under arrest and charged with treason and was stripped of all powers, rank and possessions.

Sassou-Nguesso introduced a new Constitution in July, 1979, which attempted to construct a Marxist-Leninist society in the Congo. The socialist system prevailed in the country until the end of the Cold War in 1991, when attempts were made to deconstruct socialism and introduce multi-party system. In the presidential elections of August 1992, Sassou-Nguesso conceded defeat to Professor Pascal Lissouba who was sworn into office on August 31, 1992. Between 1992 and 1996, the Congo political system experienced low-level stability but this was violated in 1997 through the instrumentality of presidential elections. The elections were marked by irregularities, tension and violence. When President Lissouba attempted to arrest his key rival,

Sassou-Nguesso, it led to a brief civil war. What compounded the problem was the invasion of Congo by Angola on behalf of Sassou-Nguesso in October 1997, and an immediate fallout of the invasion was the declaration of Sassou-Nguesso as the President of the country. Political crises continued unabated and even when Ex-President Lissouba and key members of his government were exiled and later sentenced in absentia to 30 years imprisonment, Congo did not know peace.

In 2001, a new Constitution was drafted for the country and in January 2002, it was approved in a national referendum. Under the 2002 Constitution, presidential elections were held in March 2002, in which Sassou-Nguesso was declared the winner.

The 2002 Constitution, provides for a seven-year presidential term which is limited to a maximum of two sequential terms. The country has a bicameral legislature whose members serve for 5 years. The judicial system has courts of Accounts and Budgetary Discipline, Courts of Appeal, the Constitutional Court and the Supreme Court. The country is divided into 10 Departments which are further subdivided into districts.

Economy

The Republic of the Congo is rich in mineral resources which also form the bulk of its exports. These resources include petroleum, potash (potassium chloride), gold, diamonds, lead, zinc, limestone, copper, iron ore, uranium, phosphates and natural gas. The potash deposits and oil and gas are located in the region of Pointe Noire. The Congo has the largest reserve of potash in the world. Petroleum accounts for about 90 percent of the country's export earnings. The nation's cash crops include cocoa, palm oil and kernel, tobacco, coffee and sugar. Food crops produced in the country are cassava, banana, cotton, rice, sugar, maize, groundnuts and forest products. The Congo also exports plywood and lumber.

Until the discovery of oil in the 1960s, forest products accounted for more than 60 percent of the country's total exports. Most of the Congo is covered with tropical rain forest. The Congo is the world's largest producer of limba (hard wood; terminalia superba) and the second largest producer of okume (soft wood).

Foreign Relations

Until 1991, Congo maintained cordial relations and alliance system mainly with the USSR, Eastern Europe, Angola and several socialist-inclined states. At the same time, it was a member of the OAU (now AU) and the Non-Aligned Movement. Congo is a member of the UN and its institutions, the Central African Economic and Monetary Community (CEMAC), the Economic Community of Central African States (CEEC), the Central African Customs and Economic Union (UDEAC), the African Development Bank (ADB) and the INTERPOL. In 2006, the country provided a one-year Chairmanship position of the AU and in 2006 - 2007 it held a seat on the UN Security Council.

Further Reading

African Encyclopaedia. 1974. London: Oxford University Press.
Davidson, B. 1964. *Old Africa Rediscovered.* London: Oxford University Press.
Duffy, J. 1959. *Portuguese Africa.* Harvard University Press.
Fage, J. D. 1963. *An Atlas of African History.* Arnold.
Greenberg, J. H. 1963. *Languages of Africa.* London: Indiana University Press.
International Encyclopaedia of the Social Sciences. London: Macmillan.
Murdoc G. P. 1959. *Africa: Its Peoples and their Culture History.* New York, McGraw-Hill.

CHAPTER EIGHT

Equatorial Guinea

The modern Republic of Equatorial Guinea (Republica de Guinea Equatorial) is one of the modern states of Guinea Coast. The country which was formally called Spanish Guinea was a colony of Spain. It consists of Rio Muni (also known as Mbini), on the western coast of Africa and several islands in the GoG which include Bioko (formerly Fernando Po), Corisco, Great Elobey (Elobey Grande), Little Elobey (Elobey Chico) and Annobon. The Republic has a total area of 28,051 square kilometres.

Mainland Equatorial Guinea has an area of 26,117 square kilometres and is bounded by Cameroon to the north and Gabon to the east and south. Corisco has an area of 16,000 square kilometres and the Great and Little Elobey measure less than three square kilometres. Bioko (formerly Fernando Po) which is the largest island measures 2,018 square kilometres. Annobon, which is an isolated fragment of the republic and which is a volcanic island, is about eighteen square kilometres in size. It is about 150 kilometres southwest of the island of São Tomé in São Tomé and Principe and about 644 square kilometres southwest of Bioko.

Equatorial Guinea has a population of about half a million people and the capital is Malabo on Bioko. Bata is the administrative capital of the mainland. Bioko is about 72 kilometres long and 35 kilometres wide. The highest elevation is Mount Santa Isabel with a height of 3,011 metres.

Half of the country's continental enclave is covered with forests. It has rich animal life that includes buffalo, rare species of monkeys, gorillas, chimpanzees, lions, leopards, elephants, antelope, hippopotamuses, crocodiles, snakes and rare birds.

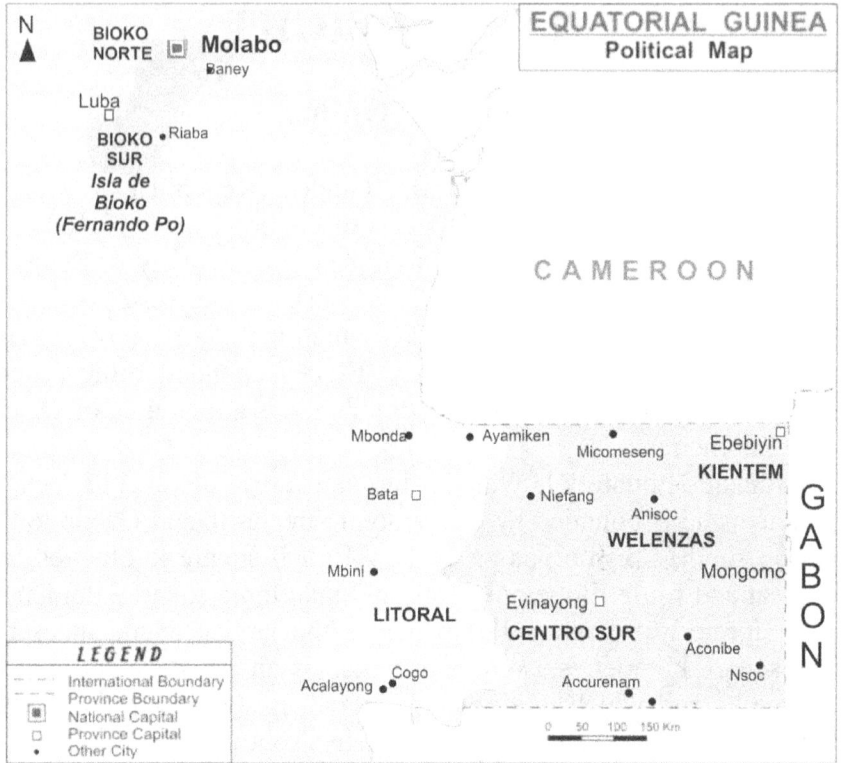

Fig. 8.1: Political Map of Equatorial Guinea

The People

Equatorial Guinea has a complex ethnic mix made up of the Africans who are majority and descendants of Europeans. The Fang people constitute about 80 percent of the mainland region. North of the Mbini River is the Ntumu Fang and to the south is the Okak Fang. Along the coast are other ethnic groups such as the Kombe, Mabea, Lengi and Benga. Both the Fang and these other groups are of Bantu origin.

The Bubi who are descendants of Bantu migrants from the mainland are the original inhabitants of Bioko. Other migrants especially in the twentieth century are the Fang of the mainland region. Other inhabitants of Bioko include the Fernandinos, who are descendants of liberated slaves by the British in the nineteenth century, emancipated Africans from Sierra Leone and Cuba.

Immigrants from other states of the GoG add up to the demographic structure of Equatorial Guinea.

As of 1914, there were 10,000 Nigerians in Bioko (Osuntokun, 1992). In 1966, the island had a total population of 100,000 people and of this number 85,000 were Nigerians. This state of affairs existed because the island depended on migratory labour which was provided by Nigerians of Ibibio and Ibo origins. And dependence on migratory labour made Bioko a no-man's island until the 1975, exodus of many Nigerians back to Nigeria on account of the repressive regime of the President of Equatorial Guinea, Macias Nguema. The immediate effect of too many Nigerians on the island made ***Pidgin*** English, and not even Spanish, to become the ***lingua franca*** of the island. Most of the inhabitants of Annobon are descendants of slaves imported by the Portuguese when the island was a dependency of São Tomé. Most of them came from the Slave Coast between the Volta River and the Niger Delta, along the present-day Togo, Benin and Nigeria.

About four-fifths of the population of Equatorial Guinea are Christians of the Roman Catholic Church mainly. The Bubi and many mainlanders practise African traditional religion and are members of the Mbwiti cult. Life expectancy in Equatorial Guinea is 62. Infant mortality rate is currently 79 per 1000 live births.

History

The modern history of Equatorial Guinea began in the late fifteenth century with the Portuguese visit to the area. Before it achieved independence in 1968, it had been administered by the Portuguese, the British and Spanish.

The island of Bioko (formerly called Fernando Po) was sighted in 1472 by a Portuguese explorer, Fernao do Po. At first it was called Formosa, meaning ***Beautiful*** but at last it was named Fernando Po in honour of the explorer. Annobon was sighted by Ruy de Sequeira in 1474. The Portuguese had exclusive rights in Africa on account of the Treaty of Tordesillas but in 1778 (see chapter two), they ceded to the Spanish the islands of Annobon and Fernando Po as well as Equatorial Guinea. The cessions were strategic because they were effected in order to give the Spanish their own source of slaves in Africa for transport to their colonies in America. In exchange Spain confirmed the rights of Portugal west of the 50°W meridian in Brazil. But daunted by yellow fever, the Spanish abandoned Fernando Po in 1781.

After the British had abolished slave trade in 1807 they required a strategic island in the GoG to assist them in the suppression of the trade. As Fernando Po was quite strategic in this direction especially as it was a striking distance from the Slave Coast, the Spanish in 1827 leased harbours in the island-Port Clarence (later Santa Isabel, now Malabo) and San Carlos Bay-to the British. The British from then administered the island where they shipped freed slaves from Africa and the West Indies to settle in it. Between 1839 and 1841 Britain made spirited attempts to buy the island from Spain but never succeeded. In frustration, it made Sierra Leone the headquarters of its antislavery activities in the GoG.

In 1844, the Spanish re-occupied the island and from there made their presence felt on the mainland. By 1877 they had occupied the entire Equatorial Guinea and from 1879 they began to use Fernando Po as a penal settlement for troublemakers deported from Cuba. The mainland received considerable attention from Spain only in the twentieth century.

Even though, by 1959, Africans and settlers in Equatorial Guinea were granted the same rights like those of the citizens in Spain by the Spanish government, political movements for independence grew strong within the same period and in 1963 self internal government was achieved. In 1968, Equatorial Guinea became fully independent. It is the only Spanish-speaking country in the GoG.

Politics and Structure of Governance

At independence in 1968, the government was led by President Macias Nguema and the National Liberation Movement. In 1972, Nguema changed the Constitution to one that allowed him to be named President for life. He equally changed the name of Fernando Po to bear his own name. Thus the island was known as Macias Nguema. President Nguema ruled with an iron fist; he controlled the press, violated human rights and banned the citizens from foreign travel. Meanwhile, many who could not flee were arrested, charged with treason or felony and summarily executed. He brought the country to a halt. During this period, especially between 1975 and 1977, the Nigerian government repatriated its citizens.

In 1979, Nguema was overthrown by his nephew, Colonel Teodoro Obiang Nguema Mbasogo through a military coup d'état. He changed the name of Fernando Po from Macias Nguema to Bioko. But in governance, the reign of terror of his uncle never departed from Equatorial Guinea. He introduced a new Constitution in 1982. The following year, he organized an election to the House of Representatives where the 41 legislators were personally picked by him. They were unopposed candidates. In 1996, the President claimed to have been re-elected with more than 99 percent of the votes. The trend continues in the political landscape of the country.

Equatorial Guinea practices democracy though of the imperial type. According to the 1982 Constitution, the system of government is presidential and elections are conducted on the basis of universal adult suffrage. The highest judicial authority is the Supreme Tribunal.

Economy

Until oil was discovered in Equatorial Guinea in the late twentieth century, the economy of the country depended on three commodities: cocoa, coffee and timber. These are also the main export commodities of Equatorial Guinea. Timber comes from its dense forest, coffee from Rio Muni and cocoa from Bioko. Bioko has the right soil and favourable climate for cocoa farming. Other agricultural products include bananas, plantain and palm oil and produce. Outside cocoa and coffee processing plants, little industrialization takes place in Equatorial Guinea. But with the promises of goodwill from oil and gas, Equatorial Guinea may well become the Oman of the GoG.

Foreign Relations

Equatorial Guinea maintains diplomatic relations with few African countries because of its lean financial base. As a former colony of Spain, it maintains cordial relations with Spain, which since independence had been balancing its budget through subsidies. Since

1981 many European nations, America and international organizations have equally been subsidizing its budget. Over the years, Equatorial Guinea has been dancing towards the French pole. As a result of deeper economic transaction with France and Francophone countries, French became a compulsory subject in schools in 1988. Already, by 1985, the country had joined the Franc zone, acquiring a freely convertible currency and more French aid.

As Equatorial Guinea is categorized as belonging geographically to the Central African sub-region, it became a member of the Customs and Economic Union of Central Africa (UDEAC) in 1983. The country is also a member of the AU and the UN.

Further Reading

African Encyclopaedia. 1974. London: Oxford University Press.
Davidson, B. 1964. *Old Africa Rediscovered.* London: Oxford University Press.
Duffy, J. 1959. *Portuguese Africa.* Harvard University Press.
Fage, J. D. 1963. *An Atlas of African History.* Arnold.
Greenberg, J. H. 1963. *Languages of Africa.* London: Indiana University Press.
International Encyclopaedia of the Social Sciences. London: Macmillan.
Murdoc G. P. 1959. *Africa: Its Peoples and their Culture History.* New York, McGraw-Hill.

CHAPTER NINE

Gabon

The Republic of Gabon which is also known as the Gabonese Republic (Republique Gabonese) is located in Central Africa, though on the west coast.

Like the Republic of the Congo it lies astride the Equator. It has an area of about 267,667 square kilometres and population of 1.5 people. The country is bordered by Equatorial Guinea and Cameroon to the north, the Republic of the Congo to the south and east and the Atlantic Ocean to the west. Situated off its coast is the island of São Tomé and Principe. Libreville (or Freetown) is the capital of Gabon. The capital owes its name to the freed slaves who landed there after 1849. Other important cities are Port-Gentil and Franceville. The country has equatorial climate.

The coast of Gabon has lagoons and mangrove swamps along a low plain which gradually rises to a plateau of about 400 metres high. Higher hills and mountains abound near the northern, eastern and western boundaries of the country. The central region is occupied by the basin of the Ogooue River and its tributaries. Most of Gabon is covered with a dense tropical forest.

The People

There are about 50 ethnic groups with different languages in Gabon. The Fang are the majority, constituting about one-third of the total population. They inhabit the region north of the Ogooue River. South of the river, the largest groups are the Punu, Sira and Nzebi. Pygmies also exist in Gabon.

About 50 percent of the population are Christians and 49 percent are adherents of the African Traditional Religion. The rest are Muslims and believers in oriental philosophy. Life expectancy in Gabon is 53 years and infant mortality rate is 51 per 1000 live births.

Gabon

Fig. 9.1: *Political Map of Gabon*

History

The earliest inhabitants of Gabon since 7,000 BC were the Pygmies who were hunters, living in small bands along the river valleys. The Bantu peoples who were mainly agriculturalists migrated from the eastern, southern and western Africa to displace them in recent centuries. The Fang people who are the Bantu sub-group and the most numerous are also found in the Cameroon and Equatorial Guinea.

Contacts with the Europeans occurred in 1472 when the Portuguese mariners led by Diego Cao visited the area. They first arrived at Estuarie du Gabon (the Gabon Estuary which they named ***Rio de Gabao***); meaning ***hooded cloak*** because of its shape. The name Gabon is derived from Gabao. Further exploration of the area by Lopo Concalves and Ruy de Sequeira led them to round Cape Lopez and to reach Pointe Sainte-Catherine.

For many years, Portuguese merchants from São Tomé used to visit the estuary coast for purposes of trade in hardwoods and ivory. Although from the outset Portuguese influence was registered in the coast, the English and French were also attracted to the region. In the rivalry for possession of territories in Gabon, the French succeeded and ultimately colonized it.

The process of colonization of Gabon started in the early nineteenth century as part of efforts to stop slave trade which had continued in the area till the end of the century. In 1839 the French through its naval officer, Captain L. E. Bouet-Willaumez in charge of anti-slave trade patrols in the Gabon area secured treaty of protection with King Denis, the chief of the communities on the south bank of the Gabon Estuary. This was followed up with a treaty with King Louis that secured the north bank in 1841. Therefore, through two swift actions, Bouet-Willaumez was able to firmly establish French influence in the Gabon region and in 1843 Fort-d'Aumale was built. Within the same period, some Christian groups established a settlement to re-settle refugee slaves. In 1489 the settlement was named Libreville (Free Town). Between 1855 and 1877, American, British and French explorers penetrated the interior of the Gabon region to claim many areas. In 1877 Pierre Savorgnan de Brazza reached the source of the Ogooue River and in 1880 established a new settlement called Franceville. In 1886 Paris appointed a French governor to Gabon. Between 1897 and 1910, the country was attached to French Congo and later it was adminis-tered as a part of French Equatorial Africa.

In 1946 Gabon was declared an overseas territory of France with its own territorial assembly. Elections were first held in the country in 1957. In 1958 Gabon became an autonomous republic within the French Community. A movement for independence was championed by Leone M'ba, whose political activities were at first suppressed by the colonial government. After much negotiations and subsequent agreements, Gabon achieved independence on August 17 1970 and Leone M'ba who was the Mayor of Libreville since 1956 became its first president.

Politics and Structure of Governance

At independence in 1960, Leone M'ba became the President of Gabon. Until his death in 1967, he dominated the political landscape of the country like a colossus. He was elected President on the platform of the *Bloc Democratiqué Gabonais (BDG)*. As President, he opted for a one-party structure for the country. This attempt led to collision with the opposition group led by his main rival, Jean-Hilaire Aubame. The protests of the group led to uprising in February 1964 and subsequent seizure of power by the military and Aubame.

Within three days President M'ba was restored by French troops on the orders of Charles de Gaulle, the President of France. In the elections that took place in April 1964, BDG won massively and had majority of seats in the National Assembly. By 1966 most of the opposition became members of the BDG and those who remained in the opposition were forbidden to take part in elections. In March 1968 the BDG was renamed the ***Parti Démocratique Gabonais*** (PDG) and with the support of Aubame, the main opposition figure, PDG was declared the only political party in Gabon.

On the death of Leone M'ba in 1967, Albert-Benard Bongo (later Omar Bongo) was made the President. Under his presidency, opposition groups were suppressed but regardless of his high-handedness, in the 1980s, an illegal opposition party, the ***Mouvement de Redressement National*** (MORENA), was formed. Despite official harassments, the party thrived and in 1985, formed a government-in-exile in Paris. On account of the pressure mounted by the opposition and the support of the international community especially in the aftermath of the Cold War, the multi-party system was introduced in 1993. In the first multi-party presidential election of November 1993, President Bongo won with 51 percent of the votes. When the main rival in that election, Paul M'ba Abessole, a Roman Catholic Priest, equally claimed victory and was set to form a rival government, Gabon experienced deep political instability. Peace was however brokered by France which led to a coalition government. In the National Assembly elections in December 1996 (into the Lower House) and February 1997 (into the Senate), PDG won majority of the seats. In 1997 the presidential term was extended by law from five to seven years. In the 1998 presidential election, Omar Bongo won with 66 percent of the vote while Paul Abessole's party, the National Rally of Woodcutters, which by now was split into two, lost. In the 2005 presidential elections, Bongo was still declared the winner.

Gabon is administered by a President who is elected by direct universal suffrage for a period of seven years and a council of Ministers appointed by the President. There is also the office of the Premier. The National Assembly is vested with legislative responsibilities and members are elected by universal suffrage. The country has a hierarchy of Courts with the Supreme Court being the highest. The country is administratively divided into 9 provinces.

Economy

Until mineral resources, especially petroleum, played major roles in the economy of Gabon in the late 1970s, forest products were the important sources of revenue for the country. About 80 percent of the country is covered with forests. The main forest regions are Booué, Fougamou, Kango, Mitzic, Moulla, and Ndjolé. Among the mineral resources of the country are: iron ore, uranium, petroleum and manganese. Gabon is the third largest producer of manganese after South Africa and Russia. Its manganese is of high quality. By far the greatest source of revenue for Gabon is petroleum which represents about 90 percent of the country's total exports. Gabon produces about 300,000 barrels of oil per day.

Foreign Relations

Gabon maintains cordial relations with its neighbours and has a special relationship with France. The country is a member of the UN, AU, African Development Bank, World Trade Organization, Central

African and Monetary Community (CEMAC), Central African Customs and Economic Union (UDEAC), the Economic Community of Central African States and the Non Aligned Movement.

Further Reading

African Encyclopaedia. 1974. London: Oxford University Press.
Davidson, B. 1964. *Old Africa Rediscovered.* London: Oxford University Press.
Duffy, J. 1959. *Portuguese Africa.* Harvard University Press.
Fage, J. D. 1963. *An Atlas of African History.* Arnold.
Greenberg, J. H. 1963. *Languages of Africa.* London: Indiana University Press.
International Encyclopaedia of the Social Sciences. London: Macmillan.
Murdoc G. P. 1959. *Africa: Its Peoples and their Culture History.* New York, McGraw-Hill.

CHAPTER TEN

São Tomé and Principe

The Republic of São Tomé and Principe is located in the Equator around the Bight of Biafra in the GoG and off the northwest coast of Gabon. São Tomé and Principe are basically two islands that are part of an extinct volcanic mountain range that extends to the north to include the island of Bioko off Equatorial Guinea and Mount Cameroon on the Cameroun coast.

São Tomé is about 51 kilometres long and 32 kilometres wide. Its highest peak is 2024 metres. The island of Principe is about 30 kilometres long and four kilometres wide. Altogether, the two islands have an area of 963 square kilometres. The capital of the Republic is São Tomé. Other cities include Angolares, Guadalupe, Neves, Santana, and Trindade in São Tomé and Santo Antonio in Principe. The population of the Republic is 167,000 with 160,000 in São Tomé and 7,000 in Principe.

The People

The people of the islands of São Tomé and Principe are migrants and descendants of ex-slaves who came in different waves to the area since 1485. The population is made up of six groups, namely:

a) Angolares: Descendants of Angolan slaves who survived a shipwreck in 1540;
b) Europeans of Portuguese origin;
c) Forros: Descendants of freed slaves after the abolition of slave trade;
d) Mestico or Mixed Blood: Descendants of African slaves who started settlement on the islands. Known as filhos da terra or sons of the land, their territories of origin are Benin, Gabon, Cameroon, Congo and Nigeria and Europe;
e) Servicais: Contract labourers from Angola, Cape Verde and Mozambique. They live temporarily on the islands;

f) Tongas: Children of servicais with ferros born on the islands.

Fig. 10.1: Political Map of São Tomé and Principe

The inhabitants of the two islands are Christian of the Roman Catholic, Evangelical Protestant or Seventh-day Adventist Churches. Life expectancy in the Republic is 66 years and infant mortality rate is 37 per 1000 live births.

History

From available records, it is highly likely that the islands of São Tomé and Principe were not inhabited until the Portuguese explorers visited them between 1469 and 1472. The first successful settlement on São

Tomé was undertaken by Alvaro Caminha in 1493. The enterprise was possible because he was given the land as a grant from the Portuguese crown. Under a similar arrangement, Principe was settled in 1500.

However, the goodwill ended when the Portuguese crown took over São Tomé in 1522 and Principe in 1573. Before the end of the fifteenth century, Lisbon had successfully turned the islands into Africa's foremost supply of sugar through the use of African slaves. After about a century's cultivation, the value of sugar declined considerably to the extent that São Tomé became merely a station to refuel ships. But the situation changed dramatically in the early nineteenth century when coffee and cocoa were introduced as the latest cash crops. As the rich volcanic soils were well suited to the cultivation of the crops, it was not surprising that by 1908 São Tomé became the largest producer of cocoa in the world.

The practice of forced labour created ill-feelings in the country and led to periodic outbreak of unrest and violence which incidentally acted as catalysts for independence. The most significant of these riots was the one that took place in 1953. The workers had rioted over oppressive labour system and unsatisfactory working conditions. In the process they clashed with the Portuguese forces which killed quite a number of them. The ***Batepa Massacre***, as the episode was called is very instructive in the history of São Tomé and Principe. For this reason, the government of the Republic observes its anniversary on February 3. Be that as it may, in the aftermath of the Batepa event, the inhabitants of the islands took steps to demand for independence from Portugal.

To actualize the dreams of independence, groups were formed for that purpose. The most prominent of them was the Movement for the Liberation of São Tomé and Principe (MLSTP). The Movement operated from neighbouring Gabon because it was not tolerated by the Portuguese authority in the islands. Even though the independence agitation grew stronger each passing year, it was the overthrow of the Salazar and Caetano regimes in Lisbon in April 1974 that laid the foundation for the independence of São Tomé and Principe.

On assuming power, the new government in Lisbon denounced colonial aspirations and indeed dissolved its overseas possessions. This being the case, the representatives of the new regime and those of the MLSTP met in Algiers, Algeria, in November 1974 to work out arrangements for the transfer of power to the MLSTP. São Tomé and Principe achieved independence on July 12 1975. Manuel Pinto da Costa who was the Secretary General of the MLSTP became the first President.

Politics and Structure of Governance

At independence in 1975, Manuel Costa of the MLSTP was the President. He established a one-party state and held the office of the President till 1990. In 1990 São Tomé and Principe embraced democratic reforms and a new Constitution drafted and ratified that year legalized opposition parties. In the 1991 presidential elections, Miguel Trovoada, who was the country's first Prime Minister and who was in exile since 1986, won as an independent candidate. In the 1996 presidential elections he was re-elected President on the platform of the Independent Democratic Action Party (ADI) that he had formed during his first term in office.

In the next presidential elections held in July 2001, Fradique de Menezes of the ADI was elected President. In July 2003 the country experienced a coup d'état in which some disgruntled elements in the military and the Christian Democratic Front made up of Sao Tomean volunteers from the apartheid-era South African Defence Force staged, but it was foiled without bloodshed. The political sparks were successfully managed within the next three years. On July 30 2006, the Republic held its fourth democratic and multi-party elections in which de Menezes was re-elected President.

The structure of governance of São Tomé and Principe recognizes independent candidates for elective offices. The President is elected to a five-year term through direct universal suffrage and a secret ballot. The President could hold office up to two consecutive terms. The party that wins a majority in the National Assembly names the Prime Minister, who must be approved by the President. Until 1990, the President of the republic was elected by the National Assembly from a list of candidates submitted to it by the MLSTP. Today, the National Assembly, made up of 55 members, is the supreme organ of the state and highest legislation institution. Under the current Constitution, the judiciary is independent and the Supreme Court is the highest judicial authority. Administratively, São Tomé and Principe is divided into six municipal districts; five in São Tomé and one in Principe.

Economy

The economy of São Tomé and Principe is based on agriculture and fishing. Agricultural goods for export include cocoa, coffee, copra and palm kernels. Cocoa which is produced on the northeast of both islands is the principal export crop. Fishing for sharks has helped the economy tremendously. On account of scenic features of the islands, the government is making serious efforts to develop the tourism industry and position it as a great revenue earner.

São Tomé and Principe is an oil producing country. Its oil is jointly produced with Nigeria in the Joint Development Zone (JDZ).

Foreign Relations

São Tomé and Principe maintains special relations with Portugal and ex-Portuguese colonies in Africa. This stems from the consideration of common language, tradition and colonial experience. In Africa, the Republic maintains cordial relations with neighbouring states such as Gabon, the Republic of the Congo and Nigeria. Outside Africa, it maintains closer ties with countries that are willing to assist it in economic development. Such countries include the US, those in Europe and Taiwan. São Tomé is a member of the UN, AU and Non Aligned Movement.

Further Reading

African Encyclopaedia. 1974. London: Oxford University Press.
Davidson, B. 1964. *Old Africa Rediscovered.* London: Oxford University Press.
Duffy, J. 1959. *Portuguese Africa.* Harvard University Press.
Fage, J. D. 1963. *An Atlas of African History.* Arnold.
Greenberg, J. H. 1963. *Languages of Africa.* London: Indiana University Press.

International Encyclopaedia of the Social Sciences. London: Macmillan.

Murdoc G. P. 1959. *Africa: Its Peoples and their Culture History.* New York, McGraw-Hill.

Section III

The Country of the Gulf of Guinea in Southern Africa

CHAPTER ELEVEN

Angola

Angola is the only country in the GoG which is located in the sub-continent of Southern Africa. The rest of the Gulf States are located in the Central and West African sub-regions. Angola is bounded to the north and east by the DR Congo, to the south-east by Zambia, and to the south by the Republic of Namibia. The country was recognized as a colony of Portugal at the Berlin West African Conference of 1884-85. Angola also includes the territory of Cabinda, which is separated from it by part of the DR Congo.

The Cabinda enclave was added to the colony by the Berlin Conference. The enclave is about 32 kilometres north of the Congo River and is bounded by the Republic of the Congo to the north and the DR Congo to the east and south. Angola has an area of 1,246,700 square kilometres and 1,650 kilometres of Atlantic Coastline, stretching from the Congo River estuary in the north to the Kunene River estuary in the south. The country has a population of about 12 million people.

Most of the country lies on a high central plateau above 1000 metres. The land rises to about 2500 metres on the Bihe Plateau in the west. There is a low narrow coastal plain which becomes broader in the north. Most of the rivers flow outwards from the highlands near the centre of the country, and many, like the Zambezi, have swamps along their valleys. Nearly all the land is desert or savanna, with hardwood forests in the north-east.

Angola had independence on November 11, 1975, after 500 years of Portuguese possession. The capital is the Port City of Luanda (full name: Sao Paulo de Luanda). Other important cities are Huambo, Lubango, Lobito and Benguela.

Fig. 11.1: Political Map of Angola

The People

There are many ethnic groups in Angola, the largest being the Ovimbundu of the central highlands, who speak Umbundu. The Mbundu people constitute the second largest group and they speak Kimbundu. They inhabit the coastal area north of Luanda down to N'gunza Kabolo. The third largest group is the Bakongo in the north who speak Kikongo language. The other groups include the Lunda-Chokwe from the east who speak Chokwe and Lunda; the Nganguela, who speak Nganguela and are spread over the east and southeast; the

Nyaneke-Humbe from the south, who speak Nyaneke and Humbe; and the Ambo.

The San (Bushmen) and the Khoikhoin (Hottentots) who speak click languages are of non-Bantu stock. Other smaller groups are the Vatua and Xindonga. About 90 percent of the population are Christians made up of the Roman Catholic Community (50 percent), Protestants (25 percent); the rest are members of Independent African Churches like Kimbanguism. About nine percent of the population are adherents of the African Traditional Religion while one percent is made up of the Muslims. Life expectancy in Angola is 38 years and infant mortality rate is 178 per 1000 live births.

History

The earliest inhabitants of Angola were the Khoisan hunter-gatherers. Between the eighth and thirteenth centuries, they were largely displaced by the Bantu language group. A small number of the Khoisan remains; they inhabit parts of southern Angola. Apparently, the Bantu came from the regions of today's Republics of Cameroun and Nigeria. The Bantu speaking immigrants were able to absorb the early inhabitants because of superior knowledge in, and revolutionary concepts of, metalworking, ceramics and agriculture. In other words, the Khoisan could not withstand the Bantu people because they were less technologically advanced than the latter.

The process of domination of the Angola area by the Bantu people took many centuries and gave rise to several ethnic groups. One of such groups was the Mbundu whose people established the Ndongo Empire. Its rulers were called *Ngola* (from which Angola derives its name). The empire had trade relations with its neighbours especially the Great Zimbabwe. In the main, articles of trade included raffia, textiles, copper, iron and salt. By the fifteenth century, slaves were added to the list of exportable goods but by this time, the importers were the Portuguese.

The Portuguese first arrived on the coast of Luanda in 1843 for trading opportunities. They were led by Diego Cao, one of Portugal's foremost navigators. They were attracted to the Angolan area by stories of availability of gold and other precious metals. When, in the final analysis, none of these commodities was available, in frustration, they turned their attention to export trade in slaves who were shipped to the sugar plantations in São Tomé and Brazil. The greatest victims of this trade were the Nganguela and Nyaneke people and the greatest beneficiaries on the African side were the Mbundu people whose king, Ngola, used the proceeds to expand his territory considerably in the sixteenth and seventeenth centuries.

It is instructive to note that for about a century, the Portuguese were not interested in colonial domination and possession but commerce. To this extent, they had cordial relations with the Ndongo Empire. Diego Cao and the early Portuguese explorers who settled in Angola brought missionaries to teach their African trading partners European concepts and values. But when the Kongo Empire decayed, collapsed and disrupted trading activities, the Portuguese had to rethink the idea of colonial domination. Consequently, they established in Angola a conquest colony similar to the ones the Spaniards had in Peru and Mexico.

To actualize the dream of colonial possession, a military base was established in Luanda. From 1576 the process of subjugation of the Ndongo Empire started and it was initiated by Paulo Dias de Novais. However, it took the Portuguese 100 years to succeed in subjugating the people. This long period accounted for series of pitched battles and wars in which no side sustained victory. But by the end of the seventeenth century, the Portuguese had established a colony which covered the areas of Benguela and the lower Kwaza valley.

The Portuguese were not the only European nation that engaged in slave trade in Angola. England, France and Holland were direct participants from the seventeenth century onward and by the end of the eighteenth century; more than a million people from Angola were ferried to the Americas, particularly South America.

When the slave trade was suspended in Brazil in the 1850s, the Portuguese diverted the direction of the trade to the cocoa estates of São Tomé in Africa. Thus by the end of the nineteenth century, Angola became one of the worst victims of slave trade which was carried out continuously for a period of four hundred years.

Be that as it may, Portugal was able to successfully claim Angola as its own colonial possession at the Berlin West African Conference of 1884-85. Even so, the claim was fiercely resisted by the people of Angola spearheaded by the Cuanhama. They fought the Portuguese for about 30 years but they lost in 1902. Indeed, the decisive campaign was the Bailundu War of that year where the power of the Ovimbundu was broken and the Bie Plateau was captured by the Portuguese.

To spread their control into the hinterland, the Portuguese started to build the Benguela railway in 1902. Even though the people of Angola did not abandon wars of resistance, European domination spread and in 1951, the country was made an overseas territory of Portugal. Consequent upon this declaration, increasing numbers of Portuguese settlers flocked to Angola and by 1960, they numbered about 200,000.

Opposition to the Portuguese rule by African peoples continued unabated and rather gained momentum after most of the British and French colonies achieved independence in 1960. Between 1961 and 1974, the history of Angola was marked by series of uprisings and wars of liberation. These episodic events started in January 1961 with a revolt in the Mbundu region against forced cotton production at a time of falling prices.

This event was followed in February by an attempted coup organized by the ***Movimento Popular de Libertacao de Angola*** (MPLA) which by now had emerged as a foremost national movement. The manner the Portuguese handled the crisis inflamed passions and led to more riots. Thus in March 1961 violence broke out in the Kongo area in the north in which hundreds of white settlers were killed. A retaliatory measure by the secret police spread the violence across northern Angola. The Kongo resistance was spearheaded by the ***Frente Nacional de Libertacao de Angola*** (FNLA) led by Holden Roberto.

By 1965 warfare had erupted in eastern Angola between the Portuguese and the MPLA led by Agostinho Neto. From the southern highlands, the Ovimbundu joined operations with the ***Nacional para a Independencia Total de Angola*** (UNITA) to resist the Portuguese. In 1972, the Portuguese government declared Angola to be a state of Portugal, but the freedom fighters were in control of large areas in the east and north of the country.

Many African leaders through the OAU used their good offices to attempt to unite the three nationalist movements so as to present a common front to confront the Portuguese but they failed as a result of the ideological differences of the movements. Besides, in the heydays of the Cold War politics, the three nationalist fronts had external patrons as supporters like the DR Congo, the apartheid South Africa, Cuba, China, the United States and the Soviet Union. In 1974 Portugal, as a result of political and financial heat generated by the guerrilla activities of the nationalist movements, recognized Angola's right to independence but never prepared the country for formal independence. Indeed, on November 11, 1975, Portugal proclaimed Angola independent and sovereign. On that date, the three major movements laid claims as the legal successor of the Portuguese government.

The MPLA anchored its claims on the fact that it controlled the strategic region of Luanda. To this extent, it proclaimed the "People's Republic of Angola" and celebrated independence with pomp and pageantry in the capital on November 11 (Akpan, 2003). The FNLA/UNITA Alliance set up a rival government of the "Socialist Democratic Republic of Angola" with Huambo as the capital. Although the MPLA eventually established control of the government, civil war broke out in the country and lasted for several decades.

Politics and the Structure of Governance

Angola gained independence in November 1975 when Portugal proclaimed it independent and sovereign. Although a civil war ensued in the aftermath of the declaration of independence, the MPLA led by Neto formed the government where Neto himself became the first President of the country.

In general administration, the President, the Vice Presidents and the Council of Ministers form the executive branch of the government of Angola. As a matter of fact, political power is concentrated in the presidency. When President Neto died in 1979, he was succeeded by Jose Eduardo do Santos who is still the President. In spite of domestic and international pressure for democratic reforms, Santos has refused to open up the political space. Again, when Jonas Savimbi, the leader of UNITA was killed in combat on February 22, 2002 and the rump of the UNITA disbanded its armed wing, ended the civil war and turned itself into an opposition party, Santos refused to effectively democratize the nation. However, a sham parliamentary election was held in September 2008 in which the MPLA was declared as the winner with 81 percent of votes and UNITA with 10 percent.

Angola has 18 provinces in which the governors are appointed by, and served at the pleasure of, the President. The legal system is based on the Portuguese and Customary laws. The Supreme Court is the highest judicial authority in the country.

Economy

Agriculture and mining form the pillars of the economy of Angola. Cash and export crops are coffee in the north-west, cotton in the Luanda-Malanje area, sisal from the North-east, sugar-cane from the northern part of the coastal plain. Maize, banana and oil palm products are also exported. Forestry resources are very important in the economy. The main food crops are cassava, groundnuts, maize and rice.

The mineral resources produced for exports in Angola include iron ore mined at Cassinga and diamonds produced in the Lunda area. Other mineral resources are copper, manganese and petroleum. Angola is the second largest producer of oil in Africa after Nigeria in the GoG and the second largest producer of diamonds after the DR Congo. The Portuguese discovered petroleum in the country in 1955. Production started in the Cuanza basin in the 1950s, in the Congo basin in the 1960s and in the Cabinda enclave in 1968. Until 1973, coffee was the largest export commodity, but it was surpassed by oil. Today, diamonds and petroleum oil constitute 60 percent of Angola's economy. The country produced 1.4 million barrels per day in 2006 and 2.9 million barrels in 2008.

The industrial sector is growing and the focus is on steel making, ship building and repairs, paper pulp processing and cement production. Others include textile manufacture from Angolan cotton and imported synthetic fibres, paints and plastics industries. There is a budding agro-industrial sector which produces quite a number of items. Between 2005 and 2007, the Angolan economy was the fastest in Africa with an average GDP growth of 20 percent.

Otoabasi Akpan
Foreign Relations

Angola maintains cordial relations with many countries in the world especially the ones that respect her worldview and interest. The country's Constitution declares adherence to the Charters of the UN and the AU and declares Angola's desire for relations of friendship and cooperation with all states on the basis of mutual respect and advantage. As a country committed to the ideals of Non-Alignment, its Constitution forbids its membership in any international military organization and prohibits foreign military bases on Angolan soil. Angola is a leading international actor in southern Africa. The country is a member of the OPEC, SADC, ADB, and many UN institutions.

Further Reading

African Encyclopaedia. 1974. London: Oxford University Press.

Clapham, C. 1998. ***African Guerrillas.*** Oxford: James Currey.

Gibson, R. 1992. ***African Liberation Movements.*** London: Oxford University Press.

Davidson, B. 1964. *Old Africa Rediscovered.* London: Oxford University Press.

Duffy, J. 1959. *Portuguese Africa.* Harvard University Press.

Fage, J. D. 1963. *An Atlas of African History*. Arnold.

Greenberg, J. H. 1963. *Languages of Africa.* London: Indiana University Press.

International Encyclopaedia of the Social Sciences. London: Macmillan.

Murdoc G. P. 1959. *Africa: Its Peoples and their Culture History.* New York, McGraw-Hill.

Olufemi, A. 1981. ***Nigeria's Recognition of Angola.*** Lagos: Nigerian Institute of International Affairs.

Soremekun , F. 1983. ***Angola: The Road to Independence.*** Ile-Ife: University of Ife Press.

Section IV

The countries of the Gulf of Guinea in the West African Sub-Region

Benin, Cape Verde, Cote d'Ivoire, Gambia, Ghana, Guinea, Guinea Bissau, Liberia, Nigeria, Senegal, Sierra Leone and Togo

CHAPTER TWELVE
Benin

The Republic of Benin (Règplique du Bènin) consists of a narrow north-south strip of land in West Africa that lies between the Equator and the Tropic of Cancer. Its latitude ranges from 6°30'N to 12°30'N and its longitude from 10'E to 3°40'E. Benin's territory extends northward for about 675 kilometres from the GoG in the Atlantic Ocean, on which it has a 120-kilometre seacoast to the River Niger, which is the limit of the country's border with the Republic of Niger. Benin has an area of about 112,600 square kilometres and a population of about 8 million people. It is bounded by Togo to the West, Burkina Faso and Niger to the north, Nigeria to the east and the Bight of Benin to the south. Although the coastline measures 121 kilometres, the country measures about 325 kilometres at its widest point. As a smaller country in the Gulf of Guinea, it is eight times smaller than Nigeria, its immediate neighbour to the east but twice as large as Togo, its neighbour to the west.

Porto Novo is its official capital but Cotonou is its largest capital city, its chief port and its *de facto* administrative capital. Benin was a colony of France. It gained independence in 1960 with the name of the Republic of Dahomey. In 1975, in line with the Marxist-Leninist tendencies of its then President, Mathieu Kèrèkou, the country was called the People's Republic of Benin.

Fig. 12.1: Political Map of Benin

From 1990, it was simply called the Republic of Benin. The name of the country is derived from the Bight of Benin in Nigeria.

Benin has five natural regions. The coastal area is low, flat and sandy, backed by tidal marshes and lagoons; in the west, the Grand-Popo Lagoon extends into Togo while the Porto-Novo Lagoon in the east provides a natural waterway to the Lagos port in Nigeria. The plateaus in the south are split by valleys running north to south along the Couffo, Zou, and Oueme rivers. An area of flat lands dotted with rocky hills with altitude of about 400 metres is observable in Nikki and Save. There is also a range of mountains which extends along the northern border and into Togo. These are the Atakora mountains with the highest point at Mont Sokbaro at 658 metres. In the south, Benin has fields of low fallow, mangroves, and large sacred forests. Some forests also line the banks of rivers. In the rest of the country, savanna is covered with thorny shrubs and baobab trees.

The People

Benin has about 42 ethnic groups. These include the Yoruba in the southeast who came from Nigeria in the twelfth century; the Dendi in the north-central area who came from Mali in the sixteenth century; the Bariba and the Fulani in the northeast; the Baetammaribe and the Somba in the Atakora Range; the Fon in the area of Abomey in South-central and the Mina, Xuede and Aja who came from Togo on the coast. The Fon make up 40 percent of the population and the next largest group is the Yoruba which are historically (related with) the Fon.

About 30 percent of the population are Christians and about 20 percent are Muslims. The rest, including nominal Christians and Muslims practise African traditional religion, mostly Voodoism, for which Benin is well known. Voodoism originated in Benin and was introduced to Brazil and the Caribbean islands by African slaves from this region of the GoG. Benin has infant mortality ratio of 61 to 1000 and life expectancy of 59 years.

History

In the pre-colonial period, Benin had a number of independent states. In the north, the most prominent state was the kingdom of Nikki, which formed part of a confederacy with Bariba states located in Nigeria today. In the south, two kingdoms had emerged; the kingdom of Allada which flourished between the sixteenth and the seventeenth centuries and the greatest of them all which was the kingdom of Dahomey. Dahomey actually replaced Allada after its collapse and flourished between the eighteenth and nineteenth centuries.

The founders of Dahomey were the Fon who were an off-shoot of the Aja people, whose homeland and primary dispersal centre were at Tado in modern Togo. The Gun of Porto Novo claims that Dahomey was founded by a Yoruba hunter, Adimola. However, what is clear is that Dahomey was a vassal state of Oyo Empire to the northeast in modern Nigeria, from about 1730. Between that period and the first decade of the nineteenth century, the Yoruba Empire of Oyo held sway in Dahomey. By the second decade of the century, Dahomey became one of the most famous military powers in the GoG. Its military instilled fear and, at the same time, admiration into all its neighbours and greatly impressed Europeans at the coast.

Dahomean rulers of this period loved to impress European visitors by massive military reviews which included corps of female warriors called the ***Amazon*** by Europeans. The kingdom attained the height of its power under the kings Gezo (1818 - 1858) and Gelele (1858-1889). Gezo defeated the Oyo army in 1823 and liberated Dahomey from its yoke. But its expansionist programmes eastward to Abeokuta in modern Nigeria in 1851 and 1864 were effectively halted by the people of Abeokuta.

The king's political power was buttressed by an elaborate cult of the deceased kings of the kingdom. These kings who were regarded as the gods were honoured by large-scale human sacrifices which were annual events performed in the public. Dahomean rulers openly championed and practiced the slave trade even after it was abolished by Britain. Because considerable royal revenue accrued from the trade the rulers refused to abandon it when no lucrative alternative was found.

In the heyday of the transatlantic slave trade, many people from Benin were sold into slavery and the sheer volume made Dahomey not only to be part of the ***Slave Coast*** but also to host at a time the biggest slave market in the GoG at Whydah. The slaves were mainly war captives. From 1840, Dahomey switched over from slave trade to export of palm oil produced by slave labour.

The first contact with the Europeans occurred in 1472 when the Portuguese explorers visited Benin. Trading with Portugal began in 1553. In the seventeenth century, the monopoly of Portugal in Benin was challenged by other European powers notably the Dutch, English and French. They all maintained trading factories in the territory but by the middle of that century, France outsmarted other European powers in Dahomey by securing treaties with its potentates. Treaties were the legal instruments that France used to ultimately colonize

Dahomey. Such treaties were negotiated with King Gezo of Dahomey in 1851; the kingdom of Porto-Novo in 1863; the kingdoms of Whydah and Porto-Novo between 1868 and 1878 and the kingdom of Nikki in 1894.

Attempts by France to annex Dahomey did not go without resistance by African rulers. King Behanzin of Dahomey, for instance, engaged the French in wars of resistance from his first year on the throne in 1889. The king was deposed and exiled while his kingdom was proclaimed a French Protectorate. The colony was at first called Benin, but in 1894 it was renamed Dahomey in honour of the kingdom of Dahomey.

By 1904, French rule had extended over all parts of Dahomey and it was ruled as part of the federation of French West Africa from Senegal. In 1946, Dahomey was declared an overseas territory of France. From that date it sent representatives to the French West African Council in Dakar. Within this period, the movement for independence developed strongly and Dahomey became internally self-governing. Full independence was achieved in 1960 with Hubert Maga as the first President.

Politics and Structure of Governance

The pattern of politics of the immediate post-independence Benin was a reflection of the politics of decolonization in the country. During this period, there were three regionally based political parties that drew support from three ethnic groups. The parties were led by Sorou-Migan Apithy, Justin Ahomadeghe and Hubert Maga. Their support came from Port-Novo, Abomey and the North respectively. Regional politics triggered long years of political instability in Benin. It is not surprising to note that the country had six successful military coups d'état between 1963 and 1972.

The last coup by Major Mathieu Kerekou introduced communism into the country when Kerekou hooked up the country to the ideology of Marxism-Leninism in the hope that it would solve his country's problems. Of course, the socialist principles afforded Benin about twenty years of fragile stability under Kerekou but economic problems triggered new political issues which were met with severe repression and violation of human rights. After Marxist ideology had failed to solve his country's myriads of economic and political problems, Kerekou abandoned it for capitalism. In 1990, Benin had a new Constitution that guaranteed human rights, freedom of association and organization of political parties, right to private property-which had hitherto been a crime-and universal franchise. The judiciary consists of a High Court of Justice, Constitutional Court and a Supreme Court.

Economy

Agriculture is the mainstay of Benin's economy. Oil palm products are the main agricultural export. In the savanna regions, groundnuts, cotton and coffee are grown for export. Cotton accounts for 40 percent of GDP and about 80 percent of official export receipts. Cattles are raised on the higher land. Benin has large plantations of coconut palms which provide the nuts and copra for export. Fishing is important on the coast and by the lagoons where fishing fleet provide shrimps and fish for export to Europe and Asia.

There are also forest resources for export. Commercial woods include iroko, mahogany, teak and samba. Benin possesses a number of important mineral resources like limestone at Onigbolo, chromium ore and gold at Natitingou, marble at Dadjo, pottery clay at Sakete and titanium at the coast. The country also has oil and gas at the coast near Cotonou. Its deep water port at Cotonou which serves the Niger Republic and Nigeria as well is a major revenue earner.

Benin is self-sufficient in staple foods like cassava, maize, millet, yams, beans and rice.

Foreign Relations

Since independence, Benin has had good relations with France, its former colonial power, many European nations and the United States of America outside Africa. In the heydays of socialism, the country strengthened ties with the Soviet Union and many socialist nations. In Africa, Benin has excellent relations with her West African neighbours and is a member of the Economic Community of West African States (ECOWAS), the AU and the UN. It has special relations with Nigeria. A part of this was reflected in Benin's policy, in the 1970s, not to join the West African Economic Community (CEAO) or for that matter any community in which Nigeria was not a member.

Today, Benin has matured diplomatically. Outside having ties with leading international organizations, it had adopted alongside Nigeria a mediating role in the political crises in Liberia, Guinea-Bissau, Sierra Leone and Togo and provided a contribution to the UN force in Haiti which practices its traditional religion, Voodooism.

Further Reading

African Encyclopaedia. 1974. London: Oxford University Press.
Akinjobin, I. A. 1967. *Dahomey and Its Neighbours.* London: Cambridge University Press.
Davidson, B. 1964. *Old Africa Rediscovered.* London: Oxford University Press.
Duffy, J. 1959. *Portuguese Africa.* Harvard University Press.
Fage, J. D. 1963. *An Atlas of African History.* Arnold.
Greenberg, J. H. 1963. *Languages of Africa.* London: Indiana University Press.
International Encyclopaedia of the Social Sciences. London: Macmillan.
Murdoc G. P. 1959. *Africa: Its Peoples and their Culture History.* New York, McGraw-Hill.

CHAPTER THIRTEEN
Cape Verde

The Republic of Cape Verde (Republica de Cabo Verde) comprises islands in the mid-Atlantic Ocean. The islands lie 620 kilometres off the west coast of Africa, between 14°30' and 17°30'N and between 22°30' and 25°30'W. It has a total land area of 4,033 square kilometres. The capital is Praia on Sao Tiago.

The country is named after the westernmost cape of Africa, which is the nearest point on the continent (Encyclopaedia Britannica, 1999). Cape Verde has 10 islands and five islets, which are divided into two groups: Windward (Barlavento) and Leeward (Sotavento). The main islands in the Barlavento group are Santo Antao, Sao Vicente, Santa Luzia, Sao Nicolau, Boa Vista, and Sal together with the islets of Raso and Branco. The Leeward Islands include Maio Sao Tiago (Santiago), Fogo, and Brava and the three islets called the Rombos-Grande, Luis Carneiro and Cima. All the islands except Santa Luzia are inhabited. Porto Grande at Mindelo on Sao Vicente is the largest port in the islands and it has deepwater harbour that accommodates medium ships.

The islands are mountainous and are volcanic in origin. Three islands of Sal, Boa Vista and Maio are level and dry. Mountains higher than 1,280 metres are found on Santiago, Fogo, Santa Antao and Sao Nicolau. Even though Cape Verde is located in the middle of the Atlantic Ocean, rainfall is irregular in the country and that explains its periodic droughts and consequent food shortages. During winter, storms from the Sahara could cloud its sky.

Cape Verde

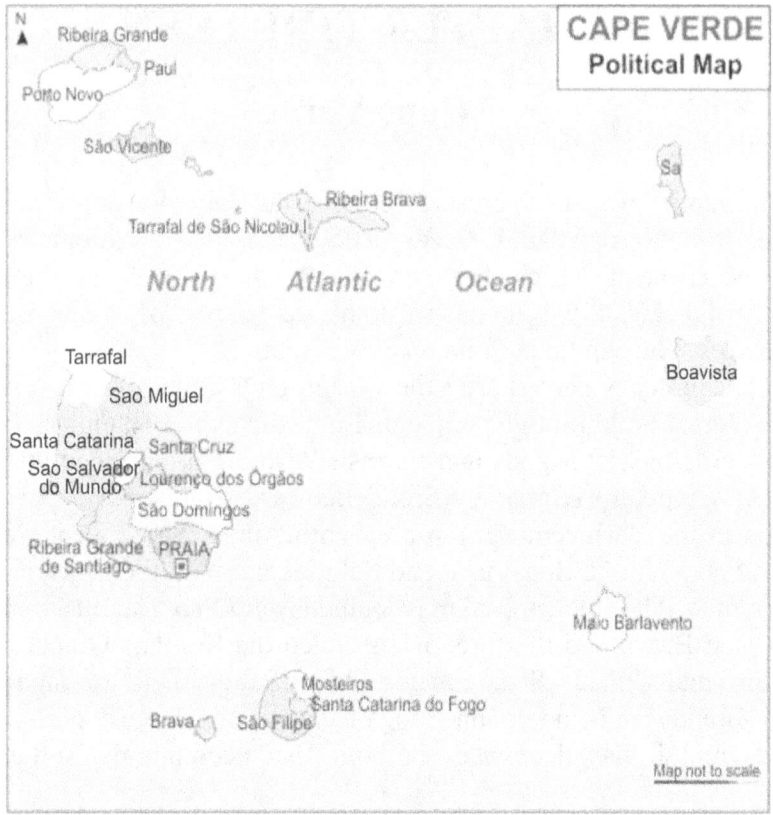

Fig. 13.1: Political Map of Cape Verde

The People

Cape Verde is a typical example of no-man's islands. By the time the Portuguese sighted the islands in 1456, they were not inhabited. The population is made up of Creole who account for about 70 percent of the citizens, 29 percent of African and one percent of Europeans. Creole are descendants of the union between Portuguese settlers and Africans who were brought as slaves in the sixteenth century to work on the plantations. These slaves were the Fulani and Mandingo people from Senegal, The Gambia and Guinea-Bissau. Crioulo is the mother tongue of these people. Though the official language of Cape Verde is Portuguese, Crioulo is the national language. African culture is very popular in the island of Santiago.

The population of the country is in the region of 500,000 and about half of this number lives outside the country as emigrant workers preferring to return home once they retire. The popular working destinations of Cape Verdeans include the United States of America, Portugal, the Netherlands, France, Italy, Senegal and São Tomé and Principe. This tradition of emigration started in the nineteenth century.

Cape Verde is a Christian state and majority of the population is Roman Catholic. Its life expectancy of 73 years is the highest in the GoG. The country's literacy rate is 77 percent and it has infant mortality rate of 25 per 1000 live births.

History

The history of this country started in 1460 when the Portuguese navigators Diogo Gomes and Antonio de Noli sighted Maio and Sao Tiago. Two years later, Portuguese settlers came and founded Ribeira Grande as the oldest European city in the tropics. In the sixteenth century, the city prospered from the transatlantic slave trade. The English under Sir Francis Drake attacked the city twice in 1585 and 1592 to seize it for the British Crown, but they were not successful ventures. In 1712, the city was abandoned on account of these attacks. After a while Portugal attempted to re-posses it.

Following the decline of the transatlantic slave trade, the country's prosperity dwindled, but its position astride mid-Atlantic shipping lanes made it an ideal place for ships to re-fuel. In the nineteenth century, its excellent harbour at Mindelo on the island of Sao Vincente made it a strategic entrepot. The Portuguese rule of Cape Verde was unified in 1587 under a governor. In 1951, the islands were made overseas territories of Portugal. In 1961, the citizens were granted full citizenship.

The gesture of full Portuguese citizenship to Cape Verdeans did not prevent the islanders from aspiring for full independent status from Portugal. The movement for independence started in 1956 when Amilcar Cabral organized armed groups in Guinea-Bissau to demand independence for Cape Verde and Guinea-Bissau. Cabral came from Cape Verde but his revolutionary vision was to free the two countries simultaneously from the Portuguese grip, hence the movement was called the African Party for the Independence of Guinea-Bissau and Cape Verde (PAIGC).

In 1960, the headquarters of PAIGC was moved to Conakry in Guinea and in 1961 armed rebellion against Portugal began. The guerilla warfare saw about 10,000 armed Africans supported by the Soviet Union and the Warsaw Pact fighting 35, 000 Portuguese and African troops. In 1972, the PAIGC controlled much of Guinea-Bissau. In 1973, it declared independence but full independence was granted in 1974. In the aftermath of independence in Guinea-Bissau, the PAIGC began its operations in Cape Verde. Pressure from the revolutionary war led to serious strains in the politics of Portugal and caused it to abandon colonial assets. On July 5, 1975, Cape Verde became an independent republic.

Its first President was Aristides Pereira who had been Secretary-General of the PAIGC since 1973. The hope of Cape Verde and Guinea-Bissau uniting into one republic in the spirit of joint revolutionary movement of the 1970s was dashed in 1980 when Guinea-Bissau experienced a military coup d'état. Relations between the two countries were severely strained to the extent that in 1981, Cape Verde dissolved its branch of the PAIGC and in its place formed the African Party for the independence of Cape Verde (PAICV) as the sole legal political party in the country. In 1990 Cape Verde abandoned its one-party system for a multiparty system. Since then the country has become fully democratic.

Politics and Structure of Governance

Political authority in Cape Verde is derived from the Constitution which was adopted in 1980 and revised in 1992, 1995 and 1999. The President is Head of State and is elected for a five-year term. The Prime Minister is Head of Government. It is the President that appoints the Prime Minister in consultation with the National Assembly. Members of the Parliament are elected by popular vote for five-year terms. Cape Verde operates a multi-party democracy.

Economy

Cape Verde is poor in natural resources and suffers from poor rainfall and fresh water. Out of the 10 main islands, only four-Santiago, Santa Antao, Fogo and Brava-support meaningful agricultural production. Its imports normally exceed exports and indeed over 90 percent of its food is imported.

The country's economy is service-oriented, with commerce, transport and public services contributing about 70 percent of the GDP. The main sources of its revenue are the Amilca Cabral International Airport on Sal, foreign aid and remittances from expatriate Cape Verdeans.

Foreign Relations

Cape Verde pursues a non-aligned and Africanist foreign policy. Because of the need for foreign aid, it cooperates with all states in the international system. It however maintains special relations with fellow Lusophone states in Africa. Cape Verde is a member of many international organizations and institutions including ECOWAS, the AU, UN, IMF and the WTO. Cape Verde also maintains special relations with the United States of America. The first US consulate in sub-Saharan Africa was established in Cape Verde in 1818.

The special relationship between the US and Cape Verde owes its origin to the eighteenth century demands for whale by the US in the Cape Verdean waters. This resulted in the US recruiting crews from Brava and Fogo to hunt whales. The tradition of emigration to the US began at this period and it is still continuing. Today, Cape Verdeans still work on American merchant ships and Boston and New England have a large immigrant community made up of thousands of people of Cape Verdean ancestry.

Further Reading

African Encyclopaedia. 1974. London: Oxford University Press.
Clapham, C. 1998. *African Guerrillas.* Oxford: James Currey.
Davidson, B. 1964. *Old Africa Rediscovered.* London: Oxford University Press.

Duffy, J. 1959. *Portuguese Africa.* Harvard University Press.
Fage, J. D. 1963. *An Atlas of African History.* Arnold.
Gibson, R. 1992. **African Liberation Movements.** London: Oxford University Press.
Greenberg, J. H. 1963. *Languages of Africa.* London: Indiana University Press.
International Encyclopaedia of the Social Sciences. London: Macmillan.
Murdoc G. P. 1959. *Africa: Its Peoples and their Culture History.* New York, McGraw-Hill.

CHAPTER FOURTEEN

Cote d'Ivoire

The Republic of Cote d'Ivoire (Repiublique de Cote d'Ivoire) which is also called Ivory Coast is a GoG state with an area of 320,763 square kilometres and a coastline of about 480 kilometres long. It is bounded to the north by Mali and Burkina Faso, to the east by Ghana, to the south by the GoG, to the southeast by Liberia and to the northwest by the Republic of Guinea. Yamoussoukro is the official capital while Abidjan, the former capital, is the economic nerve centre of the country. Other prominent cities include Bouake, Daloa, Gagnoa, Korhogo, Man and San Pedro.

The eastern part of its coastline has lagoons behind long sand-bars; the western part is more rocky and steep. There are low plains inland, which rise in the north to a plateau of about 400 metres high. To the west of Man, the Nimba Mountains rise above 1000 metres. The vegetation of Cote d'Ivoire is mainly savanna with woodland in the north and rain forest in the south. Crossing the republic from north to south are several large rivers like the Sassandra and the Comoe.

The People

Cote d'Ivoire has about 60 ethnic groups. Each of them has two unique characteristics. Firstly, they are traditionally independent of each other. Secondly, each of them has ethnic affiliations with some larger ethnic groups in the neighbouring nations. For instance, the Baule, the people east of the Bandama River and the lagoon people of the south are of the same stock with the Akan people of Ghana. The forest people of the Bandama region are of the Kru stock which is also found in Liberia. The Baule comprise the single largest group with about 20 percent of the population. They inhabit the central region around Bouake and Yamoussoukro.

In the savanna region are the Malinke and Dyula people who belong to the Mande group which is also found in Mali. The Senufo in the north, the Lobo and Bobo people are of the Voltaic stock that is found in the northeast of Cote d'Ivoire and the neighbouring nations.

Cote d'Ivoire

Fig. 14.1: *Political Map of Cote d'Ivoire*

This country of about 19 million people has more than five million non-Ivoirian Africans. Of the number, about half come from Burkina Faso; the rest are principally from Ghana, Guinea, Mali, Nigeria, Liberia, Senegal, Mauritania and Benin. The non-African expatriate community is made up of about 10,000 French and 70,000 Lebanese.

About 20 percent of the population is Christian, about 40 percent Muslim and the rest are adherents of African Traditional Religion. Life expectancy in Cote d'Ivoire is 46 years and infant mortality rate is 111 per 1,000 live births.

History

The pre-colonial history of Cote d'Ivoire relates much with the history of the ancient empires of Ghana, Mali and Songhai in Western Sudan, the Asante Empire in the Guinea Coast and the Fulani jihad of the nineteenth century in Nigeria.

From the earliest times, many groups in today's Cote d'Ivoire participated in the trans-Saharan trade and were parts of the networks of the trade associated with Ghana and Mali empires. The decline and eventual collapse of the Songhai Empire in the late sixteenth century caused a lot of strains in the political and economic development of West Africa. Economically, the trans-Saharan trade suffered a great blow from which it never really recovered.

Politically, the former empire broke into a collection of independent and warring states, each attempting to overpower the other. Most of them finally moved in different directions especially southward, founding new kingdoms in the forest zone.

In the savanna region, the development of settled communities was associated with the Dyula traders. In 1897, Samouri Toure, who was inspired by the Fulani jihad in Nigeria, destroyed the kingdoms in northern parts of the country and in their places created a Muslim empire. The emergence of the Asante in the late seventeenth century led to several wars of conquest and those who refused to be conquered, but who at the same time were not powerful enough to challenge the Asante hegemony, moved to the forest areas of Cote d'Ivoire to establish new kingdoms. One of such was the Abron kingdom of Gyaman which unfortunately was conquered by Asante in 1730. Moreover, a direct consequence of a succession struggle after the death of Opoku Ware of Asante in 1750 was the movement of one of the queens, Abla Poku and her supporters into north-central Cote d'Ivoire to found the Baule kingdom.

The process of colonization of Cote d'Ivoire was accelerated in the nineteenth century. Until then Europeans, who were mainly from Portugal and France, limited their activities to the coast where they had forts. By the 1890s, French traders led by Marcel Triech-Laplene penetrated the hinterland and along with French military officers signed treaties with African kings. In 1893, France claimed Cote d'Ivoire as a colony. The claim was challenged by Samouri Toure who engaged the French troops in a long war of resistance. In 1898, Toure was conquered and in 1918, the entire Cote d'Ivoire was pacified after fierce resistance following the imposition of forced labour and head taxes.

Between 1904 and 1958, the country was a constituent unit of the Federation of French West Africa. As a colony and an overseas territory under the French Third Republic, its affairs were administered from Paris under the French policy of *Association* which was discussed in chapter two. From the outset, France, which regarded its colonies in Africa as part and parcel of itself, never imagined that the colonies could have independence. In fact, the French Constitution of 1946 created the ***French Union*** which consisted of metropolitan France, territories designated as departments of France (in northern Africa) and overseas territories which included the colonies in sub-Saharan Africa. That Constitution even contained provisions that none of the overseas members could become independent.

But the defeat of France in the Second World War, discontentment on the part of the Africans to forced labour, imprisonment without trial, various forms of inhuman treatment, the support of French Socialist Movement in France itself and political reforms in British West Africa, inspired Africans in Francophone countries to wish for political independence. The Overseas Reform Act (Loi Cadre) quickened the process of decolonization in French colonies. The Loi Cadre transferred a number of powers from Paris to elected territorial governments in French West Africa and equally removed voting inequalities.

In December, 1958, Cote d'Ivoire became an autonomous republic within French community as a result of a referendum that brought community status to territories of the old Federation of French West Africa except Guinea, which had voted against association (see chapter seventeen). On August 7, 1960, Cote d'Ivoire became independent.

Politics and Structure of Governance

Between 1960 that Cote d'Ivoire achieved independence and 1993; its political history was associated with the career of Felix Houphouet-Boigny. Houphouet-Boigny was the President of the country for that long period. He was one of the founders of the leading pre-independence inter-territorial political party in French West African countries known as the *Rassemblement Democratique Africain (RDA)*.

After independence, the political system was controlled for 30 years by the Democratic Party of Cote d'Ivoire (PDCI) which was the only recognized party in the country. PDCI originated as a league of African farmers founded by Houphouet-Boigny at the end of the Second World War. From 1990, the country started an experiment in multi-party system.

After the death of Houphouet-Boigny in 1993, political darkness enveloped Cote d'Ivoire. Within the period of his presidency, the country had a semblance of political stability based on armed peace but intrigues followed his death because of lack of a credible succession plan. In 1999, the country experienced a coup d'état led by General Guei and in 2001 there was another coup. Though it failed it led to mass-scale protest and rebellion which prepared the political landscape of Cote d'Ivoire for a civil war. However, attempts by neighbouring countries, ECOWAS and the international community to sanitize the political system in Cote d'Ivoire were made and the prospects were bright.

Be that as it may, the contemporary structure of governance in Cote d'Ivoire is based on the 2000 Constitution of the Second Republic. It provides for a strong presidency within the framework of separation of powers. The President is elected for a five-year term and may seek re-election at the end of the tenure. The President who is the head of state selects the Prime Minister who is the head of government. The Prime Minister selects the cabinet which is responsible to him.

There is a single-house legislature, the National Assembly, with 225 members elected by direct universal suffrage for a five-year term. The highest judicial body is the Supreme Court. There are also the High Court of Justice and Independent Constitutional Council. The Council has seven members who are appointed by the President. It is responsible for the determination of eligibility of candidates for presidential and legislative elections, the announcement of final election results, the conduct of referendums and the constitutionality of legislation. Cote d'Ivoire operates the French legal system.

The country is divided into 19 regions and 90 departments. Each region is headed by a Prefect appointed by the central government but in 2002 elections were introduced to select departmental councils. There are also elected mayors to head the 196 communes in the country. Abidjan has 10 mayors.

Economy

Agriculture is the pillar of the Ivorian economy. The country is primarily noted for its forest products. It is a major exporter of tropical wood. It has about 30 species of trees that are in high demand across the world. Cocoa is another main export crop of Cote d'Ivoire. It is cultivated by about one-quarter of the population. Other commercial crops include palm oil and produce, coffee, pineapple, rubber and coconut (for copra). About 70 percent of the population is engaged in agricultural activity. Fishing is very important in the country's economy and Cote d'Ivoire is the largest African exporter of tuna. The country has two active ports in Abidjan and San Pedro. The Abidjan port is the most modern in the GoG and indeed the largest between Casablanca in North Africa and Cape Town in southern Africa.

The mining industry is not well developed, coordinated and regulated even though the country has known reserves of nickel, gold, diamond, copper, uranium, manganese and iron ore. The iron ore deposits at the slopes of Mount Nimba enrich Liberia and Guinea as well.

Foreign Relations

Cote d'Ivoire's foreign policy during the Houphouet-Boigny presidency was largely pro-Western and the Pan-Africanist content was less than one percent. Where, for instance, Africa was interested in sanctions on, and isolation of, South Africa on account of its apartheid system, Cote d'Ivoire proposed dialogue and negotiations with the evil regime. Where Africa isolated Israel on account of continuous occupation of the Sinai desert belonging to Egypt, Cote d'Ivoire re-established diplomatic relations with Israel. During the civil war in Nigeria, Cote d'Ivoire supported the Biafran regime. Its pro-Western policy favoured France considerably to the extent that though on paper Cote d'Ivoire was a sovereign state; in reality it continued to be the overseas territory of France.

Outside French understandably becoming the official language of Cote d'Ivoire as an ex-colony of France, the country operated in an undiluted manner the French legal system and hosted French marine which provided it with security alongside Ivorian troops. What is more, the former name of the country, Ivory Coast, was considered too anglicized and had to be changed to Cote d'Ivoire in order to savour the French flavour; its CFA franc currency was tied to French franc and now to the euro. France for a very long time was the country's most strategic trading partner.

The post-Houphouet-Biogny Cote d'Ivoire has reduced French influence in the country considerably and at the same time has broadened its diplomatic initiatives and engagements. Its Pan African, universalist and Non-Aligned credentials are easily noticeable. Cote d'Ivoire is a member of the ECOWAS, West African Economic and Monetary Union, Council of Entente, Communuate Financiere Africaine, Non-Aligned Movement, Non-Aggression and Defence Agreement, African Regional Satellite Organizations, Inter-African Coffee Organization, International Cocoa Organization, Alliance of Cocoa Producers, African, Caribbean and Pacific Countries (APC), Association of Coffee Producing Countries and the Organization of Islamic Conference (OIC).

Further Reading

African Encyclopaedia. 1974. London: Oxford University Press.
Besada, H. ed. 2007. *From Civil Strife to Peace Building: Examining Private Sector Involvement in West African Reconstruction.* Canada: Centre for International Governance Innovation.
Clapham, C. ed. 1982. *Private Patronage and Public Order.* London: Pinter.
Cohen, M. 1973. *The Myth of the Expanding Centre: Politics in the Ivory Coast.* **Journal of Modern African Studies.** 11 (2): 231-45.
Cohen, M. A. 1974. *Urban Policy and Political Conflict in Africa: A Study of the Ivory Coast.* Chigaco: University of Chigaco Press.
Davidson, B. 1964. *Old Africa Rediscovered.* London: Oxford University Press.

Duffy, J. 1959. *Portuguese Africa.* Harvard University Press.
Fage, J. D. 1963. *An Atlas of African History.* Arnold.
Fatton, R. 1992. *Predator Rule: Stat and Society in Africa.* Boulder: Lynner Reinner.
Greenberg, J. H. 1963. *Languages of Africa.* London: Indiana University Press.
International Encyclopaedia of the Social Sciences. London: Macmillan.
Murdoc G. P. 1959. *Africa: Its Peoples and their Culture History.* New York, McGraw-Hill.
Zartman, I. W. and Delgardo, C. eds. 1984. *Political Economy of the Ivory Coast.* New York: Praeger Books.

CHAPTER FIFTEEN

The Gambia

The Gambia is the smallest republic in the GoG. It is situated on the Atlantic coast in the Gulf and surrounded on three sides by Senegal. The country consists of a strip of land of about 470 kilometres long on the banks of the Gambia River. It is generally between 11 kilometres and 20 kilometres wide from the north to south, and the total area is 11,300 square kilometres. As stated already, except for the few kilometres of Atlantic coast, the republic is surrounded by Senegal. Its smallness in size is attributable to territorial negotiations and compromises of the nineteenth century between Britain and France. The Gambia has a population of 1.9 million. The capital is Banjul while Serekunda is the largest city.

The Gambia River is the dominant feature of the country. Its vegetation cover is savanna on the uplands, various kinds of inland swamp in the low-lying areas, and mangrove swamp along the brackish Lower Gambia River.

The People

The Gambia consists mainly of people who escaped the internecine wars in the Western Sudan in the twelfth century and migrated southwards to found new settlements. Perhaps the oldest of these groups are the Diola (Jola) people who are located in western Gambia. However, the largest group is the Malinke (Madingo) who make up about two-fifths of the population. There are other groups like the Wolof who form the largest population in Banjul, the Fula (nomadic Fulani) and Soninke, (admixture of Malinke and Fulani) who live in the upriver areas. About 90 percent of the population of the Gambia is Muslim while the rest are Christians and adherents of the African Traditional Religion. Life expectancy in Gambia is 54 years and infant mortality rate is 67 per 1000 live births.

The Gambia

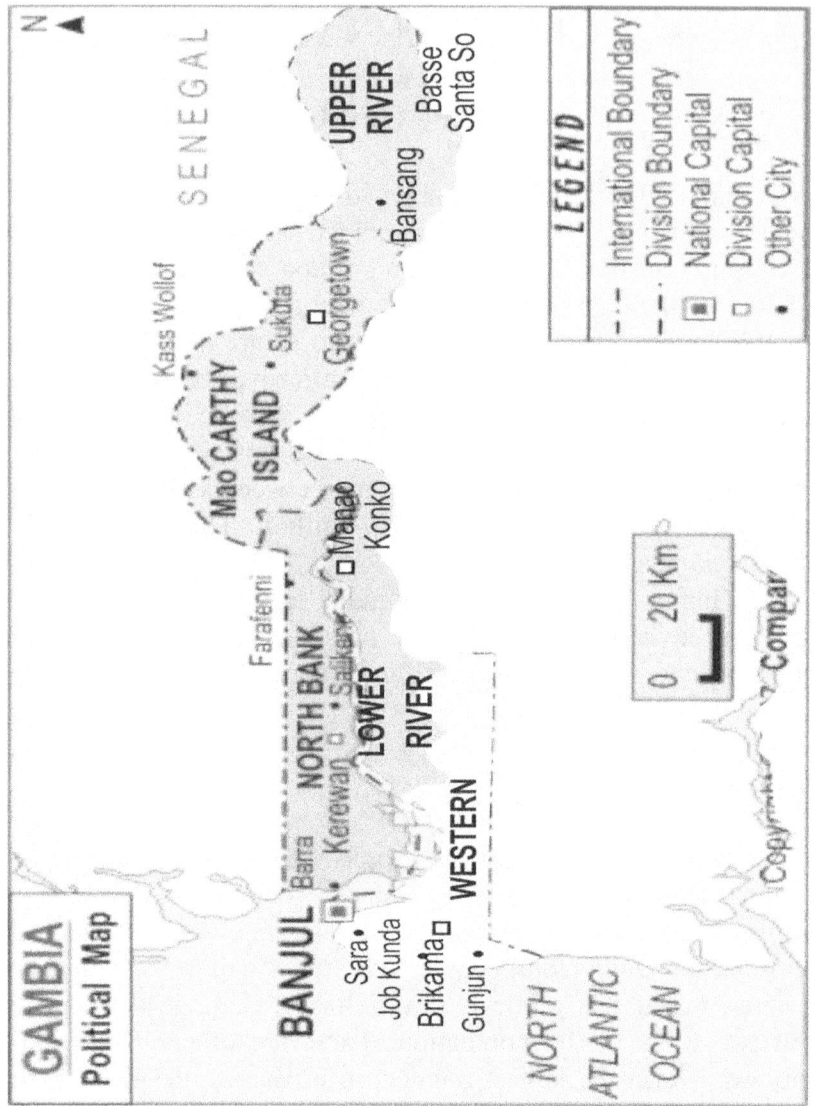

Fig. 15.1: Political Map of the Gambia

History

Two main groups of peoples who moved into the Gambia region from the earliest times had phenomenal influence on the history of modern Gambia. The cattle-rearing people who were of the Berber descent came from the north in the fifth century AD and they were followed by the Manding peoples from the east. Between the fifth and the eighth centuries, the Gambia region was part of the empire of ancient Ghana in the Western Sudan. In the thirteenth century, it became part of the empire of the ancient Mali and indeed the Malinke were the western-most peoples of that empire. The Wolof migrated from the empire of ancient Songhai while the Fulani pastoralists migrated from Futa Toro and Futa Djallon plateau of Guinea.

From the earliest times, the Mande-speaking rulers who were associated with the Mali Empire ruled the entire region of the Gambia until the period of the great upheaval in the nineteenth century in form of Fulani jihad. Even at that, the Mande-speaking peoples are still the majority ethnic group in the Gambia.

The Europeans became part of the Gambian historiography in the thirteenth century. Even though Hanno the Carthaginian had sighted the Gambian coast in 470BC on his voyage, the Portuguese were the first European visitors to the Gambia River in 1455. They established trading stations during this period but abandoned it within a century. But the commercial potentials of the Gambia made it irresistible to the English, French, Dutch, Swedish and other European nations but the contest for the control of the country was between the British and the French. From the seventeenth century, several British trading companies, the largest of them all being the Royal African Company, and the French companies struggled for the control of the country. They desired to trade in gold but ended up trading in slaves. After the war between Britain and France early in the nineteenth century, Banjul Island (St. Mary's Island), which was purchased from the king of Kombo, became a colony of Britain and was governed from Sierra Leone.

In 1816, the British sent Captain Alexander Grant to the Gambia to re-establish a naval base from which it could use to stop the slave trade. Many freed slaves especially Creoles were settled on the Banjul Island after the abolition of slave trade. Until 1889 the colony was administered as part of Sierra Leone. It is interesting to note that twice the British initiated moves to hand over the Gambia to France to be administered as part of Senegal in exchange for some French possessions elsewhere but the protests that attended the plans in Britain and the Gambia, once they were leaked, frustrated such efforts.

The Gambia

In 1901, the British protectorate of the Gambia was established and the British influence spread into the hinterland from Banjul.

Perhaps on account of its small size and population, the Gambia was late in initiating political moves towards independence unlike other British West African states. Political developments towards independence actually began with the first political party which was founded by the Reverend J.C. Faye in 1952. Political pressure made the British to give the country revised Constitutions in 1954, 1960 and 1962.

In 1962, everyone in the country was given the right to vote and in the elections that followed the People's Progressive Party (PPP) led by Sir Dawda Jawara won and formed the government. The Gambia became independent in February 1965 and was made a republic on April 24, 1970.

Politics and Structure of Governance

Between 1970 and 1994, politics in the Gambia was dominated by Dawda Kairaba Jawara, the President and his PPP. The President is constitutionally the head of government. He is elected by universal suffrage to a five-year term. The Vice President and cabinet members are appointed by the President. The highest judicial body is the Supreme Court, whose members are appointed by the President.

In July 1994, Jawara's tenure as President came to an abrupt end through a military coup d'état. It was staged by Captain Yahya Jammeh. The Constitution was suspended and political parties were banned. Jammeh promised new elections which were conducted in September 1996. In this exercise he stood for the office of the President and won. In 2001 he lifted the ban on political parties but he is the only political cock to crow in the country.

In September 2006, Jammeh, whose titles include Alhaji, Dr and Chief, won the election to return as President for a third five-year term. He repeated the feet in 2011 and may repeat it again in 2016.

Economy

The Gambian economy is based on groundnut which is the main export crop and source of revenue to the government. Oil palms are grown, and the oil and kernels are exported. Cotton is another export product. Great efforts have been made to diversify the economy through tourism, commercial fishing and rice farming.

Foreign Relations

As a country that is almost surrounded by the Francophone state of Senegal, the Gambia has special relations with Senegal and by implication France. As a former colonial territory of Britain, she maintains good relations with Britain and Anglophone states in the GoG. Its chief trading partners are Senegal, France and Britain. Additionally, she is a good player in strategic international organizations which include the Commonwealth of Nations, ECOWAS, the AU and the UN.

Further Reading

African Encyclopaedia. 1974. London: Oxford University Press.
Davidson, B. 1964. *Old Africa Rediscovered*. London: Oxford University Press.
Duffy, J. 1959. *Portuguese Africa*. Harvard University Press.
Fage, J. D. 1963. *An Atlas of African History*. Arnold.
Greenberg, J. H. 1963. *Languages of Africa*. London: Indiana University Press.
International Encyclopaedia of the Social Sciences. London: Macmillan.
Murdoc G. P. 1959. *Africa: Its Peoples and their Culture History*. New York, McGraw-Hill.

CHAPTER SIXTEEN

Ghana

Ghana is one of the countries of the Guinea Coast. It is bordered on the northwest and north by Burkina Faso, on the east by Togo, on the south by the GoG and on the west by Cote d'Ivoire. The country has an area of about 240,000 square kilometres and a population of 24 million. Though small in size and population, Ghana has since the colonial days been a leading state in the GoG. She was the first black nation in sub-Saharan Africa to achieve independence. That was in 1957.

Ghana was also the first fertile ground for the flowering of Pan-Africanism, an ideology of solidarity that is a central element in the foreign policies of many African states. She has considerable natural wealth. As a British colony, it was called the Gold Coast, a name that was given to the area by the Portuguese but at independence, it changed its name to Ghana. Its capital is Accra. Other larger cities include Kumasi, Temale, Takoradi, Teshie, Tema and Cape Coast.

The People

The indigenous population of Ghana can be classified as homoterogenous; admixture of homogeneity and heterogeneity. The people are homogenous because they belong largely to the Akan-speaking group; they are heterogeneous because within the Akan group are several sub-ethnic groups. Taking language and dialect into consideration, there are about 70 of such sub-groups the most numerous being the Akan (which include the Fante, Akyem, Ashanti, Kwahu, Akuapem, Nzema, Bono, Ahanta and Akwamu); 49.3 percent of the population, Ewe (about 11.7 percent) Ga-Dangme (which includes the Ga, Adangbe, Krobo and Ada); 7.3 percent, Guan, 4 percent, Gurma, 3.6 percent, Gurunsi, 2.6 percent, Mande-Busanga, one percent, Hausa, Zabarema and Fulani, 1.8 percent and others 1.4 percent.

About 70 percent of the population are Christians, 16 percent are Muslims and the rest are adherents of the African Traditional Religion.

Life expectancy in Ghana is 61 years and infant mortality rate is 50 per 1000 live births.

Fig. 16.1: Political Map of Ghana

History

Ghana was so named by Dr. Kwame Nkrumah at independence after the ancient empire of Western Sudan that flourished until the thirteenth century. The leadership at independence in 1957 claimed that the new Ghana was a direct descendant of the old Ghana Empire. Of course, the reasons for such claims are not hard to find. Ancient Ghana recorded some feats in the ability of the Blackman to organize himself politically, diplomatically, socially and economically at a time that most European nations were still wallowing in barbarism (Akpan, 2000). Therefore, the leadership of Gold Coast at independence being actively Pan Africanist decided to choose Ghana as the new name of the new country. This choice was justified by Nkrumah on the eve of independence in the following way:

> ... according to tradition, the peoples of the Gold Coast originally came from the great empire of Ghana, and that at the University of Sankore of the old Ghana empire there were teachers ... from all parts of the Arab world of the Middle Ages, and there was a mingling of the cultures of the peoples from the north and the south of the Sahara ... it is our earnest hope that the Ghana which is now being reborn will be like the Ghana of old, centre to which all the peoples of Africa may come ... (see Aluko, 1978:73).

This was merely an executive myth that tried to link the gold wealth of the Gold Coast with the gold wealth of ancient Ghana. The ruler of ancient Ghana was called **Lord of the Gold** on account of enormous gold resource of the empire and Gold Coast also had so much gold to warrant the region to be named after gold. Outside that, ancient Ghana was located in the areas of today's western Mali and south-eastern Mauritania.

However, the Akan-speaking peoples who inhabit the forest and coastal areas are of Mande origin. They had established themselves in the thirteenth century. Dagomba and Mamprusi in northern Ghana were established in the fifteenth century by the Hausa people. Ga and Ewe states in southeast were founded by people from Nigeria. Gonja in central Ghana was established by Mande warriors in the seventeenth century.

In the history of Ghana, these states participated in the trans-Saharan and trans-Atlantic trade. In northern Ghana, Mamprussi, Mossi and Dagomba grew rich from the trade in gold and kola nuts that went to North Africa from the forest regions. In return came salt, weapons and cloth from North Africa and the Mediterranean. In the south, the states of Akwamu and Denkyira were already powerful in the seventeenth century. But the most powerful of all the forest states was the Asante empire which was discussed in chapter one. The state profited immensely from participation in the trans-Atlantic trade.

Contacts with the Europeans took place in the fifteenth century. The Portuguese were the first Europeans to arrive on the Guinea Coast and in 1482 they built the Elmina Castle as a fortified trading post near what is now Cape Coast. The idea of the Castle was initiated by the King of Portugal, John II, who commissioned Diogo d'Azambuja to build it. Traders from other European countries soon joined in the trade in gold, slaves and ivory.

The Portuguese were followed by the English in 1553, the Dutch in 1595 and the Swedes in 1640. They also built trading forts as well. At last count, more than 30 forts and castles were built by the Portuguese, Dutch, British and Spanish merchants and buccaneers. A regular outcome of European interest in Ghana was stiff competition against each other to possess the region and exploit its seemingly endless potentials: Elmina was taken from the Portuguese by the Dutch in 1637; Christianborg (now Government House, in Accra) was built by the Swedes in 1652, was occupied by the Dutch in 1660 and was seized by the Danes thereafter.

The Africans were not left out in the competition for trade. Guns that were given to them especially by the Danes were used to sack communities and sell the captured ones as slaves. The Akwamu people led by Asomani captured Christiansburg in 1693 and John Konny, an influential African merchant held the Brandenburg forts against the Dutch in the later part of the eighteenth century.

By the nineteenth century, the British outsmarted other European powers and became the leading player in Ghana. Through treaties with the traditional rulers of Assin, Denkyra and Fanti, the British made inroads into the southern regions. In 1874, the Fanti allied with the British to defeat its Asante rivals. Even at that, the Asante continued its war of resistance with the British. In 1896, its ruler Prempeh I was arrested and exiled by the British. The British set up colonial administration in the south but when the British Governor demanded the sacred Golden Stool, the people saw it as sacrilege and renewed their war of resistance. The Golden Stool could only be used by the Asantehene. By 1900 the Asante were defeated and in 1902 the British influence spread over the entire area that was later called the Gold Coast.

Even after colonial rule was firmly in place in Ghana, the chiefs and their people resisted a number of British policies like the Indirect Rule system. Moves toward decolonization were intensified after the Second World War. Though in 1946 the Gold Coast Government was given more African representatives, the African political movement became stronger from 1947 when J.B. Danquah founded the United Gold Coast Convention (UGCC) and demanded for self-government. Meanwhile in 1949, Kwame Nkrumah, a radical politician, had established the Convention People's Party (CPP), which with popular support won all the elections between 1951 and 1957. On March 6 1957, Ghana was granted independence with Nkrumah as the Prime Minister. In 1960, Ghana became a republic with Nkrumah as the President.

Politics and Structure of Governance

At independence in 1957, Osagyefo Kwame Nkrumah and his associates in the CPP ruled Ghana. After the country became a republic in 1960, Nkrumah became the President and proclaimed himself the life President of the country. This means that opposing ideas were not tolerated; yet opposition developed against the Osagyefo. While on a state visit to China in February 1966, the army and the police mutinied, staged a coup d'état and overthrew his regime. He was replaced by Lieutenant General Joseph A. Ankrah.

When Ankrah failed to initiate political reforms that he had promised, his government was overthrown by Brigadier Akwasi Amankwaa Afrifa in 1969. Afrifa initiated political reforms which produced a Constitution. Elections were held in August 1969 through which the Progress Party led by a University Professor, Kofi Busia, won many seats in the parliament. Busia was made the Prime Minister and Ghana started the Second Republic. Busia's administration was highly unstable because of heavy foreign debt and low prices of cocoa.

As he tried to respond to these challenges, the military led by Colonel Ignatius Kutu Acheampong struck and sacked the regime in 1972. Acheampong's regime was overthrown six years later by Lieutenant General Frederick W. K. Akuffo in 1979. A year later, young and non-commissioned officers led by a radical air-force pilot, Flight Lieutenant Jerry Rawlings staged a coup which sacked the

Akuffo regime. Akuffo and Acheampong were charged for corruption and summarily executed. Rawlings handed over power to the civilians under President Hilla Limann. But failed promises by Limann forced Rawlings to seized power again in 1981. During his regime, two countercoups were attempted.

As a result of domestic and international pressure, a new Constitution was given to Ghana in 1992 where Rawlings was elected as the President on the platform of the National Democratic Congress. He won again in 1996. In the 2000 elections his Vice President, John Atta Mills ran against John Kuffour of the New Patriotic Party. Kuffour won and won again in 2004 against Atta Mills, but in the 2009 presidential elections, Atta Mills won and was sworn into office as the President of Ghana.

Ghana is in its fourth republic after many years of blight occasioned by military adventurism. The Constitution of 1992 provides clear roles and tenure for the President, Parliament, Council of state and an independent judiciary. The government is elected by universal adult suffrage.

Economy

Agriculture and mineral resources are the mainstay of the economy of Ghana. The most important cash and export crop is cocoa. The crop was introduced for cultivation in Ghana from Equatorial Guinea by Tetteh Quashie and his brother in 1879. The country has for long been the world's greatest exporter of cocoa. Other export crops include oil-palm products, coffee and groundnuts from the south, and groundnuts and tobacco from the north.

Ghana is rich in mineral resources. These minerals are found in the southern part of the country. The oldest and most prominent mineral is gold with an unbroken history dating from the fifteenth century. Ghana is still a large exporter of gold. The main gold-producing areas are Tarkwa and Obuasi. Diamonds are mined near Accra and manganese is produced at Nsuta. Manganese production in Ghana started in 1915. Another very important mineral is bauxite which is mined near Awaso for Aluminum production in Tema. The country also has iron ore and salt in which it is self-sufficient with the surplus exported to other countries.

Petroleum oil was first discovered in 1970, but it was not in commercial quantity. In 1974 and 1980 considerable amounts of natural gas were discovered offshore around Cape Three Points. In 1978 oil production began in the Salt Point area but nothing much came out of the efforts. In 2007 an oil field with about 3 billion barrels of light crude oil was discovered in Ghana and production had since started. The latest discovery has made Ghana to become an oil producing country in the GoG.

Tropical hardwoods especially mahogany and sapele are important foreign exchange earners as well. These come from the country's thick forest in the south.

Foreign Relations

From the independence period, the foreign policy of Ghana has been laced with the ideals of Pan Africanism and Non-Alignment. Ghana encourages regional political and economic blocs and is a major player in many international organizations.

From the outset, Ghana under Nkrumah espoused the ideas of continental government for Africa. He (Nkrumah) called for the establishment of the Union of African States (UAS) as one government in Africa. In 1958 Ghana joined forces with Guinea to establish the Ghana-Guinea Union and in 1961 another candidate, Mali acceded to the Union and the Ghana-Guinea-Mali Union was created. Nkrumah even went further to sign a secret agreement with Patrice Lumumba to establish a Union of Ghana and Congo as well, but the Congo crisis and the subsequent death of Lumumba ended the accord (Akpan, 2000).

In matters of decolonization of Africa, Pan Africanism, African Unity and Neo-colonialism, Ghana under Nkrumah was the chief spokesman for Africa. That is why Roland Oliver and Anthony Atmore (1994:289) conclude that the fall of Nkrumah marked a turning point in the history of independent Africa and that:

> The twenty years or so of African history from the end of the Second World War until 1965 could be called without much exaggeration, the age of Nkrumah.

Ghana through Nkrumah brought Africa to the forefront in world affairs.

After the fall of Nkrumah, his successors continued to make Ghana an active player in West Africa, Africa and the World at large. Ghana is a member of ECOWAS, the Commonwealth of Nations, the AU and the UN. Ghana produced for the world in the twentieth and twenty-first centuries, one of the finest international civil servants, Kofi Anan who was the Secretary-General of the UN between 1997 and 2006.

Further Reading

African Encyclopaedia. 1974. London: Oxford University Press.
Agbodeka, F. 1971. *African Politics and British Policy in the Gold Coast, 1868-1900.* London: Longman.
Aluko, O. 1978. *Ghana and Nigeria, 1957-70: A Study in Inter-African Discord.* London: Rex Collings.
Austin, D. 1964. *Politics in Ghana.* London: Oxford University Press.
Boahen, A. A. 1975. *Ghana.* London: Longman.
Burret, F. Y. 1960. *Ghana: The Road to Independence.* London: Oxford University Press.
Davidson, B. 1964. *Old Africa Rediscovered.* London: Oxford University Press.
Duffy, J. 1959. *Portuguese Africa.* Harvard University Press.
Dickson, K. B. 1969. A Historical Geography of Ghana. London: Cambridge University Press.
Fage, J. D. 1963. *An Atlas of African History*. Arnold.
Flint, J. 1967. *Ghana and Nigeria.* London: Oxford University Press.
Greenberg, J. H. 1963. *Languages of Africa.* London: Indiana University Press.
International Encyclopaedia of the Social Sciences. London: Macmillan.
Murdoc G. P. 1959. *Africa: Its Peoples and their Culture History.* New York, McGraw-Hill.
Kimble, D. 1963. *Political History of Ghana.* London: Oxford University Press.
Kwame, N. 1970. *I Speak of Freedom.* London: Panaf Books.
Metcalf, G. E. 1964. *Great Britain and Ghana.* London: Nelson.

Ward, W. E. F. 1966. *A History of Ghana.* London: Allen & Unwin.
Wolfson, F. *Pageant of Ghana.* London: Oxford University Press.

CHAPTER SEVENTEEN

Guinea

The Republic of Guinea (Republique de Guinee) is an independent state in the Guinea Coast. It is bordered by Guinea-Bissau, Senegal and Mali to the north and east; by Cote d'Ivoire to the southeast; and the GoG to the west. It has a population of 10 million and an area of 245,857 square kilometres. It is the source of about 22 rivers in West Africa including the Niger, Gambia and Senegal. The capital is Conakry. Other cities include Kankan, Kamasar, Boke, Kindia, N'Zerekoe, Macenta, Mamou and Faranah.

Guinea has four geographic regions, namely: the Lower Guinea (a narrow coastal belt), the Middle Guinea (the pastoral Fouta Djallon highlands), the Upper Guinea (the northern savanna) and the Forest Guinea (the south-eastern rainforest region).

The People

There are four major ethnic groups in Guinea and they are found in the four geographic regions of the country. Thus, in the Lower Guinea are found the Susu; in the Fouta Djallon are found the Fulani; in the Upper Guinea are found the Malinke while the Forest Region contains the Kpelle, Loma and Kissi. The Fulani are majority accounting for about 40 percent of the population. They are followed by Malinke with 30 percent, the Susu with 20 percent and others with 10 percent. About 85 percent of the population are Muslims and though the Christian population is merely 8 percent, it is very influential in the affairs of Guinea. About seven percent are adherents of the African Traditional Religion.

Fig. 17.1: Political Map of Guinea

History

People, who in the main were hunters and gatherers, had lived in the area that today constitutes the Republic of Guinea more than 30,000 years ago, but it was only about 1000 years ago that the Susu and Malinke people encroached and almost displaced the Baga and other people who had been living there for years before their arrival. The area of the Upper Guinea was part of the Mali Empire of Western Sudan in about the thirteenth century. In the sixteenth century, the Fulani group had already established an Islamic empire in the Fouta Djallon.

Indeed, Islam had played a significant part in the history of the region since the sixteenth century and the towns of Kankan and Labe were made centres of Islamic religion and political life. In the mid-nineteenth century, Alhaji Umah led his jihad from Dinguiray and his Fulani troops conquered Fouta Djallon before moving north-eastwards to Kaarta and Segu. From 1879 eastern Guinea became a part of the empire of Samouri Toure.

Like other states of the GoG, the Portuguese were the first Europeans to visit Guinea in the fifteenth century. They traded in slaves in the region. Until the ruler of Fouta Djallon placed his country under French protection in 1881, British and French activities were minimal in the area though the French had claimed the area as its protectorate in 1849. The protectorate was called ***Rivierers du Sud***. Even at that, the full possession of Guinea by the French was not an easy task as the Malinke state, ruled by Samouri Toure, fought them as they invaded from Senegal. Toure was only defeated in 1898 but his associates continued to resist the French into the inter-war years.

In 1895 the French Guinea, as it came to be called, was made a part of the Federation of French West Africa. In the 1930s many nationalists emerged in the French political empire in West Africa and demanded political and economic reforms. They included Lamine Gueye from Senegal, Fily Dabo Sissoko from Mali and Yacine Diallo from Guinea. As a consequence of pressure by these nationalists, in 1944 a Conference was held in Brazzaville which was the capital of French Equatorial Africa to tackle burning colonial issues. A number of resolutions were passed at the end of the Conference. The resolutions sought for more representatives to West Africans and to define future French policy with regards to the relationship between the territories and metropolitan France and the chances of decentralizing the administration of French West Africa.

In 1946 the French Union was established. The Union brought France and her overseas territories into a close association and decentralized the administration of the West African territories. But in October 1958, it was dissolved. In its place was established the French Community. By this time, the French Fifth Republic was constituted under General Charles de Gaulle. The community expected the following from member states:

1. Each member state was to be autonomous, except in the control of some common subjects including currency, external affairs, defence and higher education;
2. The President of the Community was the President of France;
3. The Executive Council was made up of the Prime Minister of France, the heads of government of the member states, and the Ministers responsible to the community for common subjects;

4. The senate consisted of delegates from the parliament of France and the member states; and
5. There was to be a court of arbitration.

The Constitution of the French Fifth Republic called for a referendum for the overseas territories to determine, by **YES** or **NO** votes, whether or not they wished to be members of the Community. Those voting **NO** were to become independent automatically.

De Gaulle toured African states to sell his idea of wanting them to remain in the French Community and emphasizing that no African country was viable enough to become independent; rather they needed French subsidy for sustenance. de Gaulle was very certain that all would vote **NO** but he was extremely disappointed at the end of the day. In the referendum of September 28, 1958, all the overseas territories voted **YES**, except Guinea which voted **NO** and opted out of the Community. On October 2 1958, it became an independent nation.

The personality behind the challenge to the French Community was Sekou Toure, a foremost Guinean nationalist who in his campaign slogan said that Guinea preferred poverty in freedom to riches in slavery. At independence, Sekou Toure became the first President of Guinea.

The consequences for Guinea in voting **NO** in the referendum were grave. The French personnel and workers left Guinea in droves but before they left they destroyed all facilities in the country including electricity poles, roads and water taps. This exercise was to serve as a punishment for Guinea for daring to confront the mother country.

Politics and Structure of Governance

Sekou Toure became the President of Guinea at independence. Under him the country became a one-party dictatorship ruled by the Democratic Party of Guinea (DPG). In governance, Toure filled strategic state institutions with his own Malinke ethnic group. Ethnicity and repression became so entrenched in the body politic that hundreds of thousands of the citizens fled the country. When the dissidents allied with Portuguese mercenaries to attack Conakry with a view to overthrowing Sekou Toure, his regime became extremely paranoid.

In the aftermath of the attack, many dissidents were tried and executed and a lot more disappeared. Sekou Toure and his PDG administered Guinea until his death on April 3, 1984. One week after his death, the military under Lieutenant Colonel Lansana Conte seized power, banned the PDG and established the Military Committee for National Recovery (CMRN). A new Constitution in 1991 led to political reforms. In 1992, Guinea legalized political parties and in the following year experimented with multiparty elections. Conte participated in the elections and won fraudulently. In 2001, Conte amended the Constitution to permit the President to run for an unlimited number of terms and to extend the presidential term from five to seven years.

Guinea operates a constitutional democracy with strong presidency. It has a unicameral legislature elected by universal suffrage.

The Economy

The backbone of Guinea's economy is agriculture which employs about 80 percent of the population. Agricultural products for export include coffee, pineapple, banana and palm produce.

Guinea is richly endowed with mineral resources. It possesses about half of the world's known reserves of bauxite. The deposits at Fria, Kinda and Boke are exploited by international consortia with the Guinea government having the controlling share. Guinea has high-grade iron ore at Mount Nimba and the Simandu Mountains. The iron ore deposits are exploited under a shipping agreement with the government of Liberia while its largest gold mining operation is a joint venture with the Ashanti Gold Fields of Ghana. There are several European and Canadian companies mining gold as well in Guinea. Diamonds are equally mined in the country.

The south-eastern rain forest has valuable species of tropical hardwoods for domestic consumption and export.

Foreign Relations

For about two decades after independence, Guinea selected countries it had to relate with in order to stabilize after the French had wreaked serious havoc on its socio-economic infrastructure. In West Africa, it related with states with radical and socialist leadership. It is not surprising that Guinea had good relations with Ghana which immediately bailed the country out of financial challenges. This special relationship made the two countries to establish a political union, the Ghana-Guinea Union in 1958. In 1961, Mali joined the Union which now became the Ghana-Guinea-Mali Union. Outside Africa, Guinea had robust relations with the Soviet bloc and China. Economic assistance came from the Eastern Europe and China.

From the mid-1970s Guinea opened up to quite a number of countries including France, Germany, the United States of America and most African countries. In 1986 the country returned to the French franc after operating a non-convertible currency since 1960. A year before, many French banks had started operations in Guinea.

Guinea is an active player in the international system. It is a member of several international organizations. The country belongs to ECOWAS, Niger River Basin (BRB), OIC, the Mano River Union (MRU), the Gambia River Basin Organization (OMVG), the Non-Aligned Movement, the AU and the UN.

Further Reading

African Encyclopaedia. 1974. London: Oxford University Press.
Davidson, B. 1964. *Old Africa Rediscovered.* London: Oxford University Press.
Duffy, J. 1959. *Portuguese Africa.* Harvard University Press.
Fage, J. D. 1963. *An Atlas of African History.* Arnold.
Greenberg, J. H. 1963. *Languages of Africa.* London: Indiana University Press.
International Encyclopaedia of the Social Sciences. London: Macmillan.
Murdoc G. P. 1959. *Africa: Its Peoples and their Culture History.* New York, McGraw-Hill.

CHAPTER EIGHTEEN

Guinea-Bissau

The Republic of Guinea-Bissau (Republica da Guiné-Bissau) which used to be known as Portuguese Guinea has an area of 36,125 square kilometres and a population of about 1.5 million. Its landmass includes its 25 Islands off the coast. The most prominent of these islands are Bolama, its former capital, and the Bijagos Archipelago. The country is bounded by Senegal to the north, Guinea to the east and south, and the Atlantic Ocean to the west. The capital and chief port is Bissau. Other cities include Bafata, Gabu, Canchungo, Farim and Cacheu. Guinea-Bissau is a low-lying coastal region of swamps, rain forests and mangrove-covered wetlands.

The People

The population of Guinea-Bissau presents a tapestry composed of different languages, customs and social structure. About 20 ethnic groups inhabit the country. The main ones are the Balanta, Fulani, Mandyako, Pepel, Bram and Malinke. The largest and the most widespread are the Balanta who constitute 30 percent of the population while the Fulani are about 20 percent of the population.

The Malinke were the ancient rulers of the Senegambia. The Mandyako and Pepel who live in the northern coastal area were the first to establish contacts with the Portuguese. About 50 percent of the population are adherents of the African Traditional Religion. Muslims make up 40 percent of the population while 10 percent are Christians. Portuguese is the official language in Guinea-Bissau but Crioulo is the lingua franca. There are also 20 languages and dialects. Life expectancy is 48 in the country and the ratio of infant mortality rate is 100 per 1000 live births.

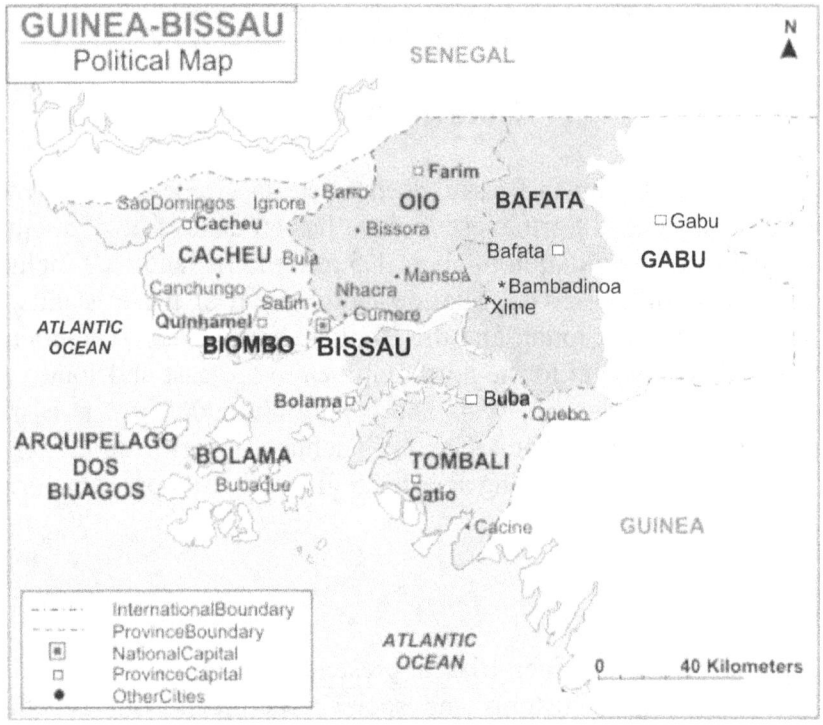

Fig. 18.1: Political Map of Guinea Bissau

History

The earliest inhabitants of Guinea-Bissau were hunting, fishing and agriculturalist peoples who had knowledge of the use of iron. In the thirteenth century, they came into contact with refugees from the dissolution of the great empire of Ghana who sought refuge in the coast. Years later, the area was part of the empire of Mali that succeeded Ghana.

The first European to visit Guinea-Bissau was the Portuguese explorer Nuno Tristao in 1446. Guinea-Bissau contributed significantly to the colonization of Cape Verde Islands during this period. Cotton and indigo plantations were established there and these needed slave labour. Skilled Guineans in weaving and dyeing were introduced in the islands and clothes made by them were sent back to the mainland for the purchase of slaves who were sent to the New World.

Other items of trade that engaged the attention of European merchants included ivory, wax, dyewood and hides but overall slaves constituted the bulk of the exports. In 1687, the Portuguese established a trading post at Bissau but it did not last. In 1792, the British established their own post in Bolama and it too turned out to be a disastrous outing. In the nineteenth century, the Portuguese re-established their Bissau base. The Portuguese territorial claim of the region was disputed by the British and the French but at last, Portugal triumphed. After wars of pacification with the indigenous population between 1913 and 1915, which was led by Joao Teixeira Pinto, the Portuguese were home and dry in their colonial bid.

In the aftermath of the Second World War, Guinea-Bissau nationalists began to demand for independence from Portugal. When Portugal renamed its colonies in Africa in 1951 as its overseas territories, the tempo of challenge to Portuguese colonial rule increased dramatically. In 1961, the nationalists led by Amilcar Cabral began to attack Portuguese administrative and military facilities. These attacks were followed by full-scale guerrilla warfare. Both the demand for independence and guerrilla warfare were carried out by the PAIGC.

In spite of the presence of about 35,000 Portuguese troops in Guinea, the PAIGC with about 10,000 men were able to control most parts of the country by 1971. In the areas it liberated and controlled, the PAIGC established local administration and conducted elections. The PAIGC announced that it would declare the independence of Guinea-Bissau in 1973. It did exactly that on September 24, 1973. Meanwhile, Amilcar Cabral who had been assassinated in that year was succeeded by his Cape Verdean half brother, Luis de Almeida Cabral. Luis subsequently became the first President of Guinea-Bissau.

Two dates should be noted about the independence of Guinea-Bissau. On September 24, 1973, independence was declared unilaterally and on September 10, 1974, it fully gained independence from Portugal. The second date was a consequence of military stalemate and the unilateral declaration of independence. On account of the two, the defeated Portuguese army overthrew the civilian regime in Portugal and asked the military commander in Guinea,

General Antonio Ribeiro de Spinola to take over power and grant independence to its African colonies.

Politics and Structure of Governance

Notwithstanding the democratic credentials that Guinea-Bissau had at independence, the country has been experiencing political tension, military coups, civil war and political intrigues.

In 1980, a coup d'état led by the Prime Minister and former armed forces commander, Joao Bernardo Veira overthrew the government of Luis Cabral and destroyed the relationship between Guinea Bissau, the mainland and Cape Verde, the islands. In 1984, a new Constitution was approved by a single-party, the National Popular Assembly. On the basis of the Constitution, Joao Veira was elected to a new five-year term. The structure of the new system was that the President served as both the head of state and government. He was also the leader of the PAIGC and Commander in chief of the armed forces.

In 1994, the first multiparty presidential elections took place. The exercise was a climax of political instability in the country that manifested itself in coup attempts in 1983, 1985 and 1993. In 1998, the army mutinied and this was followed by a civil war in Guinea-Bissau. In May 1999, the government of Veira was toppled in a military coup.

In February 2000, there was a presidential election in which Kumba Yala, the leader of the opposition party, the Social Renovation Party (PRS), won and was sworn in as President. But on September 14, 2003, the Chief of Defence, General Verrisimo Correia Seabra, led the army to force Yala to resign from office. A 25-member committee for Restoration of Democracy and Constitutional Order was established. On September 28, 2003, Henrique Rosa was sworn in as President. Two years later, a presidential election took place in which Joao Bernardo Veira won. He was sworn into office as President on September 10, 2005. On March 2, 2009, he was murdered by a group of renegade soldiers at the presidential palace. On September 8, 2009, former interim President Mallam Bacai Sanha, who had defeated former President Kumba Yala in the run-off presidential elections of July 26, was sworn into office as the President of Guinea-Bissau.

The executive branch of government in Guinea-Bissau has the President as the Chief of State and the Prime Minister as the head of government. There are other structures of executive branch as Council of State, Ministers and Secretary of state. The National Popular Assembly (ANP) with 100 members directly elected is the legislative structure of the country. In the judicial system, there is the Supreme Court as the highest court in the country. There are also lower courts.

Economy

The economy of Guinea-Bissau is largely agricultural and the country is among the worlds least developed. The main staple food is rice and export crops include groundnuts, cashews, cotton, palm products, timber and seafood (mainly fish and shrimp). The natural resources of the country are Bauxite, phosphate and offshore petroleum. Lack of capital affects the exploitation of these minerals.

Foreign Relations

Guinea-Bissau relates with a number of actors in the international system. Its immediate allies in Africa are Senegal and Guinea, which are also its neighbours. The republic also relates and cooperates with many nations across the continents of the world. It pursues a non-aligned foreign policy and at the same time is a member of several international organizations including ECOWAS, AU, OIC and the UN.

Further Reading

African Encyclopacdia. 1974. London: Oxford University Press.
Clapham, C. 1998. *African Guerrillas.* Oxford: James Currey.
Davidson, B. 1964. *Old Africa Rediscovered.* London: Oxford University Press.
Duffy, J. 1959. *Portuguese Africa.* Harvard University Press.
Fage, J. D. 1963. *An Atlas of African History.* Arnold.
Gibson, R. 1992. *African Liberation Movements.* London: Oxford University Press.

Goody, J. A. 1970. *History of the Upper Guinea Coast, 1545-1800.* London: Clarendon Press. 1970.

Greenberg, J. H. 1963. *Languages of Africa.* London: Indiana University Press.

Murdoc G. P. 1959. *Africa: Its Peoples and their Culture History.* New York, McGraw-Hill.

International Encyclopaedia of the Social Sciences. London: Macmillan.

Rodney, W. A. 1970. *History of the Upper Guinea Coast, 1545-1800.*

CHAPTER NINETEEN

Liberia

Liberia is the oldest independent republic in the GoG and indeed the sub-Saharan Africa. It is located in the western Guinea Coast. It is bounded by Sierra Leone to the northwest, Guinea and Cote d'Ivoire to the north and to the east respectively; and the Atlantic Ocean to the south and west. Liberia has a total area of 111,369 square kilometres and a population of four million.

The coastal area is made up of mangrove swamps, beaches and ridges, which rise gradually to a low plain in the interior. In the north, the level of the country rises towards the Guinea Highlands and reaches a height of 1000 metres. Rainforest and swamps cover the lowlands. Liberia has about 40 percent of West Africa's rainforest. The immediate interior has wooded hills and semi deciduous shrub.

The capital of Liberia is Monrovia. It is a port city. Monrovia was named after James Monroe, the fifth President of the United States of America. Its former name was Christopolis. Other cities in Liberia include Ganta, Buchanan, Gbarnga, Kakata and Voinjama. The name of the country (Liberia) is derived from a Latin word which means *free*.

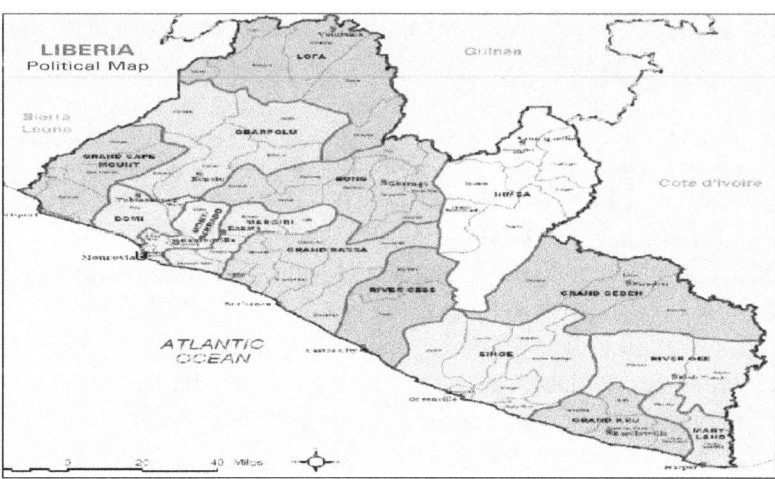

Fig. 19.1: Political Map of Liberia

The People

Three groups of people make up the ethnic and linguistic composition of Liberia. The most numerous are the indigenous people who migrated to Liberia from the Western Sudan. The second group comprises the Americo-Liberians who are descendants of freed slaves from America. These black immigrants make up about five percent of the population. Many of them came to Liberia between 1820 and 1865. The third group consists of black immigrants from the states of the GoG who arrived during the anti-slave trade campaign and European colonial rule.

A total of 16 ethnic groups make up the indigenous population. They constitute three linguistic groups, namely: the Mande, Kwa and Mel. The Mande who live in the northwest and central areas of Liberia are also found in Senegal, Mali, Guinea and Sierra Leone. The most prominent of the Mande people are the Vai, the Kpelle (who are the largest and are also found in Guinea), the Loma (who are also found in Guinea), the Gbandi, Gio, Mano, Mende and Malinke.

Occupying the southern half of Liberia are the Kwa-speaking people who are mainly Bassa, the Kru, the Grebo, the De, the Belle and Krahn. The Mel group occupy the north and the coastal areas of the northwest. The Gola and Kissi are members of the Mel group. They are the oldest settlers in Liberia and they are also found in Sierra Leone.

History

Portuguese mariners were the first Europeans to establish contacts with Liberia. That was in 1461. The Portuguese gave names to prominent coastal landmarks in the region. Such names included Grand Cape Mount, Cape Mesurado (Montserado) and Cape Palmas. The entire coastal region was eventually named the Grain Coast because of availability of Meleguta pepper seeds which, as items of trade, were as valuable as gold. In 1663 the British built several trading posts on the coast but they were destroyed by the Dutch a year later.

Thereafter, Europeans abandoned the coast. But in the early nineteenth century, the Grain Coast became a favoured settlement for freed American slaves. The establishment of settlement for free slaves on the coast was the initiative of the American Colonization Society that was founded in 1816. In 1821, the Society was granted the possession of Cape Mesurado for the enterprise. In 1822, the first American freed slaves numbering 86 landed on Providence Island at the mouth of the Mesurado River. During the following years, more freed American slaves arrived and established settlements such as Greenville and Harper. In 1839, Thomas Buchanan was named the first governor. When he died in 1841 Joseph Jenkins Roberts, a black American succeeded him.

Roberts expanded the territory more than Buchanan did. He was the one who proclaimed Liberia an independent republic on July 26, 1847. The proclamation was in response to the desire of the American Colonization Society to stop its financial assistance for the administration of the area. By 1848, more than 56 countries recognized the Liberian independence. America recognized it in 1862.

Politics and Structure of Governance

At independence, Liberia had a Constitution which was fashioned after the US Constitution. Joseph Roberts was the first elected President. He remained in office till 1856. During his presidency, he confronted the French on the Cote d'Ivoire and the British on Sierra Leone frontiers. He also confronted the opposition of the indigenous population who were excluded from the citizenship of the new country. In 1871, a new President, Edward J. Roye, took office but he did not stay long as he was deposed and jailed. Roberts was asked to administer the republic again and he did just that till 1876.

Between 1847, when Liberia was declared as an independent republic, and 1980, the country had just one political party, the Truc Whig Party (TWP). It produced Presidents as Arthur Barclay in the first decade of the twentieth century, Charles King who, together with his Vice President Allen Yancy, was forced to resign for committing crimes against humanity, William S. Tubman who had seven terms in office as President between 1943 and 1971, and William R. Tolbert who was executed by Master Sergeant (later General) Samuel Kakan Doe on April 12, 1980, after he successfully staged a coup d'état.

The killing of Tolbert ended the 133-year's domination of Liberian politics by the Americo-Liberian group. Doe's misrule of power and the appointment of people from his Krahn group to sensitive positions in the army and public service created political tensions that led to several coup attempts, civil war in Liberia and his own execution. Between 1989 and 1996, the country experienced one of the bloodiest civil wars in Africa. The ECOWAS as a sub-regional body had to intervene through its multi-national force, the ECOWAS Monitoring Group (ECOMOG).

In 1997, Charles Taylor who was Doe's procurement officer and who had been fighting Doe to seize presidential power became the President of Liberia through special elections. Taylor's political misadventure and executive ineptitude engineered armed rebellion against his government. On August 11, 2003, Taylor, bowing to international pressure, resigned from office and went into exile in Nigeria. This paved the way for political reforms in Liberia. In the 2005 presidential elections, Ellen Johnson Sirleaf became the President of Liberia. By this feat, she became Africa's first democratically elected female President.

Liberia is governed constitutionally. The country has a bicameral legislature consisting of 64 members of the House of Representatives and 30 Senators. Members of the House of Representatives serve for a six-year term while Senators serve for nine-years. The Constitution calls for a multiparty system. The country's judicial system has magistrates' courts, circuit and specialty courts and the Supreme Court. Customary Courts exist in rural areas where trial by ordeal is still practised.

Economy

Agriculture and mineral resources are the mainstay of the economy of Liberia. Rubber is the most valuable agricultural export. It is grown on plantations owned by American companies and Liberian farmers. In 1929, the Firestone Tyre and Rubber Company of America obtained a concession for rubber cultivation. Cocoa, coffee, oil palm, cotton and groundnuts are also grown for cash and export. Timber from Liberian forests is of commercial value and fishing is an important industry.

The country is Africa's greatest producer of iron ore which accounts for over 70 percent of Liberia's export by value. The ore reserves are located in four regions: Bemi Hills north of Monrovia, the Bong Rang, the Mano Hills and Mount Nimba which has the largest deposits. The country has other critical minerals like diamonds which are mined in the valley of the Loffa River, gold, lead, manganese, graphite, bauxite and barites.

Foreign Relations

Liberia is a founding member of the United Nations and its specialized agencies. This feat has given the country diplomatic clout since World War II. But it must be quickly emphasized that the country owed its international image to the actions of their leaders, especially Tubman and Tolbert who were international personalities. After their exit, nothing much was heard about Liberia in a positive way except negative stories of conflicts, killings and civil war. It is however gratifying to note that President Sirleaf is working assiduously to bring back the glory of Liberia.

Liberia is a member of ECOWAS, AU and the Non-Aligned Movement. It is also a member of the Mano River Union, a free trade group to which Guinea and Sierra Leone belong. In 2007, Liberia and Sierra Leone signed a Non-Aggression Pact in order to improve their relations. Liberia supports regional integration in West Africa in particular and Africa in general. The country relates with many Western and Asian countries as well.

Further Reading

Abasiattai, M. B. 1976. "Liberia and the Origins of the Scramble for West Africa, 1841-1891". *The Calabar Historical Journal, 1 (11)*.
Abasiattai, M. B. 1982. "Gola Resistance to Liberian Rule in the Nineteenth Century, 1835-1905". *Journal of the Historical Society of Nigeria, 11 (1&2)*.
Assis, M. 2001. *Diamonds are a Guerrilla's Best Friend: The Impact of Illicit Wealth on Insurgency Strategy. Third World Studies.* 22(3): 311-25.
African Encyclopaedia. 1974. London: Oxford University Press.

Besada, H. ed. 2007. *From Civil Strife to Peace Building: Examining Private Sector Involvement in West African Reconstruction.* Canada: Centre for International Governance Innovation.

Davidson, B. 1964. *Old Africa Rediscovered.* London: Oxford University Press.

Duffy, J. 1959. *Portuguese Africa.* Harvard University Press.

Fage, J. D. 1963. *An Atlas of African History*. Arnold.

Greenberg, J. H. 1963. *Languages of Africa.* London: Indiana University Press.

International Encyclopaedia of the Social Sciences. London: Macmillan.

Murdoc G. P. 1959. *Africa: Its Peoples and their Culture History.* New York, McGraw-Hill.

Yancy, L. J. A. 1959. *A History of Liberia.* London: Allen & Unwin

CHAPTER TWENTY

Nigeria

The Federal Republic of Nigeria is the third largest country in the GoG, the 13th largest state in the continent of Africa and the 31st largest country in the world. The country has a total area of 923,768 square kilometres and a population of 150 million. The particulars of the country's large population translate as follows: one in every four in sub-Saharan Africa is a Nigerian; one in every seven black people is a Nigerian, and about 25 percent of the world's black population are Nigerians.

The country is the eighth most populous country in the world. The name Nigeria was suggested by Miss Flora Shaw (later Mrs. Flora Lugard) who was a Press Correspondent in Cairo, Egypt. It is derived from the country's inland waterway, River Niger, which flows from the Guinean Highlands. The roots are in *Niger area* which, when pronounced conveniently, produces the noun *Nigeria* (Akpan, 2004). Nigeria is bordered on the north by Niger, on the east by Chad and Cameroon, on the south by the GoG, on the west by Benin. The country achieved independence on October 1, 1960 and became a republic in 1963. Abuja is the political and diplomatic capital of Nigeria while Lagos, the country's former capital until 1991, is the commercial capital. Other main cities include Calabar, Uyo, Ibadan, Jos, Enugu, Aba, Kano, Ilorin, Benin, Kaduna, Maiduguri, Sokoto, Warri, Benin and Port Harcourt. Lagos is the largest city in sub-Saharan Africa with a population in excess of 10 million.

Along the GoG in the country is a sandy coastline. Behind this are swamps covered with mangrove trees. Almost the entire Niger Delta region is covered with swamps. Inland, there are lowlands of less than 300 metres high that spread up to the Niger Valley to the north-west, and up to the Benue Valley to the east. In the south-west of the country, the land rises to a plateau of above 300 metres. Much of the northern part of the country is made up of another plateau over 300 metres high. It rises to above 1500 metres in Jos. The highest point is Chappal Waddi at 2419 metres. Between the mangrove swamps of the coast and the drier savanna inland is a region of rain forest. In the drier

Nigeria

parts of the north, vegetation becomes thinner, and around Lake Chad to the east and Sokoto to the west, there is only thorn-bush. The highest areas are open grassland with few trees.

The main rivers are the Niger and the Benue Rivers which converge and empty into the Niger Delta, one of the world's river deltas and a region of Central African Mangroves. At the convergent point of the two rivers is a y-shape landmark. Though located in the tropics, Nigeria has several temperate regions, the prominent ones being Obudu, Jos and Mambilla.

Fig. 20.1: Political Map of Nigeria

The People

Nigeria is not only a melting pot demographically; it is also like a sub-continent. It has about 400 ethnic groups and 521 languages. These include 510 living languages, two-second languages without native speakers and nine extinct ones. In most parts of Nigeria, some ethnic groups speak more than one language. Most of the ethnic nationalities in Nigeria have affiliations with the major ethnic groups spread across Africa.

For instance, the Arabs from the Middle East and North Africa and the Bantu from the Central Eastern and Southern parts of Africa are all represented in the peopling of Nigeria. They are found in large numbers in the northern and southeastern parts of the country respectively. In Nigeria none of the ethnic groups is large enough to dominate others. The seven largest of the 400 groups are Hausa, Yoruba, Igbo, Ibibio, Kanuri, Tiv and Ijaw. Hausa language is the most widely spoken of the Nigerian languages and it is unofficially the language of northern Nigeria which has more than 300 ethnic groups and whose population constitute about half of the population of Nigeria.

About 40 percent of Nigerians are Christians and 40 percent Muslims. Adherents of African Traditional Religion and spiritual groups and fraternities are 20 percent. The country's life expectancy is 47 years while infant mortality is 97 deaths per 1000 live births.

History

Abundant archaeological evidence confirms the presence of hunting peoples from the Stone Age. The oldest human remains found at Iwo Ileru, near Akure, were dated to about 1000 B.C. Iron tools were first made locally in the seventh century B.C. by the people of the Nok culture. The Nok culture was actually a Neolithic culture that made the transition to the Iron Age and its epicentre was the region of Central Nigeria. The Igbo Ukwu bronzes in South East Nigeria have been dated to A.D. 900.

The earliest occupants of the area that later became Nigeria settled in the forest belt and in the Niger Delta. Most of them were of the Bantu and semi-Bantu stocks who migrated from southern and central

Africa and intermingled with the Sudanese Negro who came southwards after the collapse of Mali and Songhai empires.

In the pre-colonial period, there emerged in Nigeria several kingdoms, empires and city-states. Kanem-Borno grew up in the eleventh century and by the sixteenth century had registered its mark as a great empire in the Lake Chad region. It collapsed only in the nineteenth century. The Hausa states were also prominent during this period. The centralized states of the Hausa include Daura, Gobir, Kebbi, Katsina, Kano and Zaria. Each of these states had a walled city, a market centre and a palace. One of the legendary rulers of these states was Queen Amina of Zaria whose territory included much of northern and central Nigeria and parts of Niger Republic. Islam was introduced in the area in the fourteenth century from Mali but it remained largely the religion of the court. In the nineteenth century, Usmanu dan Fodio, through jihad changed the religious landscape of northern and parts of central Nigeria.

To the south-west of the Niger and south of the Hausa states emerged the Yoruba states which had developed into powerful kingdoms from the twelfth century. The town of Oyo later developed into an empire-the Oyo Empire-with awe-inspiring military institution, controlling many neighbouring lands and peoples. Its territory once extended from western Nigeria to the Republics of Togo and Benin. On the GoG, the empire of Benin emerged in the fifteenth century. Until its collapse in the nineteenth century, it dominated not only the Edo-speaking peoples but also the region eastward to the Niger and, along the lagoon to the city of Eko in today's Lagos. Eko was the Edo name given to the territory of Lagos; Lagos is the name that was given by the Portuguese.

In most areas of the south east of Nigeria, the people did not develop centralized monarchical states but operated village democracies and Republicanism. These people were the Ibo and Ibibio who were neighbours that shared many traits except language. By the seventeenth century, some Ibibio communities along the coast and the Ijaw people developed city-states. The most prominent ones were the city-states of Old Calabar, Nembe and Bonny.

The Portuguese were the first Europeans to have contact with the peoples of Nigeria. The first contact was with the kingdom of Benin in 1494. Benin became the second most important Portuguese base after

Elmina. It was from this base that future Portuguese mariners and merchants made Lagos a strategic trading post. As recorded in chapter two, Portuguese influence in the GoG did not last long. In the Nigerian area, Britain was the European power that replaced Portugal.

Nigeria is the handiwork of the British. The process towards its creation started in the nineteenth century and by the twentieth century, the country had taken its form and structure. Therefore, by the beginning of the twentieth century, many ethnic groups numbering 400 at the very least were made part of the Nigerian nation. The process started with imperialism and ended with independence.

The development that brought the various groups into one nation started with the declaration of Lagos as a colony in 1861 and a Protectorate over the Oil Rivers in 1885, by Britain. The instruments that the British used to occupy Nigeria were varied but in the main included treaties, intrigues, deceit, blackmail and outright conquest through gunboat diplomacy. Following the passage of a law to end overseas slave trade by Britain in 1807 and the desire to substitute it with legitimate trade, she proceeded to bully, persuade or bribe other European nations, America as well as African chiefs to end the slave business. With regards to Nigeria, the British began to negotiate anti-slave trade treaties. Such treaties were signed with Brass in 1834, Bonny in 1839, Calabar in 1841 and Aboh in 1842 (Ikime, 1982).

Under the provisions of these treaties, the rulers of these states were to be paid compensation over an agreed number of years for giving up the trade in slaves. The importance of these treaties was that once signed, the British used them as the excuse to bombard Nigerian states and on the pretext that some articles of these treaties had been violated. As Obaro Ikime (1982:7) rightly notes:

> These bombardments had the same effect...weakening the states concerned, forcing them to accept the superior might of Great Britain. It is clear, therefore, that in retrospect the suppression of the overseas slave trade provided an indispensable prelude to the British occupation of Nigeria.

Outside the signing of treaties on anti-slave trade, the Niger Delta states were equally forced to sign treaties of protection which ultimately eroded their authorities. Two compelling reasons accounted for this development. First, the activities of other European powers, notably Germany and France, in the area meant swift action to block their aspirations in areas where British interest was prevalent.

Secondly, internal upheavals like succession disputes in the Niger Delta states led to instability which threatened British commerce. To nib this in the bud, the British used the diplomacy of treaty-signing to rob the people of their independence. The rulers who signed these treaties never fully understood their implications until they were dethroned by the British (Burns, 1958).

In the Western part of the country which was embroiled in fratricidal wars for many years, the British simply intervened through Missionaries and imposed their will on the people. Some of the potentates in this area were even weary of war and desired the Missionary-imposed peace. Of course, this was the very instrument that the British used to deprive them of their sovereignty.

Where it was not possible to annex the Nigerian territories through the diplomacy of treaties and peace-making, sheer coercion was used to conquer the people. The fall of the Aro in the Ibo hinterland, Benin and Brass, all in Southern Nigeria took the form of conquest.

With regards to Northern Nigeria, the British secured a foothold there through treaties to guarantee their traders access to the area. The British negotiated and concluded such treaties under the auspices of the National African Company (NAC), later called the Royal Niger Company (RNC). In order to prevent Germany and France from occupying Northern Nigeria, Britain made up its mind to declare the area a British protectorate. This aspiration was borne out of the fact that the British experienced a stiff competition from the French. Already by 1890s, France through its company, the Compagnie Française de I' Afrique Equitoriale, had established stations and presence at Gbede, Lokoja, Egga, Shonga and Raba on the Niger and Ibi and Demsa on the Benue (Burns, 1958).

In order to effect the proclamation of the Protectorate of Northern Nigeria, the British in 1899 appointed Captain Frederick Lugard as the High Commissioner. His first act in Northern Nigeria was the formal proclamation of the Protectorate on January 1, 1900 at a ceremony in Lokoja. During that occasion, the Union Jack, a symbol of the British authority in the area was hoisted in the town.

Indeed, the actions of Lugard were tantamount to a declaration of war on the people of Northern Nigeria. It is, therefore, not surprising to note that between 1900 and 1906, Lugard launched a series of wars to conquer Northern Nigeria (Arikpo, 1967). Before too long, the whole area was conquered not because the people did not resist the British encroachment on their territories, but because the enemy was better armed. While the inhabitants used simple and archaic war instruments like horses, bows and arrows, spears and old guns, the British made use of the maxim guns and modern rifles whose firepower far outweighed what the indigenous soldiers used. Already, in the words of Hilaire Belloc, Lugard would appear to have mocked Africa thus:

> Whatever happens we have got the Maxim gun and they have not (Perham, 1960:45).

At the end of the day, the Maxim gun made the difference between victory and defeat in the fight between the invading forces and the indigenous communities.

As at 1900, the British had created three countries in the present Nigeria-the Oil Rivers (later Niger Coast) Protectorate, the Lagos colony and Protectorate and the Protectorate of Northern Nigeria. These three countries were to evolve separately as new states in Africa but for the financial difficulties experienced by the Lagos colony and Protectorate and the Protectorate of Northern Nigeria.

To overcome the problems, the Niger Coast Protectorate, which was financially buoyant with lots of surpluses, was merged in 1906 with the Lagos colony and Protectorate to form the Protectorate of Southern Nigeria. Until now the Lagos colony and Protectorate was administered first from Sierra Leone and later from the Gold Coast. The merger of the Niger Coast with Lagos produced two Nigerias; Northern and Southern Nigeria. Where two countries ought to have emerged from the British endeavour, financial troubles of Northern Nigeria necessitated amalgamation with Southern Nigeria so that the financial surpluses from the former Niger Coast Protectorate could be used to solve the financial burdens of all areas of Nigeria.

On January 1, 1914, the two Nigerias were amalgamated into one. Therefore, Nigeria as a single country was created in January 1914. That same year, a legislative council was established with limited responsibilities. In 1922, a larger one was set up with elected members; three from Lagos and one from Calabar.

Agitations for independence which had started earlier in the century gathered momentum with the emergence of political parties in the 1920s. The nationalists catalogued the grievances of the people and used these to demand for self-government. Some of these grievances included forced labour, taxation without representation and the Indirect Rule system, which excluded the educated from participation in colonial administration. The colonial government responded to these demands by reforming itself.

The indirect rule system was abandoned after the Women's War of 1929 for complex constitutional adjustments which placed Nigeria on the road to independence (Akpan, 2003). Some of the Constitutions that Nigeria had included the Clifford Constitution (1922), the Bourdillion Constitution (1940), the Richards Constitution (1946), the Macpherson Constitution (1951) and the Lyttleton Constitution (1954). The last Constitution gave Nigeria full-fledged federalism with five administrative divisions, namely: the Eastern Region, the Western Region, the Northern Region, the Southern Cameroons and the Federal Territory of Lagos. The independence Constitution was not significantly different from the Lyttleton Constitution. Internal self-government was granted to the Eastern and Western Regions in 1957. On October 1, 1960 the country became independent together with the northern part of the former German Cameroons. In 1963 Nigeria became a republic.

Politics and Structure of Governance

At independence, Nigeria operated a parliamentary system of government that was bequeathed to her by the British. Political parties that won seats in the parliament were either-ethnic or regional-based. The National Council of Nigerian Citizens (NCNC) under the leadership of Dr. Nnamdi Azikiwe won in the East, the Action Group under Chief Obafemi Awolowo won in the West and the Northern People's Congress under Sir Ahmadu Bello won in the North. At independence, the new government was a coalition of two major political parties, the NPC and the NCNC. Dr. Nnamdi Azikiwe of the NCNC was sworn in as the first Governor General, later President of Nigeria, while Sir Abubakar Tafawa Balewa, the Deputy Leader of the NPC, became the Prime Minister.

In the regions, the Premiers were Dr. Michael Okpara for the East, Chief Samuel L. Akintola for the West and Sir Ahmadu Bello for the North. Chief Obafemi Awolowo of the Action Group became the opposition leader. While the President was the Head of State in the political structure, the Prime Minster was the head of government.

As soon as Nigeria achieved independence, political instability occasioned by ethnicity, nepotism, corruption, fraudulent census exercise, rigging of elections, political gerrymandering and ineptitude of the political class tasked the political system beyond elasticity. The stresses and strains produced by the instability knocked off the democratic experiment for a military regime.

The first coup took place on January 15, 1966. Nigerians immediately celebrated the coup, which liberated them from the shackles of oppression of the political class, but when the deads were counted, it was found out that the coup merely deepened the Nigerian crisis. The actors in the coup exercise were from the southern part of the country and out of the five coupists, four came from a particular region and ethnic group; the Eastern region and the Ibo ethnic group. In the exercise, western and northern political and military leaders were killed while those who carried out the coup refused to kill any of their own.

In July, 1966, Northern officers in the army carried out a counter coup which eventually threw the country into irreversible darkness and a civil war. The outcome of the second coup was that General Aguyi Ironsi; an Ibo who succeeded Balewa was killed and replaced with a junior officer of northern extraction, Lieutenant Colonel (later General) Yakubu Gowon. Lieutenant Colonel (later General) Odumegwu Ojukwu who was the military governor of the Eastern region where Ironsi came from refused to recognize Gowon.

Meanwhile in the northern region, Ibo people and non-northerners were victims of a pogrom which was carried out by the people of the region in response to the killing of their leaders in the January coup. Hundreds of thousands who were lucky to escape to the eastern region created a refugee situation in the east. As the safety of people of the eastern region could not be guaranteed in other regions of the country, Ojukwu was forced on May 30, 1967 to declare the secession of the eastern region under the name of the Republic of Biafra. This declaration was the immediate prelude to the Nigerian Civil War. The

Federal Government interpreted it as an act of rebellion and took measures to quell it. These measures which in the main were military in nature led to full scale war which lasted for 30 months and killed about one million Nigerians.

After the war, General Gowon promised to give the country a new Constitution and to hand over power to a democratically-elected government. In 1974, he postponed the 1976 target date that he had set himself. On account of this, he was overthrown on July 29, 1975 through a coup d'état masterminded by Brigadier Murtala Ramat Mohammed who himself was killed on February 13, 1976 in a failed coup d'état.

His successor, Lieutenant General Olusegun Obasanjo, facilitated the return to civil rule. On October 1, 1979, Shehu Usman Aliyu Shagari was sworn in as the President of the country's Second Republic. His government did not last for long. On December 31, 1983, he was overthrown by Major General Mohammadu Buhari who was similarly deposed on August 27, 1985 by his Chief of Army Staff, Major General Ibrahim Badamosi Babangida. Babangida promised to return Nigeria to civilian rule by the early 1990. He embarked on political reforms but in the presidential elections of June 1993 in which Chief Moshood Abiola won convincingly, he used his Armed Forces Ruling Council (AFRC) to annul the elections.

When he was faced with post-elections chaos, confusion and disorder, he quickly resigned from power after dissolving the AFRC and establishing a transitional government headed by Chief Ernest Shonekan. In November of that year the Shonekan regime was deposed by General Sani Abacha who ruled with iron fist until he dropped dead in 1998. General Abubakar who succeeded him facilitated the return to civilian rule in 1999. On May 29, 1999, General Olusegun Obasanjo (who had become Chief Obasanjo) was installed as the President of Nigeria and on that date, the country started the Fourth Republic. Before May 29, 1999, Nigeria experienced twelve military coups and seven military regimes.

Under the Constitution of 1999, Nigeria operates a presidential system of government in which the president exercises power as the Chief Executive and Head of State. The President is elected by popular vote to a maximum of two four-year terms. Nigeria has a bicameral legislative body to check the President and his team. The Senate comprises 109 members; three members from each state and one member from the capital city of Abuja. The House of Representatives has 360 members and the number of seat that a state has is determined by population. Members of the National Assembly are elected by popular vote to four-year terms.

Nigeria operates three codes of law: English law, customary law and Nigerian statute law. The courts in the country include Magistrate courts, Customary Courts, Customary Court of Appeal, Sharia Court of Appeal, High Court, High Court of Appeal and the Supreme Court.

There are three tiers of government in Nigeria: The Central (or Federal), the State Governments and the Local Governments. The country has thirty-six states and one central government. There are 774 Local Government Councils.

Economy

Nigeria is an emerging market in the GoG which practices mixed economy. It is a potential economic powerhouse in Africa if it flees from the years of mismanagement, corruption, political instability and mis-governance. For two decades after independence, agriculture was the mainstay of the economy and indeed the principal foreign exchange earner. Within this period, Nigeria was self-sufficient in agricultural needs and was the world's largest exporter of groundnuts, palm produce and cocoa. Agriculture also employed more than 70 percent of the population but today, the country is struck by the Dutch disease or most appropriately the *Abuja measles* on account of overdependence on petroleum oil. Oil has turned Nigeria into a monocultural economy and a net importer of agricultural items including palm produce. However, oil has made Nigeria to become a middle status country even though there is widespread poverty in the nation. In the West African sub-region, Nigeria is the largest economy and in the African continent it is the second, after South Africa. Its stock exchange, the Nigerian Stock Exchange, is equally the second largest in Africa.

Oil accounts for about 40 percent of the GDP and over 95 percent of government earnings. Nigeria is the twelfth largest producer of petroleum in the world, the largest in Africa, the GoG and the eighth largest exporter in the world. The country's crude oil production is about 2.2 million barrels a day, though it has the capacity to double the digits. Nigeria has about 25 billion barrels of crude oil reserves (out of Africa's proven 66 billion barrels) and gas reserves of about 200 trillion cubic feet.

Nigeria also possesses more than 50 strategic mineral resources outside oil. These include gold, iron-ore, coal, tin, zinc, lead, limestone, tantalite, barites, bauxite, uranium, gemstone, sapphire and marble. These mineral resources are largely unexploited because everybody in Nigeria worships on the altar of petroleum oil.

Foreign Relations

Since independence, Nigeria has been pro-West in its foreign policy posture but that did not prevent it from having a major broil with France over the testing of Atomic Bomb in the Sahara desert. In 1962, just two years after independence, it gave France 48 hours to close its embassy and leave Nigeria. Several western countries like the US and Britain also felt the spikes of Nigeria's foreign policy especially during the dark days of colonialism and the apartheid system in Africa. These state of affairs occurred because of the dictates of the national interest of Nigeria which is largely Afro-centric; that is, Africa is the centre-piece of Nigeria's foreign policy. In the areas of decolonization of Africa, African unity, conflict resolution and crisis management and aspirations for regionalism, the country's foreign policy always responds to Africanist elements. For these reasons, Nigeria played a leading role in the establishment of the Organisation of African Union (OAU) and the African Union (AU), the Economic Community of West African States (ECOWAS), the Economic Commission of West African States Monitoring Group (ECOMOG) and The New Partnership for Africa's Development (NEPAD). Nigeria has also played key roles in peace-keeping operations in Africa in particular and the world in general.

Nigeria is a member of the Non-Aligned Movement, the Commonwealth of Nations, the Organization of Petroleum Exporting Countries (OPEC), the AU and the UN. It maintains cordial relations with all countries in the international system especially the ones in Africa, Caribbean and the Pacific. Nigeria has a tremendous influence in the West African sub-region, Africa and the Southern Hemisphere.

Further Reading

African Encyclopaedia. 1974. London: Oxford University Press.
Akpan, N. U. 1972. *The Struggle for Secession in Nigeria. A Personal Account of the Nigerian Civil War*. London: Frank Cass and Co.
Akpan, O. E. 2000. *Regional Leadership: Nigeria and the Challenge of Post Apartheid South Africa.* Uyo: SureGod Publishers.
Arikpo, O. 1967. *The Development of Modern Nigeria*. London: Longman Press.
Balogun, O. 1973. *The Tragic Years: Nigeria in Crisis, 1966-1970*. Benin-City: Ethiope Publishing Corporation.
Burns, A. A. 1958. *History of Nigeria*. London: Faber and Faber.
Chinweizu. 1978. *The West and the Rest of us*. Lagos: Nok Publishers.
Cronje, Suzanne. 1972. *The World and Nigeria: The Diplomatic History of the Biafran War 1967-1970.* London: Macmillan Press.
Davidson, B. 1964. *Old Africa Rediscovered.* London: Oxford University Press.
Duffy, J. 1959. *Portuguese Africa.* Harvard University Press.
Fage, J. D. 1963. *An Atlas of African History*. Arnold.
Greenberg, J. H. 1963. *Languages of Africa*. London: Indiana University Press.
International Encyclopaedia of the Social Sciences. London: Macmillan.
Ikime, O. 1982. *The Fall of Nigeria: The British Conquest*. London: Heinemann Books.
Ikime, O. 1999. ed. *Groundwork of Nigerian History,* Ibadan: Heinemann Educational Books.
Iloeje, N. P. *A New Geography of Nigeria.* Ibadan: Longmans Nigeria Ltd.
Kirk-Green, A. H. M. 1971. *Crisis and Conflict in Nigeria: A documentary Source Book, 1966-1970,* Vols 1 and 2. London: Oxford University Press.
Madiebo, A. A. 1980. *The Nigerian Revolution and the Biafran War*. Enugu: Fourth Dimension.
Mackintosh, John. 1966. *Nigerian Government and Politics*. London: George Allen and Unwin Ltd.

Murdoc G. P. 1959. *Africa: Its Peoples and their Culture History.* New York, McGraw-Hill.

Perham M. (11). 1960. *Lugard: The Years of Authority, 1899-1945.* London: Oxford University Press.

Schwarz, Walter. 1968. *Nigeria.* London: Penguin Press.

St Jorre, John. 1972. *The Nigerian Civil War.* London: Longmans Ltd.

Stremlau, John. 1977. *The International Politics of the Nigerian Civil War, 1967-1970.* New Jersey: Princeton University Press.

Tamuno, T. 1982. *The Evolution of the Nigerian State: The Southern Phase, 1898-1914.* London: Longmans Group Ltd.

Uya, O. 1992. ed. *Contemporary Nigeria: Essays in Society, Politics and Economy.* Benous Aires: Edipuli SA.

CHAPTER TWENTY-ONE

Senegal

The Republic of Senegal (Republique du Sénégal) has a total area of 197,000 square kilometres and a population of about 12 million. It is bounded to the north and northeast by the Senegal River which marks its boundary with Mauritania, to the east by Mali, to the south by Guinea-Bissau and Guinea; and to the west by the Atlantic Ocean. The Gambia penetrates into Senegal for more than 320 kilometres; she surrounds the Gambia on three sides. Dakar, which is the country's capital, is the westernmost point in the continent. Other cities include Rufisque, Thies, St. Louis, Matam, Tambacounda, Fatick, Kedougou and Kaolack.

Senegal is a low-lying country with forests in the southwest and semi-desert in the north and northeast. The main rivers are Senegal in the north and Casamance in the south.

The People

Senegal has about seven major ethnic groups and several smaller ones. These include Wolof, Fulani, Bambara, Malinke, Serer, Soninke, Dyula, Lebu, Tend and Diola. Most of these groups were parts of the ancient empires of Ghana, Mali and Songhai which later spilled into the neighbouring states in the Gulf of Guinea.

The Wolof constitutes about 43 percent of the population and their language is used in most parts of Senegal. The Serer are mostly found in the western part of the Ferlo region. They make about 15 percent of the population. The Fulani who constitute about 23 percent of the population are found in all parts of the country but are mostly located in the Ferlo, the Upper Casamance and Oualo regions. The Tukulor live around the Senegal, the Gambia and Saloum rivers. The Diola are found in the regions of lower Casamance and the Gambia vallies. The Malinke are distributed around the regions of the Gambia, Upper Casamance and Saloum river valleys. The Soninke who are of Berber descent came into Senegal from Mali.

About 95 percent of the population are Muslims. Christians constitute 4 percent and 1 percent are adherents of the African Traditional Religion. The country has life expectancy of 60 years and infant mortality rate of 60 per 1000 live births.

Fig. 21.1: Political Map of Senegal

History

Senegal has been inhabited for centuries. In the eleventh century, parts of the country were occupied by Tukulor. The name of the country is a corrupted name of **Zenega** from the Zenega Berbers of Mauritania whose activities in Senegal were noticed since the eleventh century. In the twelfth century, the kingdom of Jolof was founded but in the sixteenth century, it disintegrated and became four Wolof states of Jolof, Walo, Cayor and Bawol. At about the same time, the Serer also established their kingdoms. In the late eighteenth century, Tukulor Muslims established a theocratic state in Fouta-Toro.

Overseas contact with the people of Senegal began in about 1444 when the Portuguese came to the coast and began to trade with the states of the region. In the sixteenth century, the Dutch built a trading post on Goree Island, off Cape Verde. The French and the British also came to the coast to trade. By the seventeenth century, trade in slaves and gum Arabic had developed phenomenally. By this period too, France became the most influential power on the coast spreading its tentacles from the fort of St Louis on the Senegal River.

Even at that, the British later occupied St. Louis and Goree twice but returned them to France in 1816. In 1854, the French traders requested their Emperor, Napoleon III to establish military presence in some parts of Senegal. General Louis-Leon-Caser Faidherbe was appointed as governor of St. Louis to take charge of the military operations in the area. French military interest clashed with the military might of Al-Hajj Umah, the head of the Tijaniyah Brotherhood, who had established an Islamic empire in the Upper Niger Valley. The military clash resulted in a stalemate and the consequence of the stalemate was a truce of coexistence. But through astute diplomatic intercourse, the French expanded their sphere of influence to the extent that by 1895, they had established French West Africa and in 1902 ,Dakar became its capital.

Senegal was one French colony in the GoG that benefited from the French policy of assimilation. The inhabitants of the four *communes* of St. Louis, Goree, Dakar and Rufisque were granted French citizenship and treated quite differently from the rest of French West Africa. Through the efforts of Blaise Diagne, the first West African elected as a Deputy to the French National Assembly, children of African-French descent became French citizens in 1916. Elections into French National Assembly signposted the necessity of political participation of the people of Senegal in their affairs.

By 1946 they began to take prominent roles in politics, and one of the first African political parties was the **Convention Africaine** led by Leopold Sedar Senghor who allied with several Muslim fraternities to vote in favour of the country's membership of the French community. A year before the **Yes** or **No** referendum, Senegal had gained local self-government under Mamadou Dia and a year after the referendum, the country and the French Sudan (Mali) merged to form the Mali Federation, which became fully independent on June 20 1960.

The Federation did not survive on account of internal political stresses and strains; it broke up on August 20 1960, just three months after its creation. Consequently, Senegal and French Sudan, which was now, renamed the Republic of Mali, proclaimed independence. In that same August, Senghor was elected the country's first President while Mamadou Dia was appointed the Prime Minister.

Politics and Structure of Governance

After the dissolution of the Mali Federation and the independence of Senegal, Senghor, the President and Dia, the Prime Minister, governed the country under a parliamentary system. In 1962 Dia was arrested and accused of plotting against the state. Consequently, Senegal proclaimed a new Constitution that consolidated the President's power. In 1980 Senghor retired from office and handed over power unilaterally to his political godson, Abdou Diouf, who was President between 1981 and 2000.

Though Senghor had in 1976, authorized the formation of two opposition parties, Diouf encouraged broader participation. As a mark of political tolerance, when he was defeated in the 2000 elections by opposition leader Abdoulaye Wade, he readily accepted defeat. It is instructive to note that Wade of the Senegalese Democratic Party (PDS) had been an opposition leader in Senegal for 25 years and the party he defeated, the Socialist Party (SP) had been in existence for 40 years.

Though Senegal is a predominantly Muslim state, it is a secular republic. Its Constitution provides for a strongly centralized presidency. The President is elected by universal adult suffrage to a five-year term. The President appoints the Prime Minister who in turn appoints Ministers but in consultation with the President. The National Assembly is bicameral with 150 members of the lower parliament and 100 Senators; 35 of whom are elected and 65 chosen by the President.

The judiciary is independent with ***Cour de Cessation*** being the highest Appeals Court. The country has 14 administrative regions, each headed by a governor appointed by the President. The governors are equally responsible to the President. Senegal is one of the few countries in Africa that has not been menaced by the afflictions of coup d'état. However, it experiences a violent secessionist movement in the southern region of Casamance.

The Economy

The country runs an agrarian and a single crop economy. It depends on the groundnut trade which is conditioned by climatic factors and world commodity prices. Other export items include fish products, cotton and phosphates. Fish is fast becoming Senegal's leading exportable item. In 2007 the sector contributed 22 percent of the country's export earnings and employed about 15 percent of the population. The main food crops are millet, rice, beans, corn and cassava.

Senegal is poor in mineral resources. The few ones are phosphates, iron ore and petroleum.

Other sources of revenue for the country include remittances, tourism and economic assistance from France and other Western nations. Tourism is the second major source of foreign exchange contributing in most cases about 7 percent of the GDP yearly. The country has about 400 first class hotels for tourists and tourism employs more than 100,000 citizens. About 1 million tourists visit Senegal yearly. France and the US assist the country economically. Remittances also assist the country financially. In 2007 the country earned about $1 billion from these sources.

Foreign Relations

Senegal maintains cordial relations with its neighbours and attaches importance to diplomatic dialogue as an instrument of international conflict resolution. However, in 1981 its soldiers entered the Gambia to suppress a coup and in the aftermath proclaimed a Senegambian Confederation which in any case was short-lived as it was dissolved in 1989. Senegal has good relationship with many states in Africa and international organizations. It is a member of the ECOWAS, the AU and the UN. Outside Africa, Senegal has close relations with France and her allies. France provides the country with economic assistance annually to shore up its economy.

Further Reading

Adloff, R. 1964. *West Africa: The French Speaking Nations.* New York: Reinhart & Winston.
African Encyclopaedia. 1974. London: Oxford University Press.
Crowder, M. 1962. *A Study of French Assimilation Policy.* London: Faber & Faber
Davidson, B. 1964. *Old Africa Rediscovered.* London: Oxford University Press.
Duffy, J. 1959. *Portuguese Africa.* Harvard University Press.
Fage, J. D. 1963. *An Atlas of African History.* Arnold.
Greenberg, J. H. 1963. *Languages of Africa.* London: Indiana University Press.
International Encyclopaedia of the Social Sciences. London: Macmillan.
Murdoc G. P. 1959. *Africa: Its Peoples and their Culture History.* New York, McGraw-Hill.
Neres, P. 1962: *French Speaking West Africa.* London: Oxford University Press.

CHAPTER TWENTY-TWO

Sierra Leone

The Republic of Sierra Leone is an independent country in the GoG. It is bordered on the north and east by Guinea, on the south by Liberia, and on the west by the Atlantic Ocean. It has an area of 73,000 square kilometres and a population of about five million. The name of the country was given by a Portuguese explorer, Pedro de Sintra, who first sighted and mapped Freetown harbour. He called it Serra Lyoa, in Portuguese, which means in English Lions Mountain. This referred to the range of hills that surrounds Freetown harbour. The name Sierra Leone is a corrupted form of Serra Lyoa. Freetown, which has one of the world's largest natural harbours, is the capital. Other cities include Bo, Kenema and Makeni.

Most of the coast is made up of lagoons and low islands except near Freetown, where steep and Rocky Mountains are close to the sea. The coastal swamp region is extensive. It spreads up to the river valleys from the sea into the coastal plain covering about 320 kilometres. In the interior, the land rises to plateaus which are about 500 metres high and Mount Bintimati in the Loma Mountains is over 2,000 metres high. The major rivers are the Great and Little Scarcies, the Rokel and the Sewa. There is the rain forest on the coastal plain and wooded savanna in the interior.

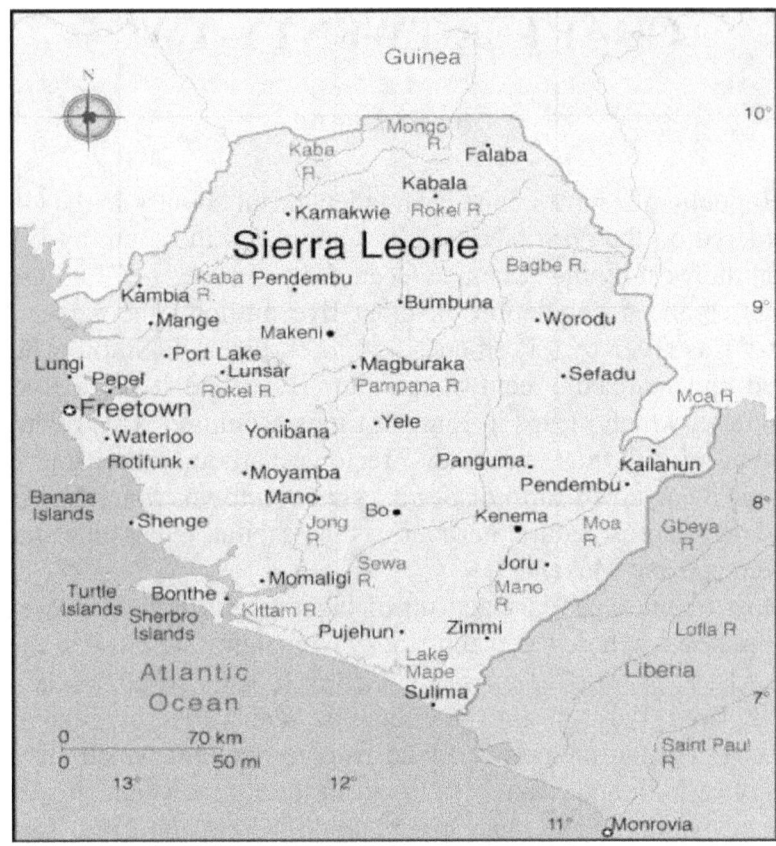

Fig. 22.1: Political Map of Sierra Leone

The People

Sierra Leone has about 20 African ethnic groups and the descendants of freed slaves. The Temne in the north and the Mende in the south are the largest. Other major groups are the Limba, Kuranko, Susu, Yalunka, and Loko in the north; the Kono and Kissi in the east; and the Shebro in the southwest. Minor groups include the Bullum, Vai and Krim and the Fulani and Malinke immigrants from Guinea. They are mainly found in the north and east.

Most of the groups in Sierra Leone are part of larger ethnic networks extending into several countries in West Africa. About two percent of the population are the Krio (Creoles) who are descendants of free blacks from the United Kingdom and the United States of

America. They are mainly found in Freetown. About 60 percent of the population are Muslims while Christians constitute 30 percent. The rest are adherents of the African Traditional Religion. Sierra Leone has life expectancy of 56 years and infant mortality rate of 80 per 1000 live births.

History

For centuries, the area of Sierra Leone has been inhabited by agricultural, pastoral and fishing peoples. The knowledge of iron working came to the area in the seventh century. The earliest inhabitants of the interior were the Limba. The Temne and Shebro people occupied the coastal areas in the fifteenth century. A century later the Mende people came from the southeast. They organized themselves in small political units where they practiced village democracy. The rulers did not have absolute power as they were checked by village councils. Secret societies notably the Poro society exerted wide-ranging political influence in these chiefdoms and taught youths the art of warfare and bravery. Islam was introduced by Muslim traders, first into the north and from there spread through the entire country.

Contacts with Europeans occurred in the fifteenth century when in 1460 Sierra Leone estuary was reached by the Portuguese who wished to trade in ivory. They were followed later by the English. During the trans-Atlantic slave trade era, thousands of Africans were sold into slavery and taken to the plantations of the United States of America. In 1787, a group of freed slaves from England arrived Sierra Leone to establish a settlement.

The project failed but was revived by the Sierra Leone Company, a commercial company which was sponsored by English opponents of the evil trade. Freed slaves from Nova Scotia in the US were brought to Sierra Leone where they started a new settlement named Freetown or Province of Freedom. Other freed slaves from the West Indies, especially Jamaica, joined the settlers in Freetown. When slave trade was declared illegal in 1807, Freetown became a naval base for the British against continuous trade in slaves.

In the course of time, about 50,000 slaves were rescued in the Atlantic Ocean and brought to settle in Freetown. Most of them came from Nigeria and became known in their new homes as the Aku. From the Aku community emerged phenomenal personalities some of whom returned to Nigeria to hold responsible positions in government, the Church and the educational sector.

In the early nineteenth century, Freetown served as the centre from which the British ruled the Gold Coast, the Gambia and the Lagos Colony and Protectorate in Nigeria. It also served as the educational centre of British West Africa. Fourah Bay College, which was established in 1827, became a centre of academic excellence on the Guinea Coast for more than a century.

Attempts by the British to colonize Sierra Leone were met with stiff resistance by the indigenous people who mounted several revolts against the British rule and the Krio domination. The most successful leader of the battle against the British was Bai Bureh. He was eventually defeated in 1898, and in that year, the British proclaimed the area a protectorate. Already, by 1807, the British had declared the settlements in Freetown as a Crown Colony. In the protectorate the Chiefs ruled under the supervision of British officials. This was Indirect Rule in practice. In the colony, the settlers held senior administrative positions. But the colony and protectorate were governed directly by British officials.

After the Second World War, the demand for independence, which had started decades earlier, grew in the colony and the protectorate areas. The British responded to the demand by constituting democratic institutions. The nationalists in the colony wished to take over power from the British but at independence power went to the protectorate. The process of independence started with the 1951 Constitution. In that year, Dr. Milton Margai with the leaders from the protectorate and the colony founded the Sierra Leone People's Party (SLPP) for the independence and unity of both the colony and the protectorate. On April 27, 1961 Sierra Leone became an independent state with Sir Milton Margai as the Prime Minister.

Politics and the Structure of Governance

The SLPP led Sierra Leone to independence and the first general elections in May 1962 under universal adult franchise. In 1964, Sir Milton Margai died and was succeeded by his brother, Sir Albert

Margai, as Prime Minister. In the next election in March 1967, the opposition party, the All-Peoples' Congress (APC) led by Siaka Stevens won a plurality of the parliamentary seats. Stevens was declared as the new Prime Minister. A few hours after the declaration, the military led by Brigadier David Lansana staged a coup d'état and placed both Margai and Stevens under house arrest.

These officers were overthrown two days later through another coup and the military formed the National Reformation Council (NRC) to rule the country. After a year, there was yet a third coup where the privates and non-commissioned officers mutinied, imprisoned their superiors and restored parliamentary democracy under Stevens and his APC. Between 1968 and 1985 that Steven ruled, all political parties, except the APC, were banned. The amended Constitution of 1978 legalized the ban.

In 1985, Stevens retired but chose his successor in the person of Joseph Saidu Momoh who was the army chief. On April 29, 1992, the Momoh government was overthrown through a coup led by Captain Valentine Strasser. Meanwhile, a rebellion led by Foday Sankoh, which had started a year before the coup, had threatened the very foundation of Sierra Leone. The government responded to this threat by hiring mercenaries from the Private Military Company (PMC), the Executive Outcomes. By 1995, the government and the PMC could not dislodge the rebellion. In 1996, the Strasser government bowed to international pressure and organized elections to hand over power to democratically-elected government.

In the elections held in April 1996, Ahmad Tejan Kabbah, a weather-beaten diplomat won as President. But on May 25, 1997, Major Jonny Paul Koroma overthrew Kabbah in a coup d'état. In March 1998 ECOMOG forces led by Nigeria threw Koroma out of the presidential palace and reinstated President Kabbah. After an unsuccessful coup attempt in January 1999, civil war ensued in Sierra Leone. With the assistance of ECOMOG and the United Nations Mission in Sierra Leone (UNAMSIL), the civil war was brought to an end in 2002. In fact, on January 18 2002 Kabbah declared the civil war over in the country. In May 2002 he was elected to a five-year term.

Economy

Like most countries in the GoG, Sierra Leone advertises an agrarian economy. The main food crop is rice. Swamp rice is cultivated in the low marshy river valleys. Upland rice is grown in the wetter region inland. Other food crops include maize, yams, cassava, sweet potatoes and plantains. For export, the main agricultural items include palm oil and kernels, cocoa, ginger, coffee, piassava (fibre from the raffia palm), kola nuts, groundnuts and banana.

Sierra Leone is rich in mineral resources. Diamonds which are the most valuable products are exploited in the Upper Sewa valley and Kono. Iron is mined at Marampa and Bonthe. Bauxite is mined at Moyamba. The country has the world's largest known deposits of rutile, an ore of the metal titanium. Rutile is used for making paint, plastics, paper, welding rod coatings and cloth. Sierra Leone earns much from the export of rutile.

Tourism is a thriving industry in Sierra Leone. Many people visit the Game Reserve at Kabala in the north. The country also has oil and gas.

Foreign Relations

Sierra Leone maintains cordial relations with many countries especially in Africa, Europe and Asia. It has special relations with the United Kingdom and the United States of America.

The country is a member of leading international organizations including ECOWAS, the AU, the MRU, the OIC, the Non-Aligned Movement, the Commonwealth and the UN and its specialized agencies.

Further Reading

African Encyclopaedia. 1974. London: Oxford University Press.
Ayissi, A. and R. E. Poulton. eds. 2006. *Bound to Cooperate: Conflict, Peace, and People in Sierra Leone*. New York: UN Institute for Disarmament Research.

Besada, H. ed. 2007. *From Civil Strife to Peace Building: Examining Private Sector Involvement in West African Reconstruction.* Canada: Centre for International Governance Innovation.

Cartwright, J. R. 1970. *Politics in Sierra Leone, 1947-1967.* Toronto: University of Toronto Press.

Conteh-Morgan, E. and M. Dixon-Fyle. 1999. *Sierra Leone at the End of the Twentieth Century: History, Politics and Society.* New York: Peter Lang.

Davidson, B. 1964. *Old Africa Rediscovered.* London: Oxford University Press.

Duffy, J. 1959. *Portuguese Africa.* Harvard University Press.

Fage, J. D. 1963. *An Atlas of African History.* Arnold.

Fyfe, C. 1964. *A History of Sierra Leone.* London: Oxford University Press.

Greenberg, J. H. 1963. *Languages of Africa.* London: Indiana University Press.

International Encyclopaedia of the Social Sciences. London: Macmillan.

Murdoc G. P. 1959. *Africa: Its Peoples and their Culture History.* New York, McGraw-Hill.

Kpundeh, S. J. 1995. *Politics and Corruption in Africa: A Case Study of Sierra Leone.*

Kup, A. P. 1961. *A History of Sierra Leone, 1400-1787.* London: Cambridge University Press.

Lander, R. 1967. *Records of Captain Clapperton's Last Expedition to Africa.* London: Frank Cass & Co. Ltd.

Little, K. 1967. *The Mende of Sierra Leone.* London: Routledge & Kegan Paul.

Reno, W. 1997. *Privatizing War in Sierra Leone.* **Current History.** 1997. 96 (610). 230.

CHAPTER TWENTY-THREE

Togo

The Republic of Togo (Republique Togolaise) is one of the smallest countries of the GoG. It has a total area of 57 square kilometres and a population of six million. Togo is bounded by Ghana to the west, Burkina Faso to the north, Benin to the east and the GoG to the south. It stretches 579 kilometres north from the Gulf and is 160 kilometres wide at the broadest point. Togo consists of the part of the former German colony of Togo land that was made French mandated territory after the First World War. Lome which is the largest city and port is the capital. Other cities are Sekode, Kara, Atakpame and Dapaong.

Togo has six geographic regions. The coast has sand-bars and lagoons, and there is low clay plain inland. The Atacora Mountains extending west from Benin Republic reach a height of about 1100 metres. In the north, the country becomes lower again near the valley of the Oti River, one of the main tributaries of the Volta.

The People

Togo is composed of about 30 ethnic groups and many of these groups are immigrants from other parts of West Africa. The two major groups are the Ewe in the south and the Kabye in the north. Other groups in the north include the Gurma, the Natemba, Dye, Bu-Bankam, Bu-Kombong, and Kokomba, the Tamberma, the Basari, the Moba, the Naudemba, the Kabre and Logba, the Namba, Fulani and the Kebu. In the southwest and central Togo are the Akposo, the Adele and the Ahlo.

The Ewe who forms the single-largest group emigrated from the Niger River valley in Nigeria and moved into Togo between the twelfth and fourteenth centuries. The Yoruba group called Ana also came from Nigeria. Emigrants from Ghana and Cote d'Ivoire who came in the seventeenth century are the Ane, the Ga-Adagme, the Kpelle and the Anyana, the Chakossi and the Dagomba. Emigrants from Burkina Faso, who live mainly in the north of Togo, include Gurma and Mossi and Kotokoli and Temba.

About 50 percent of the population are Christians, 15 percent Muslims and the rest are adherents of the African Traditional Religion. Life expectancy in Togo is 60 years and infant mortality rate is 56 per 1,000 live births.

Fig. 23.1: Political Map of Togo

History

Until the Portuguese explorers and traders visited the coast of Togo between the fifteenth and the sixteenth centuries, the Togo along with Ghana and Cote d'Ivoire constituted the southern termini of the important trans-Saharan trade routes. The Ewe people had already migrated to the region from Nigeria and were direct participants in the trade. The consequence of the Portuguese trading venture was that the direction of trade shifted to the coast. The items of trade were mainly ivory and slaves. So many slaves were taken from Togo that, together with the Niger Delta and Benin, the region was called the Slave Coast.

The process of European colonization of Togo started in 1847, when German missionaries arrived in Ewe territory. Closely on the heels of the missionaries came German traders who established their settlement at Anecho. In 1884, Gustav Nachtigal, on instructions from the German government, signed treaties of protection with the coastal chiefs. German military expeditions followed between 1888 and 1897. On the successful conclusions of the military exercises, Lome was in 1897 made the colonial capital. Colonization began that same year. Though thoroughly harsh and brutal, German administration was efficient.

From 1914, Togo was a pawn in the European diplomatic chess board. On 7 August, 1914 when the First World War began, a combined troops from the Gold Coast (British colony) and Dahomey (French colony) invaded Togo land. On August 26, the Germans surrendered. In the aftermath of this invasion, Britain and France divided the country into two with the western part taken by Britain and the eastern part taken by France. In 1922, the League of Nations issued mandates to Britain and France to administer the two territories of Togo in their control. British Togo was administered as part of the Gold Coast while French Togo was administered as a distinct unit. As French colony, it sent a deputy to the French National Assembly, a Councillor to the Assembly of the French Union and two Senators to the French Council.

In 1946, Britain and France placed their territories under UN trusteeship. On May 9, 1956, a plebiscite was organized by the UN to determine how the people of the two territories needed to be governed. British Togo voted to remain in the Gold Coast and on December 13, 1956, it was incorporated into the Gold Coast.

In 1957, Kwame Nkrumah named the Gold Coast and British Togo land Ghana. For the French Togo, opportunity for independence came in April 1958, when the UN asked for elections in the territory, which already had a Premier, Nicholas Grunitzky who was appointed by the French government. In the April elections the people of French Togo voted for complete independence. They also rejected Grunitzky and elected to be led by Sylvanus Olympio. On April 27, 1960, Togo became independent, severed its Constitutional ties with France and at the same time shed its UN trusteeship status. In the 1961 elections, Togo established a presidential form of government and Olympio became its first President.

Politics and Structure of Governance

The 1961 Constitution in Togo created an executive President to be elected for seven years by universal suffrage. The President was given the legal rights to appoint ministers and dissolve the National Assembly. In the 1961 elections, Togo had four political parties- Togolese Youth Movement, the *Union Democratique des Populations Togolaises* (UDPT), the *Parti Togolais Du Progress* (PTP) and the *Comite Unite Togolaise* (CUT). Olympio who won represented the CUT, and Grunitzky's PTP was disqualified and disallowed from participating in the 1961 elections. In 1962, Olympio dissolved all political parties in the country. On January 13, 1963, he was assassinated. Two days later, Grunitzky who had gone into exile returned to head a provisional government as Prime Minister. A new Constitution was adopted on May 5, 1963. That Constitution restored the multiparty system in the country and in the election which followed, Nicolas Grunitzky was elected as President.

He stayed in office for three years. On November 21, 1966, he was overthrown by the military in a bloodless coup led by Lieutenant Colonel Etienne Eyadema (later General Gnassingbe Eyadema). Eyadema assumed the presidency of Togo and suspended all political parties. He ruled for 38 years as one of Africa's longest serving rulers. He died on February 5, 2005. A day after his death, the military in a brazen manner and as if they carried out the *Will* of General Eyadema, installed his son Faure Gnassingbe to serve out his term. But domestic protest and external pressure including sanctions by ECOWAS and the AU forced Faure Gnassingbe to step down on February 25, 2005. In a deeply flawed presidential election of April 2005, Faure was announced the winner.

In the aftermath of the show of shame, the international community pressurized him to form a government of national unity. He first named one of the opposition leaders, Edem Kodjo, as his

Prime Minister in 2005. In 2006, Yawovi Agboyibio was appointed as the next Prime Minister. In 2007, Komlan Mally was appointed Prime Minister and when he resigned on September 5, 2008, Gilbert Fossoun Houngbo was named as the Prime Minister. These frequent changes of the position of the Prime Minister are a reflection of political instability that besets Togo.

Economy

Agriculture is the backbone of the economy of Togo. The main food crops are corn, cassava, yams, guinea-corn, millet and groundnuts while the agricultural exports include cocoa and coffee from the mountain region, and oil palm products, cotton, sheanuts, and copra (from coconuts) from the southern lowlands. At the lagoons, rivers and at the coast, fishing is important.

The country's leading export commodity is phosphate, which is mined near the coast east of Lome. Togo is the world's largest producer of phosphate. Other mineral resources of note in Togo include limestone, bauxite, iron ore, uranium, chromite, gold, diamond, manganese oxide, kaolin and rutile. It is little wonder that the country's industry is dominated by mining and quarrying.

Foreign Relations

Although a small country by all standards, Togo is an active player in the international system. Togo has cordial relations with its neighbours and Germany and France on account of historical ties. It relates with many countries in Africa, Europe, Asia and Latin America. In the West African sub-continent, Togo and Nigeria facilitated the establishment of ECOWAS in 1975, through the famous *Nigeria-Togo Initiative*.

Togo is a member of many international organizations including the Non-Aligned Movement, ECOWAS, AU and the UN.

Further Reading

African Encyclopaedia. 1974. London: Oxford University Press.
Davidson, B. 1964. *Old Africa Rediscovered.* London: Oxford University Press.
Duffy, J. 1959. *Portuguese Africa.* Harvard University Press.
Fage, J. D. 1963. *An Atlas of African History.* Arnold.
Greenberg, J. H. 1963. *Languages of Africa.* London: Indiana University Press.
International Encyclopaedia of the Social Sciences. London: Macmillan.
Murdoc G. P. 1959. *Africa: Its Peoples and their Culture History.* New York, McGraw-Hill.

Section V

Making Africa Visible Actor in the International System

The Strategic Future of the Gulf of GuineaHistory, Geo-Politics and the African Desideratum

CHAPTER TWENTY-FOUR

The Strategic Future of the Gulf of Guinea

As documented in the Introduction, the GoG is the single richest region in Africa. Region here is taken to mean "an area within which the combination of environmental and demographic factors have created a homogeneity of economic and social structure" (Beujeu-Garnier, 1976:79). In terms of geographical location, historical experience, economic and social structure, the GoG is a region.

Although the states are grouped into Central Africa, Southern Africa and West Africa, geographically speaking, they are all located in West Africa. Historically, all the states of the GoG were parts of the Portuguese empire in Africa. Economically, the states of the GoG are rich in critical mineral resources that have the capacities to turn the region into one large self-reliant and developed economy. These mineral resources range from oil that everybody needs to diamonds, gold, bauxite and cobalt that sustain the economies of the developed world. Socially, the citizens of the GoG are linguistic cousins; majority are of the Bantu African origin or products of inter-marriage with the Bantu group.

These profiles were used, and are still being used, to prop up the global economy but the region that assisted, and still assists the world to develop thus far is in penury and highly de-developed. An examination of the historical evolution of the region, including its political economy and politics, reveals the germs of its de-development; a complete state of opposite of development which is worse than underdevelopment. The state of underdevelopment conveys a message of a standard of development that is below conventional expectations but in the state of de-development, the states are simply writing their histories backwards; into the woods.

The resources that made the region the darling of the Portuguese and later of all European citizens are seemingly inexhaustible, beginning with the human resources that developed the world economy through slave trade and slavery to critical mineral resources. If the region is to have any strategic future, it has to develop these resources to serve its needs. This means that it should stop, through active industrialization, wholesale exportation of raw resources in cheap forms only to buy them back in expensive forms after value are added by the Euro-American world.

During its first contact with the European world, the region exported its human resources in form of slaves. The slaves worked the plantations of the Americas and produced the capital for Europe to launch its industrial revolution which was later employed to colonize the people of the GoG and create in their environments ready market for these industrial goods.

Already, slave trade led to the rise of port cities in Europe like Birmingham, Manchester, Bristol, Nantes, Seville, Liverpool, Bordeaux and Marseilles and these cities acted as catalysts of the new industrial world. No equivalent of such cities existed in Africa. When slave trade ended, these cities became triggers of agglomeration economies, urbanization economies and localization economies. With these, Europe had a head-start over other continents of the world.

Ordinarily, the continent that it earned so much resources and goodwill from ought to have benefited tremendously from such contacts. But this was not so. If in the relative age of innocence, the GoG never fared well from contacts with Europe, there is nothing in logic or historical experience to assume that it will ever fare well. Therefore, for the GoG in particular and Africa in general, the choice is clear: they have to evolve African-compliant strategies to overcome the challenges of de-development.

This calls for the use of the same techniques that made the Euro-American World to subjugate the citizens of the region for ages and continue to manipulate their political and economic systems to its own advantage. These techniques revolve around three discernible areas, namely: Human Security, Human Resources Development and the Creation of the orbit (s) of modern civilization for political stability.

The Necessity for Human Security Agenda

There is no doubt that insecurity is the norm in Africa. Like other developing zones of the world, fundamental security challenges include perennial threats of interstate war and communal violence, poverty and famine, weapons proliferation and crime, political instability, social breakdown, economic failure and in extreme cases complete state collapse (Jackson, 2007). Added to these negative profile are concrete cases of internally displaced persons or refugees, internal political violence, such as coups or rebellions, ethnic or religious violence, campaigns of hate and terrorism, riots and disorder, threats of small arms and light weapons (SALWs), people dying everyday from hunger and diseases such as diarrhoea, HIV-AIDS, influenza, tuberculosis and leprosy-diseases that are taken for granted in the developed world.

Furthermore, "tens of millions more suffer from chronic poverty, lack of employment opportunities, inadequate health, declining educational standards and environmental ruin" (Jackson, 2007:147). These security challenges occur because the elite, particularly members of the ruling class, are after regime security as against national security. Regime security is the condition where governing elites are secure from violent challenges to their rule whereas national security is the condition where the institutions, processes and structures of the state are able to continue functioning effectively in spite of the make-up of the ruling elite (Jackson, 2007).

The states of the GoG in particular and Africa in general should re-think their national security arrangements and engagements and move decisively and deliberately to embrace the provisions of human security. The term ***human security*** was given form and currency by the UN since the 1990s and till today it remains the best attempt to re-think and indeed broaden the concept of security in line with the aspirations of man. In its 1994 Report, the United Nations Development Programme (UNDP) describes human security as a condition where people are given relief from the traumas that besiege human development. Accordingly, human security means (UNDP, 1994:23):

> First safety from such chronic threats as hunger, diseases and repression. And second, it means protection from sudden hurtful disruptions in the patterns of daily life-whether in homes, in jobs or in communities.

To ensure human security, the UNDP calls attention to seven critical areas to be addressed. These include economic, food, health, environment, personal, community and political security.

The fulcrum of human security is economic development and to ensure success in economic endea-vours, African states should create and sustain legal-rational institutions to promote development. Strong institutions would guarantee states infrastructural power with which to strengthen state capacity and make them to overcome the burdens of insecurity, including regime insecurity which African potentates are scared of.

Infrastructural power, according to C. Thomas (1989), refers to the effectiveness and legitimacy of the state's institutions and its ability to rule through consensus. This is contrasted with despotic power which refers to the state's coercive abilities and the exercise of force to impose its rule on the people. Throughout Africa, despotic power is over-developed and, in most cases, over-resisted at the same time by the people. It is the clash between despotism and struggles for liberation that is at the heart of human tragedy in Africa. Therefore, the first step towards human security in the continent is the institutionalization of political liberalization.

Human Resources Development

Human beings are clear agents of development. All states in the international system have human beings who are their citizens. To be sure it is not all human beings that are agents of development. The category of human beings that constitutes agents of development is the one whose capacities and resources are well developed. Human beings, and by implication population, fall within the category of natural sources of power.

Ideally, there are three natural sources of power and these are geography, population and natural resources. They are called natural sources because they are direct endowments of nature; resources that are not man-made. But it has to be noted that nature, regardless of its opulence, is wild and merciless when not tamed, re-configured and re-directed towards desired ends. That is why nations that get the best from nature are the ones that have developed nature itself by way of adding value to it. In other words, in its pure state, nature is but a critical platform for man to excite his ingenuity for greatness and comfort.

Nations that are great and have achieved a high level of comfort for their citizens are those that have employed the ingenuity of their citizens to challenge, and tinker with, nature. Of all the resources of nature, only man is the credible agent of change and at the same time endowed with resources for ingenuity. This is because man alone has rational faculty. But man in a pure state of nature is brute, whose behaviour is hardly distinguishable from that of an animal. Therefore, to make him serve a higher need of nature, his resources have to be developed.

Contemporary developing countries are poor, underdeveloped and de-developed because they lag behind in human resources development and endowment. Their populations are less developed, less informed, less experienced and less skilled (Todaro & Smith, 2004). In this direction, Paul Romer argues that the developing countries "are poor because their citizens do not have access to the ideas that are used in industrial nations to generate economic value" (see Todaro & Smith, 2004:92). In his view, the technology gap between the rich and the developing nations can be divided into two components, "a physical object gap, involving factories, roads, and modern machinery, and an idea gap, including knowledge about marketing, distribution, inventory control, transactions processing, and worker motivation" (see Todaro & Smith, 2004:92).

It is this idea gap thesis that accounts for the difference between the rich and poor nations. Thomas Homer-Dickson calls this gap the ingenuity gap; that is, the ability to apply innovative ideas to solve practical social and technical problems. All in all, the knowledge gap (because in the final analysis that is what it is) must be bridged if Africa seriously desires to get out of the woods. As Todaro and Smith (2004:92) have aptly emphasized:

> The ability of a country to exploit its natural resources and to initiate and sustain long-term economic growth is dependent on, among other things, the ingenuity and the managerial and technical skills of its people and its access to critical market and product information at minimal cost.

In chapter three on the political economy of the GoG, it is documented that the natural resources of the region have the capacities to banish poverty and want in the Gulf. For instance, on account of possession of natural resources, the DR Congo is potentially the richest country in the world but despite these endowments, the country's name is registered on the last page of the poorest nations in the international community. Similarly, Nigeria is in a class of its own on account of the trinity of large size, big population and abundant natural resources; but despite these, its status is only slightly better than that of the DR Congo. This continuous state of poverty in the midst of plenty is largely caused by the state of human resources of the two states. To start with, their natural resources are mined by foreign companies that are not engaged on charity schemes but profit-making and, in most cases, the profits so-declared are accepted by these states because they do not have the technology to either harness the resources themselves or track the entire operations. Therefore, in the GoG foreign technologies have constituted modern-day imperialism to the extent that because of corporate interests, foreign companies sometimes collude with local political actors to inspire secessionist agenda and to cause political nightmares for the states.

To overcome the new imperialism, the states of the GoG should confront these challenges the way they confronted colonialism. Unlike their forbearers, today's leadership has the advantages of sovereignty and unfettered decision-making processes. Therefore, deliberate efforts should be made to develop the human resources of the continent in the critical areas that would serve the needs of the region.

The Imperatives of the Creation of Orbit(s) of Modern Civilization in Africa

In a continent full of despots, unimaginable crimes, conflicts and crises, humanitarian disasters, population explosion, low life expectancy, low standard of living and weak state status, how can it advance materially and develop? These questions have bothered many scholars in Africa and elsewhere. Mohammed Ayoob, for instance, has utilized state-making theories to explain the predicament and to project a stable future for Africa.

According to him, the negative events in Africa represent a normal stage in a long-term state-building process from which the continent will come out stronger (Ayoob, 1995). Making historical parallels with the European experience whose state-building process took centuries of chaos, confusion, disorder and bloodshed in order to weld disparate groups into a single national identity, Ayoob persuasively argues that nothing is wrong in Africa. But Ayoob's confidence is not shared by many. Pointing out the obstacles that were absent during the European experience even though they had a bloody and tortuous process, Richard Jackson (2004:158) writes:

> ...unlike European states, today's weak states have to cope with the ongoing effects of colonial rule, which includes: the imposition of alien doctrines and institutions of statehood; irrational territorial boundaries and the lack of national identity; societies divided along class, religious and ethnic lines; stunted and dependent economies; and an entrenched culture of political violence. These factors make the state-building process even more difficult than it might have been. The contemporary state-building process is also constrained by a shortened time-frame. Unlike European states, weak states today are expected to become effective, fully functioning, democratic states within a few decades. Moreover, they are expected to do it without the violence, corruption and human rights abuses that accompanied the European state-building process. Established international norms and rules, such as the protection of minority and human rights and the right of self-determination (which often encourages ethnic rebellion), also complicates the state-building process. A particularly problematic norm is the inviolability of statehood. Once a state achieves independence and is admitted to the United Nations, its status cannot be revoked or its territory subsumed into another state, no matter how unviable it proves to be in practice. Thus, unlike European entities such as Burgundy and Aragon which could not complete the state-building process and were absorbed into larger, more viable units, today's weak states must struggle on indefinitely.

The logic of this critique is that Africa is in trouble and perhaps has no future and if it has at all the prospect is located in the distant future; centuries away. This prospect makes Richard Jackson (2007:158) to finally lament thus:

> In short, according to this approach, we can expect weak states to experience a great deal more bloodshed and violence over an extended period until stronger, more representative states emerge. Until then, they will remain 'quasi-states'-states possessing the nominal features of

statehood, such as international recognition, but lacking the infrastructural capacities to create and secure a sense of genuine national identity.

On the basis of the dilemma which hinges on prolonged crises in Africa, some scholars have argued that state-building should be abandoned in favour of alternative forms of political structure based on either smaller units like city-states or clans or large units such as the European Union (EU) (Jackson, 2007).

The first option is tantamount to creating a state of anarchy in the continent. The second option is the key to overcoming the burdens of underdevelopment provided conditions of modern civilization are formulated and made pre-conditions for participation and membership. This is what we call ***orbit of modern civilization*** where two or few democratic states are encouraged by the international community to establish a regional organization with a set of civilized rules and standards for initial members and thereafter admit others on the basis of compliance with the rules.

The EU model is the best approach for Africa. Civilization here is taken to mean tritely a state of human society that is effectively developed and efficiently organized to achieve security, peace and stability in line with the aspirations and worldview of members of the society, while at the same time incorporating positive conventional norms and culture. So far, democracy is the best element in contemporary civilization and it is evidently an instrument of conflict resolution in plural societies. The democratic peace theory acknowledges the fact that pacific unions exist effectively between liberal democracies and once established, democratic peace would spread through spill over dynamics, international socialization and positive feedback (Harrison, 2002; Mitchell, 2002).

The history of the EU shows that it was started in 1952 by six democratic countries: Belgium, France, Germany, Italy, Luxembourg, and the Netherlands. Success brought new members. Denmark, Ireland and Britain joined in 1973. Greece became the tenth member in 1981; Spain and Portugal were admitted in 1981. In 1995 Austria, Finland and Sweden became members. By the turn of the twentieth century, Bulgaria, Cyprus, the Czech Republic, Estonia, Hungary, Latvia, Lithuania, Malta, Poland, Romania, Slovakia, Slovenia and Turkey had applied to join the EU. For a country to be admitted into the Union, it has to pass through stringent conditions rooted in human security and fundamental human rights. Africa should take a cue from the EU.

If the OAU had had stringent conditions based on human security and human rights for states in Africa to attain before membership, the continent would have been developed by 2002 A.D., the year it had a cosmetic change in its name but not in its content and character. In that year, it transmuted itself from the OAU into the AU with despotic characters like the late Omar Bongo of Gabon (ruling for 41 years), Robert Mugabe of Zimbabwe (ruling for 32 years), the late Muammar Ghadaffi of Libya (ruling for 42 years), Paul Biya of Cameroon (ruling for 30 years) and Jose Eduardo do Santos of Angola (ruling for 33 years).

In the same vein, if the UN had set stringent civilized conditions for new members in 1945 when it was founded, the world would have attained a higher degree of peace and security by the time it celebrated its Golden Jubilee in 1995. Indeed, with strong orbits of civilization, the world would have saved for mankind and development purposes $246 billion it used in the Korean war; $347 billion it expended on the Vietnam war; $ 61 billion that was engaged in the Persian Gulf war; $500 billion that was wasted on the Iraq war; $1 billion a day that the US spent on the war on terrorism in the Afghanistan-Pakistan corridor and over $50 billion a year that the same country spends for security in the Middle East.

For the GoG, which does not have a *region-wide* international governmental organization (except the Gulf of Guinea Commission (GGC) which is very limited in scope, membership and operations and, indeed, a league of dictators, outside Nigeria), a minimum of two states should establish either a GoG Union (GGU) or a Union of African States (UAS). If the former is established, its future should be limited to the states of the GoG and if the later is established, the orbit should incorporate as well the states flanking the Gulf to the north, except Sudan.

As a matter of fact, Africa should have a maximum of four Unions; that is, four orbits of modern civilization under the League of African Nations (LAN). These should be:

1) The Magrib Union
2) The Nile Union
3) The Union of African Republics and
4) The Union of African States. Table 24.1 shows the particulars of states under each proposedUnion.

Table 24.1 Proposed Unions and Membership in Africa

Unions	Sovereign States
The Magrib Union	Libya Mauritania Morocco Tunisia Western Sahara Headquarters: Morocco Notes: (Six States): Mauritania has since withdrawn from ECOWAS and it is now in the Magrib Union. Excluding Egypt, these are Arab States in Africa. Outside Morocco, Algeria, Libya and Tunisia were administered by the Ottoman Empire in the pre-colonial period. Morocco, Western Sahara and Mauritania belong to the Almoravid culture. Their geo-politics require a separate Union.
The Nile Union	Burundi Djibouti Egypt Eritrea Ethiopia Kenya Rwanda Somalia Sudan Tanzania Uganda Headquarters: Ethiopia Notes: (Eleven States) These are the states of the Blue and White Nile (the Nile Basin). The Nile River runs through these states and they collectively depend on it for survival.
Unions	Sovereign States

The Union of African Republics (UARs)	Botswana Comoros Lesotho Madagascar Malawi Mauritius Mozambique Namibia Seychelles South Africa Swaziland Zambia Headquarters: South Africa Notes: (Twelve States) Comoros, Madagascar, Mauritius and Seychelles are located on the Indian Ocean in the same manner with most states of the proposed UARs, which are located on the Coast of the Indian Ocean.
The Union of African States (UAS)	Angola Benin Burkina Faso Cameroon Cape Verde Congo Republic Cote d'Ivoire Central African Republic (CAR) Chad DR Congo Equatorial Guinea Gabon The Gambia Ghana Guinea Guinea Bissau Liberia Mali Niger Nigeria São Tomé & Principe Senegal Sierra Leone Togo Headquarters: Nigeria Notes: Twenty Four States; Nineteen States of the Gulf of Guinea plus five of their neighbouring land-locked states

Conditions for Membership

Conditions for membership should include, but not limited to, the following:

a) Constitutional Democracy with term(s) of the Heads of State not exceeding 10 years
b) Operation of federalism as distinct strategy for conflict resolution on account of the multi-ethnic and religious nature of the continent
c) Common foreign policy
d) Common defence policy
e) Prohibition of foreign military base(s) in member states
f) Common currency. E.g. Afrik, Guinea, Magrib and the Nile; Africa has no business having more than four currencies
g) Implementation of the UN Convention on Human Rights and the African Charter on Human Rights
h) Inter-member trade and Co-ordination of development plans
i) Industrial promotion and regional integration
j) Setting a time-frame for withdrawal of membership from existing inter-governmental organizations other than the GGU or UAS, or other Unions as the case may be; Africa has the highest number of IGOs with some working at cross-purposes
k) The development of legal-rational institutions of governance and
l) When conditions i-xi are fulfilled, membership of new states should be effected on the basis of referendum conducted within the states that apply for membership.

As it is known African states are members of quite a number of IGOs but none of them is effective and functional. In the final analysis, there are more than 100 IGOs in Africa and the West African sub-region alone has about 40. Up till today, the problems that confronted them in their formative years in the 1980s still persist.

Conducting a research on the contributions of the Economic Commission for Africa (ECA) to the establishment of ECOWAS,

Otoabasi Akpan (1986:138) wrote thus about the challenges of multiplicity of the IGOs in West Africa:

> ... What is lacking in them is that their activities tend to overlap and are not coordinated, thereby imposing enormous human and financial burdens on member countries. Added to this is the fact that there is no well-planned, system-wide and sustained attack on West African problems ... in most cases, what led many to as many organizations as they like was the anxiety not to be left out in what might turn out to be a viable means of securing aid and or assistance. A cost-benefit analysis did not in any way come within the purview of their calculation and the result is still diffuse loyalty and lack of focus.

For instance, Niger and Burkina Faso which are poor land-locked countries belong to 30 and 25 IGOs respectively. That is why Africa should be saved from itself by getting them to concentrate on just a single IGO or few IGOs.

The international community, especially the advanced economies, should assist Africa to get out of the woods by encouraging them to create *orbit(s) of modern civilization* in the region. As bait, they should direct Foreign Direct Investment, Foreign Aid and Technical Assistance to the *orbit(s)* to encourage others to straighten up their socio-political systems and join; meanwhile, non-members should be left to stew in their own juice.

This way, Africa will achieve peace and security within a quarter of a century as against centuries of continuous bloodshed and violence before effective state building. Indeed, a stable Africa will reduce the world's security challenges by half and if orbits of modern civilization are developed in several regions of the world, global peace and security would be guaranteed.

History shows that African states readily embrace a new order that promises positive transformation. They embraced the conditionality of the SAPs wholeheartedly and democratic reforms half-heartedly because of absence of legal-rational institutions and not because they do not desire them. If external pressure is introduced, they would easily accept conditions of orbit(s) of modern civilization and participate in such arrangements. And the international community would be better for it.

The imperial powers in Africa actually started the whole idea of regional organizations and cooperation in Africa during the period of colonial rule but at independence "even contiguous territories found it extremely difficult to sacrifice the charms of national sovereignty in favour of collective decision making" (see Akpan, 1986:6). Mention could be made of the Central African Federation created in 1945 between Malawi, Zambia, and Zimbabwe which collapsed in 1964; the Mali Federation formed in January 1959 between Senegal and Mali which collapsed in 1960; the French West Africa created in 1895 between Benin, Cote d'Ivoire, Guinea, Mali, Mauritania, Niger and Senegal which collapsed in 1960; the French Equatorial Africa created in 1910 between Gabon, the Central African Republic, Chad, the Republic of Congo and the Republic of Cameroon (since 1919) which collapsed in 1960; the East African Community created in 1948 by the British between Kenya, Uganda and Tanzania which collapsed in 1973, and the Anglo West African Common Institutions created in 1874 between Nigeria, Ghana, The Gambia and Sierra Leone which collapsed in 1960. The case of Burkina Faso is instructive. In 1920, Burkina Faso was partitioned between Cote d'Ivoire, Mali and Niger by the French and in 1947, it was re-established to become an overseas territory of the French Union. It achieved independence on August 5, 1960.

The imperial powers embarked on the process of creating larger political units in Africa because they after all realized that they were dealing with twisted states that were individually not viable enough to develop. It is instructive to note that in 1950 all imperial powers in the sub-Saharan Africa created a common organ of cooperation among themselves called the Commission for Technical Cooperation in Africa South of the Sahara, or ***Commission de Cooperation Technique en Afrique au sud du Sahara (CCTA).***

Even after independence, attempts were made by some countries to integrate politically but such attempts did not last long. Typical examples include the Senegambian Confederation created in 1981 between Senegal and The Gambia which collapsed in 1989. Before then there was the Ghana-Guinea Union which was created in 1958 between Ghana and Guinea; in 1961, Mali joined and it became the Ghana-Guinea-Mali Union but it collapsed in 1966. The Union which was the initiative of President Kwame Nkrumah of Ghana was to become the nucleus of the Union of African States (UAS) which he advocated. With the UAS platform, Nkrumah wanted immediate political Union in Africa with a single government, "which he saw as a means of solving the pressing problems of the African people" (Akpan, 1986:5).

A case for political unity in Africa is a noble dream. Indeed, an argument for the political integration of Africa is less convincing because it flies in the face of political reality (Akpan, 1986). What Africa should do, and what the international community should wish for the continent, is to create *orbit(s) of modern civilization* based not on immediate supra-national political authority but union of states in the mould of the EU. To be sure, absolute sovereignty will give way to shared sovereignty but in the final analysis, Africa will be better for it.

The past of Africa should be used as a guide for the future of the continent. The creators of modern Africa were no fools when they created Federations and, or Unions, as enlarged political frontiers to serve their interests. The past is like a shadow where no entity can divorce or separate from. The attempts by modern states in Africa to go alone constitute the greatest bane of the continent. The past Federations or Unions should be reconstructed and given contemporary twists for development and security. Africa should not forget the warning of the ECA in the very month the OAU was created, that:

> The present cash market of most African countries individually is not larger than that of a moderately-sized European town.

The situation has not changed and the African condition is now worse than it was at independence. It is only *orbit(s) of modern civilization* that can constitute the needed masterstroke and talisman for Africa.

Further Reading

Ayoob, M. 1995. *The Third World Security Predicament: State Making Regional Conflict, and the International System.* Boulder, CO: Lynne Rienner.

Buzan B. 1991. *People, States and Fear: An Agenda for International Security Studies in Post Cold War Era.* Boulder, CO: Lynne Rienner.

Clampham, C. 1996. *Africa and the International System: The Politics of State Survival.* Cambridge: Cambridge University Press.

Collier, P 2003. *Breaking the Conflict Trap. Civil War and Development Policy.* Oxford: Oxford University Press.

Davidson, B. 1964. *Old Africa Rediscovered.* London: Oxford University Press.

Duffy, J. 1959. *Portuguese Africa.* Harvard University Press.

Fage, J. D. 1963. *An Atlas of African History.* Arnold.

Falk, R and Mendlovitz S. (eds.). 1973. *Regional Politics and World Order.* San Francisco: W. H. Freeman and Company.

Greenberg, J. H. 1963. *Languages of Africa.* London: Indiana University Press.

Green, R. H. and Seidman, A. 1968. *Unity or Poverty? The Economic of Pan-Africanism.* England: Penguin Books Ltd.

Gruhn, I. V. 1979. *Regionalism Reconsidered: The Economic Commission for Africa.* Columbia: Wesviews Press.

Holsti, K. J. 1996. *The State, War, and the State of War.* Cambridge: Cambridge University Press.

Hampson, F. O. *et al.* 2002. *Madness in the Multitude.* Toronto: Oxford University Press.

Human Security Centre. 2005. *Human Security Report.* Oxford University Press.

Huxtable, P. A. eds. 1998. *The African State at a Critical Juncture: Between Disintegration and Reconfiguration.* Boulder: Lynne Reinner.

Hazlewood, A. (ed.) 1967. *African Integration and Disintegration: Case Studies in Economic and Political Union.* London: Oxford University Press.

Jackson, R. H. 1990. *Quasi-State: Sovereignty, International Relations and the Third World.* Cambridge: Cambridge University Press.

Job, B. (ed.) 1992. *The Insecurity Dilemma: National Security of the Third World States.* Boulder, Co: Lynne Rienner.

Kaldor, M. 1999. *New and Old Wars: Organized Violence in a Global Era.* Cambridge: Polity Press.

Keller, E. J. and D. Rothchild. Eds. 1996. *Africa in the International Order: Rethinking State Sovereignty and Regional Security.* Boulder: Lynne Reinner.

Mutarika, B. W. T. 1972. *Towards Multinational Cooperation in Africa.* New York: Praeger Publishers.

Murdoc G. P. 1959. *Africa: Its Peoples and their Culture History.* New York, McGraw-Hill.

Musah, A and Kayode F. J. (eds.) 2000. *Mercenaries: An African Security Dilemma.* London: Pluto.

Reno, W. 1998. *Warlord Politics and African States.* Boulder, Co: Lynne Rienner.

Rich, P. B (ed.) 1999. *Warlords in International Relations.* London: Macmillan.

Robson, P. 1968. *Economic Integration in Africa.* London: George Allen and Unwin Ltd.

Thakur, R. and Newman, E. (eds.) 2004. *Broadening Asia's Security and Discourse Agenda.* Tokyo: University Nations University Press.

Thomas, C. 1987. *In Search of Security: The Third World in International Relations.* Boulder, Co: Lynne Rienner.

Thomas, C. 2000. *Global Governance, Development and Human Security.* London: Pluto Press.

United Nations Development Programme. 2005. *UNDP Human Development Report, 2005.* Oxford: Oxford University Press.

Wallerstein, I. 1967. Africa: *The Politics of Unity.* London: The Pallmall Press.

Zartman, I. W. (ed.) 1995. *Collapse States: The Disintegration and Restoration of Legitimate Authority.* Boulder, Co: Lynne Rienner.

CHAPTER TWENTY-FIVE

History, Geo-Politics and the African Desideratum

Without doubt, the African desideratum is the creation of an orbit of modern civilization in the GoG, or orbits in the sub-Saharan Africa, or better still, the entire continent of Africa. It is no longer debatable that all the states in Africa are individually not viable; not even broad-arced countries like Algeria, Nigeria, Angola and the DR Congo. History bears out the simple conclusion that Africa has no strategic future except it creates modern Union(s) of states and cloth same with civilized standards and culture that would guarantee the continent peace, security and stability.

With regards to the GoG, an examination of its peoples, history, political economy, politics, economy and foreign relations reveals that the region has reagents to quicken the process of the establishment of a union of states. Historically, the area is not new to such strategic arrangements; politically there are democratic states in the Gulf, though tottering, that can be strengthened and reconfigured to constitute the nucleus of the Union and geo-politically the states of the GoG have over the years been relating bilaterally and multilaterally. Taken together, the visible states to form the nucleus of the African desideratum should be six; namely: Benin, Ghana, Liberia, Nigeria, Sierra Leone and Togo.

The six states or a combination of the six have the necessary particulars to create a nucleus of an orbit of modern civilization for Africa especially in the GoG. In addition to what is already known about them in the book, there is need to examine briefly their geo-politics which can act as a foundation for a viable Union.

Benin

As a GoG state, Benin was created by France and though France assists her through grants, the national interest of Benin responds very much to environmental determinism which hinges seriously on its pre-colonial history and requirements of the geo-politics of the West African sub-region. Writing about a part of these requirements, Emeka Nwokedi (1992:121) documents thus:

> Of the four countries that share territorial contiguity with Nigeria, the Republic of Benin (ex-Dahomey and ex-People's Republic) is the smallest in both land mass and population size and appears, together with the Republic of Togo, like a wedge between the Nigerian colossus and the rest of the space on the Atlantic coast-line. This strategic position permits Benin to play with remarkable dexterity the role of a transit territory for all its immediate northern and eastern neighbours. Benin's position or rather predicament is a consequence of the Anglo-French rivalry and, indeed, of the arbitrariness which characterized boundary delimitation in colonial West Africa. This has ensured that several ethnic groups straddle the international borders between Benin and all its neighbours. With Nigeria, for instance, it shares the Goun and the Yoruba in the South-east, and the Bariba and the Hausa in the North-east of its international frontiers.

On account of strategic needs, both countries have been positively cautious in dealing with each other. For instance, when Nigeria severed diplomatic relations with France in 1961 and banned French aircrafts and ships from her territory, Benin, Chad and Niger were the worst hit. Benin, for one, depended on the Lagos port for heavy equipment from France which was needed for the construction of the Contonou harbour. But as a result of solicitation from Benin, Niger and Chad, Nigeria was persuaded to lift the embargo on French aircraft and ships (Nwokedi, 1992).

Furthermore, when Mathieu Kerekou seized power through a coup d'état in 1972, one of his first duties in office was to revive the proposal for the establishment of a Benin Union between Benin, Togo and Nigeria which was first proposed in the 1960s (Africa Confidential, 1973; Nwokedi, 1992). The proposed Benin Union was an outcome of series of negotiations by the Foreign Ministers of Benin, Nigeria and Togo in the 1960s. Ghana was also to become a member of the Union.

The Union did not materialize because of the political idiosyncrasy of Tafawa Balewa, Nigeria's Prime Minister, who was not favourably disposed to a Union that would expose the country as pursuing *pax Nigeriana.* But in 1982, when the ECA came to the conclusion that the ECOWAS project had failed, it suggested the creation of zonal organizations within ECOWAS in order to strengthen it and one of such organizations was the Benin Union. Parts of the ECA proposal read:

> It is observable that both MRU and CEAO constitute roughly two economic zones, the other basically a forest zone. Another economic zone may be created to comprise Nigeria, Benin, Togo and Ghana. This may be called the Benin Union, which for purposes of sub-regional planning, may be treated as another (forest) zone. No administrative structure need to be set up now ... the question of a separate Benin Union can be left for the future (ECA, 1982:68)

Nevertheless, the Kerekou regime in Benin was overtly pro-Nigeria in its foreign policy. When George Pompidou, the French President cancelled a state visit to Benin in 1972, Kerekou lambasted him and the immediate consequence was reduction of French influence in Benin. A new military agreement was substituted for a Defence pact.

Although Nigeria and Benin signed a military Cooperation Agreement in April 1979, Nigeria refused to upgrade it to a Defence Pact years after when Benin demanded for it. Nigeria rejected the Pact because she was not comfortable with Kerekou's Marxist inclinations and his romance with radical states such as Cuba, Libya, North Korea and the USSR. Meanwhile, the military Cooperation Agreement ensured the training of Benin's military in Nigeria, joint naval and air patrol of the two states and their borders.

In chapter twelve, it is recorded that Benin's policy in the 1970s was not to join any IGO in which Nigeria was not a member. A typical example was the all -Francophone West African Economic Community (CEAO) which was engineered by France to counter Nigeria's influence, size and population. When the country was pressurized to become a member of the CEAO, it opted for an observer status. It was not until 1988 that it agreed to adhere to the 1973 Abidjan Treaty which established the group.

Over the years, Benin has had many bilateral agreements and treaties with Nigeria; just as it has with Togo and Ghana. At a multilateral level in Africa, Benin is a member of ECOWAS, the AU and NEPAD. Ghana, Liberia, Nigeria, Sierra Leone and Togo are also members of most multilateral institutions and agencies that Benin belongs to and these can further provide the six countries the platform to launch a political Union. Above all, Benin is a multi-party democratic state in the GoG.

Ghana

Ghana is one active state in the GoG that has an impressive pedigree in African Unity. Together with Nigeria, Sierra Leone and the Gambia, they shared colonial heritage, early cooperation and common inter-territorial institutions. In the first instance, the Lagos Colony and Protectorate, which today constitutes a geo-political region in Nigeria, was first administered from Sierra Leone and later from Ghana. Indeed, in 1874, the Lagos dependency was annexed to the Gold Coast though it still retained its own administrator. This arrangement, however, changed in 1883 when the post of the administrator was abolished and the Lagos Colony and Protectorate were merged into the administration of the Gold Coast. In 1886, the arrangement was discontinued but throughout the period that it lasted, it strengthened the bond of unity between the two countries (Aluko, 1978). The sense of oneness was further expressed in 1942 when the Governor of the Gold Coast, Sir Alan Burns, (in addition to being the Governor of the Gold Coast) also acted as Governor of Nigeria.

It is instructive to note that from the 1930s the British government encouraged uniform laws in both Ghana and Nigeria and indeed in British West Africa to cover many subjects. Aside from the British government, Nigerians and Gold Coasters, as they were then called, cooperated in a number of ways especially in African nationalism. Politically, they started the concept of a united West Africa. For this reason, six representatives from Nigeria, three from Sierra Leone, one from the Gambia and 40 from the Gold Coast met in Accra in 1920 and inaugurated a political party to cover the territories of British West Africa. This party was the National Congress of British West Africa (NCBWA) led by J. E. Casely-Hayford. According to Olajide Aluko, the idea behind the Conference in which the NCBWA was inaugurated was suggested by a Nigerian, Dr. R. A. Savage who was the editor of

The Gold Coast Leader (Aluko, 1978). The fourth Congress of the party was held in Lagos between December 1929 and January 1930. It was supported by the Nigerian National Democratic Party (NNDP) whose member included Mr. Winifred Tete-Ansa from the Gold Coast.

Among the Nigerian editors of newspapers in the Gold Coast was Dr. Nnamdi Azikiwe who on December 22, 1934 produced the first issue of his paper, the ***African Morning Post***. He used the paper to call for Dominion status for the Gold Coast and to demand for self-governing federation of all the four Anglo-West African territories.

In students' activism in the United Kingdom and Africa, Ghana and Nigeria presented a common platform. A typical example was the West African Students' Union (WASU) which was the fusion of the Gold Coast Students' Progress Union with the Nigerian Progressive Union in London.

Outside efforts of individuals and associations, Ghana and Nigeria had common administrative structures, institutions and services. These included Common Marketing Board (the West African Produce Control Board since 1941), Common Judicial Institution (the West African Court of Appeal since 1866); Common Military Institution (the West Africa Frontier Force (WAFF) since 1873), Common Air Transport (the West African Airways Corporation since 1946), Common Currency (Shilling and Pence since 1912), Common Research Institutions (the West African Institution of Trypanosomiasis, 1947; the West African Cocoa Research Institute (WACRI), 1944; the West African Institute for Oil Palm Research (WAIFOR), 1951, the West African Council for Medical Research (WACMAR), 1954 and the West African Examinations Council (WAEC) since 1953.

Of these institutions, only the WAEC survives. Others were deliberately consigned to the dustbin of history by later-day elements of African nationalism. Lack of foresight, micro-nationalism, the lure of political positions and the excitements of independence were some of the reasons that led to the destruction of these common institutions.

Even though at independence, the Ghanaian Constitution contained clear provisions that mandated Ghana to surrender its sovereignty for a Union of States in Africa, Kwame Nkrumah, the President of Ghana who was a leading Pan Africanist also became a leading destroyer of the common institutions. In April 1955, two years before its independence, Ghana signified its intention to set up its own Central Bank to issue its currency. Justifying the aspiration, its Finance Minister, K. A. Gbedemah announced that:

> The issue by this country of its own currency will be one of the more significant marks of its own attainment of full nationhood (see Aluko, 1978:64).

The next victim was the WAFF. Ghana withdrew from the institution in 1959. A. E. Inkumsah, a Minister of State justified the country's action by arguing that the WAFF:

> Was raised and maintained as a colonial force, and it is from that aspect of it that we wish to dissociate ourselves, so as to emphasize that the Ghana Army is the independent Army of an independent state (see Aluko, 1978:64).

Meanwhile, Nigeria within the same period also harboured grand designs to withdraw from the common institutions. The government in 1952, in anticipation of full self-government, had set up a commission to propose the establishment of a Nigerian Central Bank. The following year, a negative report on the possibility was submitted. Not meeting the pre-conceived intention of government, it set up another commission in 1954. It was this commission that turned in a "favourable" report and on the basis of it Nigeria started the process of establishing its own Central Bank with powers to issue and controls its own currency.

Aside from the activities of the later-day elements of African nationalism that chose to practise micro-nationalism based on individual states, four other factors accounted for the dissolution of most of these institutions. Firstly, Nigeria and Ghana were locked up on the issue of mutual jealousy since the pre-independence period. Secondly, based on the trinity of big size, large population and abundant natural resources, Nigeria picked the bills of maintaining those institutions and never had a major voice in deciding their destinies. Thirdly and closely related to the second factor was the fact that Nigeria was not comfortable that Ghana hosted the headquarters of the most sensitive institutions. Fourthly, there was the issue of air of superiority that Ghanaian leaders had which Nigerian leaders abhorred. On this aspect, Olajide Aluko (1978:65) writes:

> The Gold Coast leaders felt superior to the Nigerians for three main reasons. Firstly, the Gold Coast had the advantage of higher education earlier than Nigeria. Secondly, most of the Nigerians trading and working in Ghana till the early fifties were largely uneducated and unskilled labour, and 'farm hands'. Thirdly, the faster rate of the decolonization process in the Gold Coast, which started with the 1946 Constitution, made its leaders feel more important than the Nigerians. The result of all this was the Gold Coast did not want to be in any position subordinate to Nigeria. Thus in the mid-forties the Gold Coast refused to accept the decision of the Secretary of State for the Colonies that only a single University should be established in Nigeria to serve the needs of all the British West African colonies, as recommended by the minority report of the Elliot Commission on Higher Education in West Africa in 1945. Instead the Gold Coast leaders chose to have their own separate university. And to this the Colonial Secretary agreed on the understanding that it would be endowed largely from local resources. Thus in 1948 two separate universities were established in Ibadan and Achimota.

Generally, Ghana-Nigeria relations during the times of Kwame Nkrumah in Ghana and Tafawa Balewa in Nigeria were akin to Cold War where each side tried to sabotage and run down the other. It was not until the period of military leadership in the two countries, beginning from 1966, that Ghana and Nigeria increased the level of interactions. For this reason, Ghana exhausted its diplomatic goodwill to make sure that the Nigerian political crises in 1966 and 1967 did not snowball into a civil war. Even when the war eventually started, Ghana supported Nigeria diplomatically so as to escape dismemberment.

A study of Ghana-Nigeria relations in the immediate post independence period reveals the fact that despite availability of common administrative and technical facilities, it never responded to the functionalist theories of international integration of Ernest Haas and David Mittrany. As defined by Haas (1958:16), international integration is:

> The process whereby political actors in several distinct national settings are persuaded to shift their loyalties, expectations, and political activities towards a new and larger centre, whose institutions possess or demand jurisdiction over the pre-existing national states.

On the other hand, it responded to the idea of Albert Eistein who wrote in 1921 that: "Nationalism is an infantile disease. It is the measles of the mind" (see Rourke, 2008:158). These measles cost West Africa from the earliest stage of independence a Union of states which ECOWAS cannot even pretend to give because it does not have the capacity.

The geo-politics of the relations between the Anglo-phone West African States which started in the pre-independence period should be reconfigured based on mutual respect and interest to establish a Union of states in the GoG.

Liberia

Liberia is the only country in the GoG that was never colonized. This fact gave it a peculiar clout in (West) African international relations. From 1960, the Africa year of independence, Liberia became a visible actor in African politics. Its role was most noticeable in the diplomacy of African unity in the 1960s especially when the continent needed an inter-state organization to champion and fine-tune its relations.

At the preparatory stage, three ideological blocs emerged in Africa. The first was the Brazzaville group which was championed by Houphouet-Boigny of Cote d'Ivoire. It was made up of newly independent French-speaking African states and the immediate aim was to formulate a common position on African issues before the UN. The second was the Casablanca group which was made up of radical states like Morocco, Ghana, Guinea, Mali, Egypt, Algeria and Libya. The other states that never belonged to either of the group coalesced into the Monrovia group. Such states included Nigeria, Liberia, Sierra Leone, Niger, Togo and Ethiopia. The Monrovia group was formed in Liberia on May 8, 1961. When the Second Conference of the Monrovia bloc was held in Lagos in January 1962, members adopted the following proposal which, with slight amendment, formed the embodiment of the charter that established the OAU in May 1963:

1. Absolute equality of African and Malagasy states whatever may be the size of their territories, the density of their populations, or the value of their possessions;
2. Non-interference in the internal affairs of states;
3. Respect for the sovereignty of each state and its inalienable right to existence and development of its personality;
4. Unqualified condemnation of outside subversive action by neighbouring states;
5. Promotion of co-operation throughout Africa based upon tolerance, solidarity and good neighbour relations, periodical exchange of views, and non-acceptance of any leadership;
6. The unity that is aimed to be achieved at the moment is not the political integration of sovereign African states, but unity of aspirations and of action considered from the point of view of African social solidarity and political identity (African Summit in Monrovia, 1961:18).

After the formation of the OAU and after the thrust of the ECA became increasingly sub-regional in the early 1960s, Liberia played a crucial role in West African politics, especially in the area of regional cooperation and integration. The country hosted many Conferences that were to come up with proposals for the establishment of multi-national cooperation in West Africa. For example, a West African Conference on transport was held in Monrovia from October 23 to 27, to examine the ECA proposals on sub-regional transport network.

The greatest efforts of Liberia towards the creation of a regional group in West Africa were the hosting of the Heads of States Conference in Monrovia from April 23-24, 1968. The Summit Conference was declared open by the Liberian President, Mr. William Tubman, where he stressed the need for economic integration in West Africa. According to him, of all developing countries in the world, African states were the least developed and that was why he urged:

> We must now mobilize our search for effective and practicable cooperation measures which can be taken together not in some distant future, but in the months immediately ahead. I hope that the specific practical cooperative steps we may take will move us towards our ultimate goal of full and

effective cooperation among the Nations of the West African sub-region (Africa Research Bulletin, 1968:995).

After commending the valuable professional role and research programme of the ECA, he launched a fierce attack on "the powerful elements within and without the West African sub-region which have in the past tended to thwart all meaningful efforts at cooperation (Africa Research Bulletin, 1968:995). Unmistakenly, President Tubman was referring, on the one hand to some of the leaders of the French West African states, who were sometimes more patriotic in their devotion to France than even many of the French citizens themselves and on the other hand to France which did not want to see an all-embracing Community in West Africa.

Nevertheless, the group was the precursor to ECOWAS. Even after the Nigeria-Togo initiative had re-kindled the hope of the establishment of a multi-national economic group in West Africa, and the CEAO states had stalled its emergence in 1974, it was Liberia that came to the rescue of the initiative. After the Accra meeting of February 16, 1974, which formalized arrangements for the launching of the group, Niger was to host the next meeting and when it could not, Mali was contacted. Mali at the last minute refused to host the next meeting and thereafter, it appeared as if the meeting would be postponed *sine die,* like its predecessor, the West African Regional Group. Nigeria took the initiative for another venue. Liberia agreed to provide facilities for the meeting. President Tolbert's acceptance, therefore, saved the Nigeria-Togo initiative and cleared the way for the formation of ECOWAS. The Ministerial meeting took place in Monrovia on 27-30 January, 1975, where the final text of the draft treaty was prepared.

In the mid- and early 1970s, Liberia again was on hand to promote economic cooperation in Africa, especially the "Revised Framework of Principles for the Implementation of the New International Economic Order for Africa, 1976-1986," which was also referred to as ECO 90. ECO 90 examined critically the backward nature of most African economies and the fragmented national market for industrial products and suggested that under these circumstances, inter-states cooperation was essential to socio-economic change of the continent.

This new development priority led to the Monrovia Colloquium in July, 1979. The Monrovia Conference was to produce guidelines and measures for national and collective self-reliance in development and for the establishment of a NIEO (New International Economic Order). The Monrovia strategy as it was called ultimately led to the Lagos Summit of 1980 and the adoption of what was now called the Lagos Plan of Action and its companion, the Final Act of Lagos. The two seminal documents, which themselves carried further the analysis and argument of the Revised Framework of 1976, constituted an important guiding light for the economic and social struggle for the continent.

In the 1980s, 1990s and up to 2003 Liberia was to interact with West African states through the instrumentality of the ECOWAS' multi-national force (ECOMOG) which was set up to intervene in the Liberian crisis and restore order. As Carl Von Clausewitz rightly said that war is a continuation of relations by other means; Liberia provided a typical case where states in West Africa deepened their relations with her through war. Liberia is a good player for cooperative endeavours and she is a democratic state. Having experienced a civil war, she realizes the value of democratic peace and multi-national approach to security challenges.

Nigeria

Nigeria may be in aggregate terms the biggest state in the GoG but she is not a bully. The Balewa doctrine which was the foundation of Nigeria's foreign policy made sure that African countries were treated on the basis of equality, regardless of their size, population and natural resources. An embodiment of this doctrine was contained in Balewa's speech during the Summit proceedings that established the OAU. According to him:

> Nigeria's stand is that if we want unity in Africa, we must first agree to certain essential things; the first is that African states must respect one another. There must be acceptance of equality by all the states. No matter whether they are big or small, they are all sovereigns and sovereignty is sovereignty. The size of state, its population or its wealth should not be the criteria. It has been pointed out many times that the smaller states in Africa have no right to exist because they are too small. We in Nigeria do not

agree. It was unfortunate that African states have been broken up into different groups by the Colonial powers. In some cases, a single tribe has been broken up into four different states. You might find a section in Guinea, a section in Mali, a section in Sierra Leone and perhaps a section in Liberia. That was not our fault because, for over sixty years, these different units have been existing and any attempt on the part of any country to disregard this fact might bring trouble to this continent. This is the thing we want to avoid (Stremlau, 1977:17)

On account of the Balewa doctrine, Nigeria has been cautious in its geo-politics in Africa especially when dealing with its contiguous Lilliputian neighbours. Indeed, it is the Balewa doctrine that saved Mauritania and Togo from the jaws of Morocco and Ghana respectively, which wanted to reclaim these countries as theirs. Even the military that ruled Nigeria for about three decades toed the line of the Balewa doctrine. In its geo-politics, Nigeria is a team player and strategic partner.

However, in choosing to sponsor the establishment of ECOWAS, it made strategic mistakes which are haunting the organization till today. The initial attempt was to establish the community with few states which were to become its nucleus, until new members agreed to join but at the end of the day, fifteen states started ECOWAS and turned it into "a grand debating forum for mere expression of views" (ECA, 1982:23).

While on a state visit to Togo on May 1, 1972, General Gowon, the then Nigerian Head of State, signed a joint communiqué in which the two countries agreed to establish an economic grouping which would form the nucleus of a West African economic community. Speaking at a state dinner held in his honour in Lome on April 30, 1972, Gowon said that he did not think it was necessary for all the countries in the sub-region to come together at the same time. According to him:

Let those who are ready and willing come together to form the nucleus of a community which can be expanded as new members come in (New Nigerian, May 2, 1972:2)

Even the ECA thought the same way. For this, it's Secretary General, Professor Adebayo Adedeji said:

> An economic community must be allowed to grow over a number of years. It must start modestly and achieve some successes...of all the sub-regions in Africa, it is in West Africa ... that economic cooperation has been most elusive...the reasons for the failure of the past attempts have been due to the fact that we have hitherto tried to build a closely-knit economic community when we have not yet acquired the experience of working closely together. We have adopted holistic approach which has required that all the fifteen countries be members at one go and for all levels or types of economic cooperation to be embarked upon at the same time. Indeed, we are trying to run before we have learnt the intricacies of walking (Adedeji, 1975:5).

As it turned out to be, when other member-states in West Africa were persuaded to join the group, they repudiated the Nigeria-Togo proposals. Mauritania, for instance, which eventually withdrew its membership from ECOWAS, did not want the proposed community to threaten the existence of the CEAO. In Dakar, President Senghor's reaction was that Senegal would prefer a West African Economic Community stretching from Nouakchott (Mauritania) to Kinshasa (Zaire) rather than the 15 - Nation grouping "now being planned" (Africa Research Bulletin, 1974:2965).

The real ECOWAS was killed by the CEAO states to satisfy the national interest of France in Africa; what subsists now is its shadow. Needless to add here, that a shadow cannot be as effective as the real thing. Therefore, Nigeria together with Togo and other democratic states should re-engineer a new multilingual and inter-state Union based on historical experience and conventional realities.

Sierra Leone

The historical assets of Sierra Leone are so robust that for many years they fertilized the country's geo-politics. The modern state of Sierra Leone was founded as a settlement for freed slaves most of whom came from the United Kingdom and the New World. They started to arrive in the country from 1787. After the abolition of slave trade in Britain in 1807, the British government took control of the settlement and made it a naval base as well as a centre for slaves captured in the Atlantic. By mid-1860s, more than 50,000 of such recaptured slaves were settled in Sierra Leone and as recorded in chapter twenty two, they came from the slave coast; that is, the region of today's Nigeria, Benin and Togo. The descendants of these recaptured slaves make a sizeable group in the demography of Sierra Leone.

It is instructive to note that Sierra Leone was made the headquarters of British administration in West Africa. To this extent, the Gambia, Ghana and Nigeria were first administered for years from Sierra Leone before they had separate administrative structures. In the course of operating from Sierra Leone, the British made it the magnet of West Africa. Nationals of other territories in West Africa were attracted to the country on account of its cosmopolitan nature and educational institution. People and communities of note sent their children for training in Fourah Bay College, a centre of educational excellence in British West Africa.

Fourah Bay College was founded in 1814 to train teachers and catechists. In 1827, it developed into a college. In 1876, it became the first University College in West Africa and was affiliated to Durham University in the United Kingdom. It retained this relationship until 1961 when it became the University of Sierra Leone.

The products of Fourah Bay had phenomenal impact on West African history. John Ezzido, a recaptured slave of Northern Nigerian origin was a known merchant across West Africa; James Africanus Horton, a descendant of Igbo recaptives had a successful medical practice in Ghana, played a significant role in the early African-nationalist movements and wrote a classical book entitled ***West African Countries and Its Peoples***; Samuel Johnson of Yoruba recaptives wrote the much revered ***History of the Yoruba***; and Joseph E. Casely Hayford was the founder and moving spirit of the NCBWA. Among the scholars of the College who laid the foundation of linguistic studies of some of the West African languages were J. C. Taylor on Igbo, P. T. Williams on the Egbirra, C. Paul on the Nupe and Bishop Ajayi Crowther on the Yoruba (Buah, 1977). Ajayi's *magnum opus* is Grammar and Vocabulary of the Yoruba language. This work was quite influential in the study of the Yoruba language. Ajayi also translated the Holy Bible into Yoruba.

Unlike its immediate neighbour, Liberia, Sierra Leone never played much active role in African international relations as a result of years of political instability, but like the case of Liberia, West African states interacted with it during its civil war. Its post-civil war policy has a high dosage of peace and democracy.

Togo

Togo has a long history of cooperation with Benin and Nigeria because of her location. In 1934, the French established an economic union between Togo and Benin, but after two years it was replaced by integration with French West Africa. The integration lasted for ten years only. Since independence, Togo has been interacting with Benin on bilateral and multilateral levels.

As a country that was first colonized by Germany and which was later a mandated territory of the League of Nations as well as under the UN Trusteeship, it is not as Francophonied as territories that were originally colonized by France. For this reason, Togo was not a member of the Brazzaville group in African politics, but rather elected to belong to the Monrovia group which had Nigeria and Liberia as members. As Balewa was the leader of the Monrovia group, he reached out to all African states to intimate them on the position of Nigeria and the Monrovia bloc on the politics of African unity. Nigeria's closest ally in this direction was Togo which Balewa also used to reach out to many African states as well. On January 6, 1963, he sent a message to Sylvanus Olympio of Togo through Jaja Nwachukwu, Nigeria's External Affairs Minister, but on January 13, seven days after, Olympio was assassinated in a coup d'état.

The killing of Olympio more than any thing else destroyed the iron curtain that acted as a barrier to African unity. This is because the killing elicited sympathetic reactions from African Heads of States and statesmen. In unison, they condemned the mode of political change in Togo which was violent and indeed strange in post-colonial Africa. Meanwhile, Nigeria initiated a Conference of Heads of States in Lagos to look at the circumstances surrounding the assassination.

The Conference opened on 24 January, 1963 and among the countries present were: Cameroon, Congo (Kinshasa), Chad, the Central African Republic, Ethiopia, Gabon, Ivory Coast, Benin, Liberia, Mauritania, Madagascar, Niger, Nigeria, Senegal, Sierra

Leone and Upper Volta. Togo was represented by two rival groups, one sent by the new regime and the other, a remnant of the old regime.

At the end of the day, Nigeria intervened diplo-matically in the politics of Togo and successfully brought stability to the country. It was on account of the long history of cooperation with Nigeria dating back to the time of Balewa (see Onwuka, 1982) that Nigeria and Togo agreed on May 1, 1972 to establish an economic grouping which "would hopefully form the nucleus of a West African economic community" (Akpan, 1986:98). This agreement led to the famous Nigeria-Togo Initiative which ultimately gave birth to ECOWAS on May 28, 1975.

Togo, therefore, is an active player in the West African politics that Nigeria could ally with to establish a new Union in the GoG in line with the vision of the Nigeria-Togo initiative. The Nigeria-Togo Initiative which was compromised by the CEAO states was revolutionary enough to solve the economic and security problems of West Africa. Built into it were proposals like the creation of payment union, together with the adoption of a common account currency, a committee of permanent representatives and a system of political consultation aimed at promoting friendship (Akpan, 1986).

Strategic Challenges and Prospects

A number of challenges will confront attempts to establish GGU or UAS. In the first place, the six states whose particulars are examined above are ECOWAS states. The implication is that ECOWAS would go the way of the dinosaur. Of the 19 states of the GoG, 12 are members of ECOWAS and about half of them are democratic; the rest are autocratic. Yet democracy should be the first foundation of a new Union in Africa. To this extent, it behoves on the states that would form the nucleus of the Union to set a time-table for themselves to dissolve ECOWAS.

At the time ECOWAS was formed in 1975, it had the following lofty ideas:

* The elimination as between member states of customs duties and other charges of equivalent effect in respect of the importation of goods
* The abolition of quantitative and administrative restrictions on trade among the member states
* The establishment of a common customs tariff and a common commercial policy towards third countries
* The abolition as between the member states of the obstacles to the free movement of persons, services and capitals
* The harmonization of the agricultural policies and the promotion of common projects in the member states, notably in the fields of marketing, research and agro-industrial enterprises
* The implementation of schemes for the joint development of transport, communication, energy and other infrastructural facilities, as well as the evolution of a customs policy in these fields
* The harmonization of the economic and industrial policies of the member states and the elimination of disparities in the level of development of member states and
* The establishment of a fund for cooperation, compensation and development.

A transitional period of fifteen years was made in the treaty for the realization of these aims. The implication is that the aims of ECOWAS ought to have been realized in 1990. But despite a number of protocols to its Treaty and in spite of innovative mechanisms like the ECOWAS Parliament, Court of Justice, ECOWAS Commission and ECOMOG, ECOWAS is a gargantuan failure, three decades after its establishment.

It suffers mainly from the trinity of multiplicity of IGOs, multiplicity of non-convertible currencies and lack of intra-African trade. If the first two problems are not overcome, the third cannot be confronted and if the three cannot be dealt with successfully, then the ECOWAS project cannot succeed even in the next century. Already, the multiplicity of IGOs has reduced the effectiveness of ECOWAS as members are more loyal to them than the multilingual body. With regards to multiplicity of currency, it should be noted that it acts as a major barrier to trade and economic cooperation in West Africa. A major weakness in the existence of these currencies is that most of them are not convertible and are not actively traded in organized foreign exchange markets. Apart from the CFA *(Communuate Financiere Africaine)* francs used by seven Francophone West African countries -Benin, Burkina Faso, Ivory Coast, Niger, Senegal, Togo and Mali-there is the Liberian Dollar, the Nigerian Naira, the Ghanaian Cedi, the Sierra Leonian Leone, the Gambian Dalasi, the Pesetos of Guinea-Bissau, the Escudos of Cape Verde and the Guinean Syli.

The effect of these inconvertible currencies in the sub-region is considerable. In the first place, the governments of the Anglophone states (mainly) whose currencies are inconvertible cannot defend the official rates of their national currencies because they are openly exchanged on the markets-mostly black markets-of Togo, Benin, Niger and Ivory Coast which largely benefit from the situation. Herein also lies a major incentive for smuggling and unrecorded trade links between West African states.

Moreover, this unhealthy situation usually produces another effect, which is closure of borders. Border closure itself is counter productive to economic cooperation because freedom of movement of persons, goods and capitals would be affected and once this situation exists, then the basis of economic cooperation is violated. Indeed, pre-colonial West Africa was by far better than ECOWAS' West Africa for the simple reason that it experienced free movement of persons, goods and services, a high volume of intra-African trade, resourceful diplomacy and international law and at a stage common currency. Today, the ECOWAS-inspired West Africa is a ghost of the old vibrant West Africa.

The only strategic path to get over the myriads of problems plaguing West Africa and indeed the GoG states is to start a fresh regional integration agenda. Luckily, the GoG as a region does not have any region-wide international organization unlike the Persian Gulf in the Middle East which has the Gulf Cooperation Council (GCC). Therefore, the vacuum should be filled and the initiators which should be few in number should set for themselves modern civilized standards, consolidate the gains that would attend these for at least a decade before accepting others to join on the basis of application and referendum.

Externally, big powers in the international system would not be disinterested in any attempt to establish a region-wide Union in the GoG. This is because the GoG is of critical importance to the strategic calculations of the Western World and China. Outside France, the other permanent members of the UN Security Council (UNSC) would not be averse to the idea so long as it would guarantee security and stability of the region. The permanent members of the UNSC are Britain, China, France, Russia and the United States of America.

Strategically speaking, the end of the Cold War in 1991 also signalled the end of Russia's influence in Africa. The Soviet Union was no longer there to act as patron to socialist states and those that claimed to practise socialism. So long as this state of affairs prevailed in Africa, the US whose mission was to contain communism relaxed the policy and the immediate result was that Africa was downgraded strategically (Thompson, 2004). However, the US wishes to see Africa that is democratic, politically stable, with strong legal-rational institutions, secure and at the same time promoting fundamental human rights. And because a Union of states properly packaged will achieve all of these, it would have the support of the US. The US policy in Africa as articulated by Susan Rice, a top American Diplomat in 1998 still holds water. According to her (1998:4):

> The United States must continue to work in concert with Africans to help secure the continent's future if we are to be smart about securing our own. If Africa succeeds, we all-Africans and Americans-stand to benefit. If Africa fails, we will all pay the price ... if we hold back until the whole of Africa is on even footing, we will concede important opportunities to our competitors and worse still, leave doors open to our adversaries ... we must invest the United States commitment, talent, resources, and energy in Africa in order to promote lasting peace, security, and prosperity here at home.

Peace and security in the GoG and, by extension, Africa would be of symbiotic value to the US interests in the region. The alternative source of energy to the US is located in the GoG. It is predicted that by 2020 A.D., the region's oil production would surpass the value of the Persian Gulf nations-by producing 25 percent of global requirement as against 22 percent from the nine states of the Persian Gulf. The Persian Gulf states are: Bahrain, Kuwait, Iran, Iraq, Oman, Qatar, Saudi Arabia, United Arab Emirates and Yemen.

For Britain, most of the post-independence and, indeed, the immediate post Cold War era in Africa were regarded as a "source of trouble rather than opportunity" (Clapham, 1996:88; Thompson, 2004:162). Regardless of this stance, the UK has since the twenty first century renewed its interest in Africa. It has been calling for good governance and change in the continent. The governments of John Mayor and Tony Blair initiated and consolidated the moves to bring debt relief to Africa. It is to the credit of the UK that it placed before the G8 of industrialized nations the agenda for the debt relief in the 1990s.

Given the degree of poverty and instability in Africa, Tony Blair was moved to call Africa "a scar on the conscience of the world" (see Thompson, 2004:163). Blair added that Africa needed a Marshall Plan to come out of the valley of poverty. For Jack Straw, the then Foreign Secretary for Africa: "It matters if you want to produce a stable world. You can't have four continents going forward and one going backwards" (Thompson, 2004:163). Therefore, for Britain a Union of states in Africa would symbolize a Marshall Plan which would push Africa forward and which would need its diplomatic and financial support.

Theoretically, China's foreign policy is rooted in the Five Principles of Peaceful Co-existence, formulated in 1954, thereby setting out the guidelines for its geo-politics. The Principles are:

a) Mutual respect for each other's territorial integrity
b) Non-aggression
c) Non-interference in each other's internal affairs
d) Equality and mutual benefits and
e) Peaceful co-existence.

Regardless of the Westphalian peace message of the Chinese Foreign Policy, in practice Africa is a neo-colonial field to explore to its own advantage; indeed the name of its game in the continent is communist capitalism. On account of its miraculous expansion, China is on the threshold of a superpower status. This status comes with heavy cost on its environment at home and has turned it from being a net exporter of petroleum oil to a net importer.

Like the Western World, its newfound status is oiled by oil and without oil; China would go back to the rank it just left. As US corporate interests dominate the Middle East and for fear of denial control, China has turned its attention to the GoG for oil and market. It is oiling deals in the region with soft loans and in doing this it undercuts the IFIs and bolsters tottering dictatorships. In the GoG, China has announced its presence in Angola, the DR Congo, Gabon, Equatorial Guinea, the Republic of the Congo and Nigeria. The sources of attraction are natural resources and market.

China needs the GoG for its destiny and in spite of the fact that it does not care about domestic politics in the countries that it operates in, it needs peace, stability and security to sustain its strategic interest. Taken together, China would support a Union of states in Africa.

The case of France in Africa is quite peculiar. It had the largest number of colonies in the continent and they were administered as overseas territories of France. Therefore, from the outset the colonial arrangement tied the colonies to Paris. At independence, Charles de Gaulle, the President of France envisaged the construction of the **Communuate Franco-africaine**, a confederal system with France at the centre and the colonies as peripheries; but the forces of African nationalism shocked him and woke him from the dream of French empire in Africa. However, the shock did not prevent Paris from instituting *la francophone*, the French-speaking Commonwealth where even its non-ex-colonies like the DR Congo, Equatorial Guinea, Guinea-Bissau, Rwanda and Burundi were recruited into.

France's masterstroke in Africa is attributed to three factors by Christopher Clapham. These are people, money and force (Clapham, 1996:88). Bassey Ate adds the facts of "the numerous bilateral economic, financial, cultural and military arrangements under Cooperation Agreements" (Ate, 1992:13). Ate's points could well be accommodated within the Clapham thesis. In terms of people, Paris showered diplomatic and financial resources on its ex-colonies than all the big powers in the international system. The project was coordinated by a dedicated department within the Elysee Palace.

Today, there is an African cell in the palace that takes important decisions regarding Africa. The cell is composed of a highly decentralized decision-making unit outside parliamentary influence, built around the French President, informed, controlled and made up of numerous "fous d'Afrique", members of the military and secret services, African sympathisers, and various actors of the infamous networks of the Franafrique (Hugeux, 2007). In addition, regular Franco-African Summits were held and there were also numerous occasions of exchange of state visits.

Financially, France supports its Commonwealth tremendously. For a start, its treasury guarantees the ***Communuate Financiere Africaine (CFA)*** franc. This makes the states that use the CFA to have a fully convertible currency tied to the French currency. Of course, this comes with a price as their sovereignty is compromised by France and, indeed, reduced by more than half their value.

In terms of force, France has Military and Defence Pacts with many francophone states. The country has on African soil troops in excess of 10,000 and more than 500 military advisers attached to their government houses. But it should be quickly noted that France bestrides the post-independence Africa like a colossus because there is no alternative power with strategic resources in Africa to fill the vacuum. The forces of African nationalism are more powerful than the three sources of French influence in Africa.

In most cases, extra-African powers have always been deluding themselves into thinking that they can always think for Africa, but they forget that there are occasions when African nationalism would dictate the pace for any project to succeed in the continent. For example, in trying to act as the Godfather for both Somalia and Ethiopia in the 1970s, Moscow inspired Fidel Castro to suggest that the two hostile "Marxist" states in the Horn of Africa join, together with Djibouti and South Yemen, in a confederation of "progressive states". But as James Dougherty notes, this ***Pax Sovieta*** showed that the Kremlin had "grossly over-estimated the centripetal power of Marxist internationalism against the centrifugal force of nationalism" (Dougherty, 1979:29).

It is the same African nationalism that threw the American AFRICOM (the United States African Command of the US DoD) project out of gear. Therefore, should a power emerge from among the African states with sufficient capacity and willingness to deploy its capability, France would abandon its idea of ***chasse gardee.*** The age of African leaders like Felix Houphouet-Boigny of Cote d' Ivoire and Leopold Senghor of Senegal who were the purveyors of French cultural influence on the continent is gone and buried in their graves. Some of these leaders served as deputies in the French National Assembly while some were ministers in the national government in France before ruling their countries at independence. It is not surprising that they acted as facilitators of French influence in Francophone states in Africa.

The modern-day African leaders are Africanist in their thinking but the missing gap in their aspirations in this direction is lack of state capacity. On the question of force, it should be noted that military means have so far not solved any problems in Africa. Rather they compound the already complex problems. For example, since 1961, force has not been able to solve the myriad of challenges in the DR Congo which is the biggest and richest country in sub-Saharan Africa. On a more fundamental note, democratic Africa does not need force or military intervention anymore. Conversely, it needs positive means of strengthening democratic traditions and state capacity.

Taken together, it should be in the overall interest of France to enter into strategic partnership with the leading democratic states in Africa in order to set a new agenda for the continent. The new agenda calls for a Union of states for which France is undoubtedly a strategic master. History bears her out in this direction. French Equatorial Africa which comprised five states and the French West Africa which was composed of seven states are excellent legacies of France in Africa.

Outside Africa, France is remotely the architect of the EU which has today given her absolute security in Europe. Her citizens led by Jean Monet who was fondly called Mr. Europe championed an integrated Europe so as to take care of the security challenges of France. And what were these challenges? The unification of Germany and its emergence in 1870 as a continental power in Europe overstretched the Balance of Power in that continent and cast a dark shadow of insecurity on France. This shadow which came with her defeat in the Franco-Prussian war manifested in series of more defeats and security challenges in the inter-war years. After its defeat in the First World War, the imperatives of multilateral approach to its security were explored. Outside the League of Nations mechanisms, the imperatives led to the Dawes Plan of 1924, the Geneva Protocol of 1924, Locarno Treaty of 1925 and the Kellogg-Briand Pact of 1928, among other measures. E. H. Carr (1963:27) calls these imperatives "the system of guarantees" and "the system of alliances" (1963:30).

Even when the systems did not prevent the outbreak of the Second World War in which France was the first victim, they provided platforms for multilateral approach to tackle security challenges that beset nations of Europe. In the aftermath of the Second World War, French Foreign Minister Robert Schuman acted on Mr. Europe's proposal and issued a plan for a supranational authority for the Coal and Steel industries (Hauss, 2000). That plan was the foundation of the EU. Two of Mr. Europe's declarations are worth noting (Rourke, 2008:196):

a) There will be no peace in Europe if the states rebuild themselves (after World War II) on the basis of national sovereignty, with its implications of prestige politics and economic protection

b) The countries of Europe are not strong enough individually to be able to guarantee prosperity and social development for their peoples. The states of Europe must ... form a federation or a European entity that would make them into a common economic unit.

To these declarations could be added the sentiment of former French President Jacques Chirac who urged French voters in 2005 to ratify the EU Constitution as a way of avoiding an:

Anglo-Saxon, Atlanticist Europe ... dominated by America ... We (cannot) defend our interests alone. We can only defend them collectively, and if Europe is united ... Otherwise, we'll be swept away (see Rourke, 2008:230)

Africa of today needs these declarations even more than Europe of yesterday. Therefore, in Africa, France has a moral obligation to support a Union of states so as to guarantee security and development in the continent. It is the Union of states in Europe, the EU, that has given France active security insurance in Europe. Overall, the Western World has a moral duty to re-construct Africa and the most effective means would be through a Union of few democratic states; an orbit of modern civilization.

In the aftermath, all foreign aid and financial assistance to Africa should be directed to the orbit to encourage others to reform and join. So long as foreign assistance in whatever form is directed to individual states in Africa, there would be no progress and development in the continent. It is instructive to note that:

> ... The United States decided that it would not allot Marshall Plan aid through a series of bilateral agreements with the European governments. Instead, it preferred working through the Organization for European Economic Cooperation (OEEC), predecessor of today's (OECD) Organization for Economic Cooperation and Development (Hauss, 2000:171).

It is equally worth noting that since 1960, Africa's year of independence, Africa has received more than $600 billion in foreign aid (Posner, 2007) but it is still taking a southward dive towards the precipice. Therefore, Africa expects from the international community a unionized approach to development.

Nigeria and the Geo-Politics of the Gulf of Guinea

Nigeria has historical resources and cultural assets to initiate a process to institute the much-needed orbit of modern civilization in the GoG or sub-Saharan Africa, or Africa as a whole. These resources and assets constitute the country's power, but the critical type that is called *soft power*. The concept of soft power was given currency by Harvard political scientist, Joseph S. Nye. Soft power concerns the notion that non-traditional forces such as culture and commercial goods can exert influence in world affairs (Nye, 2000:55). Soft power is also called persuasive power (Rourke, & Boyer, 2002:188).

This type of power owes its existence to the dynamic nature of power itself which is changing at a fast rate. Scholars contend that military and other assets that contribute to *coercive power* (also called hard power) are declining in importance as military force and economic sanctions become more costly and less effective (Rourke & Boyer, 2002:188). Simultaneously, scholars maintain that soft power which gives moral authority and excellence and at the same time enhances a country's image of leadership is increasing in importance.

For Nigeria, the ethno-cultural links it has in Africa promise to be the most important asset if explored and exploited by the Nigerian leadership and people. Geo-strategically, Nigeria is situated on the West Coast of Africa by the GoG; that is, almost in the centre of the Western curve made by the continent of Africa. This feature makes the country nearly equidistant from the extreme corners of the continent. To this extent, it takes a relatively very short time to travel by air to or from any place in Africa. Indeed, the location of Nigeria makes the distinction between West and Central Africa very fluid (Akpan, 2000:87). With about 500 different nations which have affiliations with the major ethnic groups across Africa, Nigeria is not only a melting pot demographically; it is also a sub-continent.

Indeed, in Nigeria, there is a whole continent in one country (Akpan, 2000:87). The Arabs from the Northern part of Africa and the Bantu from the Southern part are all represented in Nigeria. They are found in large numbers in the Northern and South Eastern parts of Nigeria respectively. Culturally, Nigeria possesses uniquely what Ali Mazrui calls the three parts of the soul of Africa. According to him (1983:139):

> ... We have an African country which best encompasses within itself the three parts of the soul of Africa – the indigenous, the Euro-Christian and the Islamic. All three forces are strong in Nigeria.

For instance, the Sokoto Caliphate in North West Nigeria is the headquarters of Islamic activities in sub-Saharan Africa and almost all pre-colonial jihads in the region had the imprimatur of Sokoto. Additionally, the single-most followers of the Christian-faith and adherents of the African Traditional Religion in Africa are found in Nigeria.

It is worth noting that there used to be West African Governors' Conference for Governors of British West African colonies. The first

Conference took place in Lagos from 10 to 18 August 1939. At the Conference, it was decided that the Governor of Nigeria should be the permanent chairman of the Governors' Conferences, and that Nigeria should host its secretariat permanently. The main aims of the Conference included coordination of matters of common interest and concern in areas such as immigration, subversive propaganda, research pro-grammes, higher research programmes, higher education, culture and agriculture.

A combination of these sources of soft power should strengthen Nigeria to be a leading state in Africa to confront the challenges of Africa in league with willing democratic states in the region, beginning from the GoG. She should start with a strategic permutation of two, four or six with the six democratic states already discussed. If she starts with two states, the states should be either Togo or Ghana; if she starts with four states, the states should be the states of the proposed Benin Union-Nigeria, Togo, Benin and Ghana; otherwise the states to form the nucleus of a new Union of states in Africa should be the six states of Nigeria, Togo, Benin, Ghana, Liberia and Sierra Leone.

To bring seriousness to the project, a Department for its realization and sustenance should be created in Aso Rock (Presidential Villa) and directed by committed experts of the states to form the nucleus of the Union. Outside the original founders, membership of the Union should be based on application and results of referendum. The necessity of a referendum for new applicants warrants extended analysis.

Fundamentally, there is some truth in the assertion that while political will is essential for any regional economic endeavour to start at all, its survival will require a more broad-based support (Renninger, 1979). For this to happen, there is, therefore, the need to create and sustain in the general population of the country an awareness of the necessity for economic cooperation, and, additionally, nationals should be encouraged to participate in inter-state programmes.

Awareness of efforts at economic cooperation is very poor among the generality of population in the various countries in Africa. This public apathy only serves to reinforce government reluctance. For instance, while conducting a research on what ECOWAS meant to the people in 1985, *West Africa* came to the conclusion that:

> To ask a man in the street here what he thinks about ECOWAS is to be met with a blank stare and even government officials will tell you that ECOWAS is a matter for the experts and has no bearing on everyday life (Adesola, 1985:1063).

Similarly, the ECA mission to West Africa within the same period met with the same amusing interpretation of ECOWAS. According to the team, some people thought that ECOWAS was one of the following: a football team, a department of government (in the particular country), an organ of the OAU based in Accra, Ghana, and a movement to fight *apartheid* in South Africa. The pointer here is to the fact that efforts at economic cooperation in West Africa are largely an affair of government and not quite of the people; yet at the end of the day, the fruits of economic cooperation would permeate down to the people.

Up till today, the citizens of Africa do not have knowledge of cooperative endeavours in the continent. In Nigeria, most people think NEPAD means NEPA, the moribund electricity authority – the Nigerian Electricity Power Authority (NEPA) and across West Africa, people take ECOWAS to be a team in the Spanish *La Liga*. Without sufficient knowledge about regional bodies and multilateral institutions, nobody can be mobilized to help them develop. Herein lies the basis for referendum where the citizens of countries that want to join the Union should be sensitized about their future needs, roles and expectations with regards to membership.

At this juncture, it is necessary to point out that ECOWAS to which the six countries belong should undergo the needed surgery by way of transformation and change. Change is the only permanent issue in history and, therefore, ECOWAS should be made to experience the change that the European Economic Community (EEC) experienced in the course of its transformation to the EU.

Writing on the stages of these transformation and new names that Shakespear in *Romeo and Juliet* asked "what's in a name?", John T. Rourke (2004:223) notes:

> The EU's genesis began in 1952 when Belgium, France, (West) Germany, Italy, Luxembourg, and the Netherlands created a common market for coal,

iron, and steel products, called the European Coal and Steel Community (ECSC). Its success prompted the six countries to sign the Treaty of Rome on March 25, 1957, which established the European Economic Community (EEC) to facilitate trade in many additional areas and the European Atomic Energy Community (EURATOM) to coordinate matters in that realm. Continued economic success led the six countries to found an overarching organization, the European Communities (EC), in 1967. Each of the three pre-existing organizations became subordinate parts of the EC. Then in 1993 a new name, the European Union, was adopted to denote both the existing advanced degree of integration and the EU's goal of becoming a single economic entity. Even more significant was the adoption of a single currency, the euro, by most of the EU's members in 2002. As the financial transactions among the EU's countries rapidly grew, it became clear that continually converting currencies from one to another made little sense. Therefore in the early 1990s, the EU agreed to move toward a common currency. Once the new currency was ready for launch, only those countries that met certain criteria for sound governmental financial management (such as limited inflation and budget deficits) could adopt the euro. With a few exceptions, all countries are required to move toward that point and to adopt the euro. In 2002 it went into general circulation in countries using it, while their traditional currencies ceased to be legal tender. As of the EU's 50th birthday in 2007, 13 of the EU countries were using the euro, and a number of small, non-EU countries such as Monaco, had also adopted it. Of the older EU members, Great Britain, Denmark, and Sweden still do not use the euro for various reasons. Of the countries that have joined the EU since 2004, Slovenia already uses the euro, and the rest of the newer members are slated to transition to the euro once they achieve the required benchmarks of financial stability. Creating the euro was important both economically and politically. Economically, it has tied the EU members even closer together by eliminating one of the hallmarks of an independent economy, a national currency. Adding to the economic importance of adopting a common currency that may well one day overspread an entire continent, there is great political symbolism in the replacement of Germany's Deutcsche Mark, France's franc, Italy's lira, and other countries' national currencies with a common currency. Adding to the EU momentum provided by its new currency, 10 new members joined it in 2004 and 2 more in 2007, bringing the total of 27.

Africa as the least developed continent has to take a cue from other continents of the world, especially Europe that colonized it, if it cares to develop. When Japan was in isolation and believed that it had attained the highest civilization and was, indeed, the centre of the earth, it took America's adventurism and imperialism to shake her off the delusion. Surprised that there was another centre of higher civilization, Japan immediately imitated America in the fields of science, education and democracy. And today, possessing practically no mineral resources and even enough land for its citizens, Japan is able to use the trinity of science, education and democracy-the very trinity that conferred on America higher status-to conquer her vicissitudes of life. Africa must look up to European history to transform itself and Nigeria should take the lead. So far, as presently constituted, ECOWAS, NEPAD and the AU do not have the capacities to civilize Africa and take it out of the woods.

Further Reading

Adedeji, Adebayo. 1974. *The Evolution of a West African Community*. Ibadan: Ibadan University Press.

Adedeji, A. 1975. *The West African Economic Community: Ideals and Reality*. Lagos: April.

Ademoyega, A. 1981. *Why We Struck*. Ibadan: Evans Brothers Ltd.

Akinyemi, A.B. 1986. *Foreign Policy and Federalism: The Nigerian Experience*. Ibadan: Ibadan University Press.

Akinyemi, A. B, Agbi, S. O. and Oyunbanjo. 1989 eds. *International Relations; Nigeria since Independence, The First 25 Years*. Ibadan: Ibadan University Press.

Akinyemi, A. B. 1984. *Readings and Documents in ECOWAS*. Lagos: Nigeria Institute of International Affairs.

Akpan, O. E. 2000. *Regional Leadership: Nigeria and the Challenge of Post Apartheid South Africa*. Uyo: SureGod Publishers.

Aluko, O. 1977. *The Foreign Policy of African States*. London: Hodder and Stoughton.

Aluko, O. 1981. *Essays in Nigerian Foreign Policy*. London: Longmans Ltd.

Bach, Daniel. 1983. "The politics of West African Economic Cooperation: CEAO and ECOWAS" The *Journal of Modern African Studies*, Vol.21, No.4.

Charlton, Michael. 1990. *The Last Colony in Africa: Diplomacy and the Independence of Rhodesia*. Cambridge: Basil Blackwell.

Davidson, B. 1964. *Old Africa Rediscovered.* London: Oxford University Press.

Duffy, J. 1959. *Portuguese Africa.* Harvard University Press.

Elias, T. O. 1965. "The Charter of the Organization of African Unity (OAU), *American Journal of International Law* 59 (2), April.

Fage, J. D. 1963. *An Atlas of African History*. Arnold.

Gambari, Sule. 1980. *Party Politics and Foreign Policy: Nigeria Under The First Republic*. Zaria: Baraka Press.

Garba, Joseph. 1991. *Diplomatic Soldiering*. Ibadan: Spectrum Publishers.

Gibson, Richard. 1992. *African Liberation Movements*. London: Oxford University Press.

Greenberg, J. H. 1963. *Languages of Africa*. London: Indiana University Press.

Idang, Gordon. 1973. *Nigeria: Internal Politics and Foreign Policy, 1960-1966.* Ibadan: Ibadan University Press.

Jalaoso, Olujimi. 1991. *In the Shadows: Recollections of a Pioneer Diplomat.* Lagos: Malthouse Press.

Mazrui, A. A. *Africa's International Relations. The Diplomacy of Dependency and Change*. London: Heinemann.

Murdoc G. P. 1959. *Africa: Its Peoples and their Culture History.* New York, McGraw-Hill.

Ofoegbu, Ray. 1978. *The Nigerian Foreign Policy*. Enugu: Star Printing and Publishing Co.

Ogunsanwo, Alaba. 1986. *Our Friends, Their Friends: Nigeria External Relations, 1960-1985*. Lagos: Alfa Communications Ltd.

Ogwu, Joy. 1986. *Nigerian Foreign Policy: Alternative Futures*. Lagos: Nigerian Institute of International Affairs.

Olufemi, Abiodun. 1981. *Nigeria's Recognition of Angola*. Lagos: Nigerian Institute of International Affairs.

Olusanya, G. O. and Akindele R. A. 1986. eds. *Nigeria's External Relations: The First 25 Years*. Lagos: Nigerian Institute of International Affairs.

Olusanya, G. O. and Akindele R. A. 1990. eds. *The Structure and Processes of Foreign Policy Making and Implementation in Nigeria 1960-1990*. Ibadan: Vantage Publishers International Ltd.

Onwuka, Ralph. 1986. ***Development and Integration in West Africa: ECOWAS***. Ife: Ife University Press.

Phillips, Claude. 1964. ***The Development of Nigerian Foreign Policy***. London: Longmans Group.

Soremekun, Fola. 1983. ***Angola: The Road to Independence***. Ile-Ife: University of Ife Press Ltd.

St Jorre, John. 1972. ***The Nigerian Civil War***.London: Longmans Ltd.

Stremlau, John. 1977. ***The International Politics of the Nigerian Civil War, 1967-1970***. New Jersey: Princeton University Press.

Wayas, Joseph. 1979. ***Nigeria's Leadership Role in Africa***. London: The Macmillan Press Ltd.

Wolfers, Michael. 1976. ***Politics in the Organization of African Charter***. London: Oxford University Press.

References

Ake, C. 2002. *A Political Economy of Africa*. London: Longman Group Ltd.

Akpan, O. E. 1986. ***The Economic Commission for Africa (ECA) and Economic Cooperation in West Africa***. M.A. Dissertation, University of Ibadan.

Akpan, O. E. 1989. ***Militarization and Regional Security: A Case of the Horn of Africa***. MSc. Dissertation, University of Jos.

Akpan, O. E. 2000. ***Regional Leadership: Nigeria and the Challenge of Post-Apartheid South Africa***. *Uyo*: Sure God Publishers.

Akpan, O. E. 2003. ***Nigeria's Diplomatic Initiatives in Africa, 1960-1979***. Ph.D Dissertation, University of Port Harcourt.

Akpan, O. E. 2004. ***First Among Equals: A Chronicle of Pioneering Efforts of Akwa Ibom in National Development***. Calabar: Saesprint Publishers.

Akpan, O. E. 2004. The Evolution of the Nigerian State: Pre-Colonial to Independence Period. In: Akpan, A. U. and A. J. Oluwabamide. Eds. ***Nigerians and their Cultural Heritage***. Lagos: Lisjohnson Resources Publishers.

Akpan, O. E. 2005. *French Colonial Policy in Africa*. In Okereke, O. O. ed. ***Issues in African Politics***. Abakaliki: Williy Rose and Appleseed Publishing Company: 79-86.

Alagoa, E. J. 1999. The Eastern Niger Delta and the Hinterland in the 19th Century. In Ikime, O. ed. *Groundwork of Nigerian History*: 249-261.

Albright, D. E. 1980. *Africa and International Communism.* London: Macmillan Press.

Alden, C. 2007. *China and Africa.* London: Zed.

Aluko, O. 1978. *Ghana and Nigeria, 1957-1970: A Study in Inter-African Discord.* London: Rex Collings.

Anene, J. C. 1966. Slavery and Slave Trade. In: Anene, J. C. and G. N. Brown. eds. *Africa in the Nineteenth and Twentieth Centuries.* Ibadan: Ibadan University Press: 92-109.

Asirvatham, E. and K. K. Misra. 2009. Political Theory. *New Delhi.* S. Chand and Company Ltd.

Ate, B. 1992. *The Presence of France in West-Central Africa as a Fundamental problem to Nigeria.* In: Ate, B. and B. A. Akinterewa: ed. *Nigeria and Its Immediate Neighbours: Constraints and Prospects of Sub-Regional Security in the 19990s.* Lagos: Nigerian Institute of International Affairs.

Ayandele, E. A; A. E. Afigbo, R. J. Gavin and J. D. Omer-Cooper. 1971. *The Growth of African Civilization: The Making of Modern Africa.* London: Longmans Ltd.

Ayoob, M. 1995. *The Third World Security Predicament: State Making, Regional Conflict, and the International System.* Boulder, Co: Lynne Rienner.

Ballentine, K. and J. Sherman. 2003. *The Political Economy of Armed Conflict: Beyond Greed and Grievance.* Boulder, CO: Lynne Rienner.

Berdal, M., and D. M. Malone, eds. 2000. *Greed & Grievance: Economic Agendas in Civil Wars.* Boulder, Co: Lynne Rienner.

Bhagwati, J. 1964. The Pure Theory of International Trade. *The Economic Journal.* LXXIV (293).

Buah, F. K. 1981. *West Africa Since AD 1000: The People and Outsiders.* London: Macmillan Educational Ltd.

Charbonneau, B. 2008. *France and New Imperialism: Security Policy in Sub-Saharan Africa.* Aldershot: Ashgate.

Chinweizu. 1980. *The West and the Rest of Us.* London: Nok Publishers Ltd.

Clapham, C. 1996. *Africa and the International System: The Politics of State Survival.* Cambridge: Cambridge University Press.

Collier, P. and A. Hoeffler. 2004. *Greed and Grievance in Civil War.* Oxford Economic Papers 56(4): 563 - 595.

Crowder, M. 1976. *West Africa Under Colonial Rule.* Benin City: Ethiope Publishing Company.

ECOWAS.2008. Conflict Prevention Framework. Abuja: ECOWAS Commission.

Ekpe, A. E. and O. O. Okereke. 2002. *Development and Underdevelopment: Politics of the North-South Divide.* Enugu: John Jacob's Systems.

Elias, T. O. 1956. *The Nature of African Customary Law.* Manchester.

Fearon, J. D. 2005. Primary Commodities Exports and Civil War. *Journal of Conflict Resolution* 49(4):483 - 507.

Fearon, J. D. and D. D. Latin. 2003. Ethnicity, Insurgency, and Civil War. *American Political Science Review* 97(1):1 - 16.

Finer, S. E. 1962. *The Man on Horseback: The Role of the Military in Politics.* London: Pall Mall.

First, R. 1970. *The Barrel of a Gun: Political Power in Africa and the Coup d'état.* London: The Penguin Press.

Hauss, C. 2000. *Comparative Politics: Domestic Responses to Global Challenges.* New York: Waldsworth.

Hopkins, A.J. 1977. *An Economic History of West Africa.* London: Longman Group Ltd.

Huntington, S. 1968. *Political Order in Changing Societies.* New Haven: Yale University Press.

Hussy, W. D. 1977. *Discovery Expansion and Empire.* London: Cambridge University Press.

Ikpe, E. 2000. *Europe in the Early Modern Period, 1400-1700.* Darlington and Sons, Lagos.

Kanet, R. E. 1974. *The Soviet Union and the Developing Nations.* Baltimore: The John Hopkins University Press.

Jackson, R. 2007. Regime Security. In Collins, A. ed. *Contemporary Security Studies.* London: Oxford University Press.

Janowitz, M. 1977. *Military Institutions and Coercion in the Developing Nations.* Chicago: University of Chicago Press.

Klare, M. T. 2001. Resource Wars: ***The New Lanscape of Global Conflict.*** New York: Henry Holt and Company: Metropolitian Books.

Mazrui, A. 1983. ***Africa's International Relations: The Diplomacy of Dependency and Change.*** London: Heinemann Group.

Mistry, P. S. 1991. ***African Debt Re-Visited: Procrastination or Progress? African Development Review.*** 3 (2).

Nkrumah, K. 1974. ***Neo-Colonialism: The Last State of Imperialism.*** London: Panaf Press.

Noah, M. 1980. ***Old Calabar: The City State and the Europeans, 1800-1885.*** Uyo: Scholars Press Ltd.

Noah, M. 2002. ***Ibibio Pioneers in Modern Nigerian History.*** Uyo: Scholars Press Ltd.

Okonjo, I. M. 1974. ***British Administration in Nigeria, 1900-1950: A Nigerian View.*** London: Nok Publishers.

Olsen, G. R. 1997. Western Europe's Relations with Africa since the End of the Cold War. ***Journal of Modern African Studies.*** 35(2): 299-319.

Oliver, R. and A. Atmore. 1996. ***Africa Since 1800.*** London: Cambridge University Press.

Osuntokun, J. 1992. The Dynamics of Nigerian-Equatorial Guinea Relations from Colonial Times to the Present. In: Bassey, E. A and B. A. Akinterinwa. eds. ***Nigeria and Its Immediate Neighbours: Constraints and Prospects of Sub-Regional Security in the 1990s.*** Lagos: The Nigerian Institute of International Affairs.

Rodney, W. 1970. ***A History of the Upper Guinea Coast, 1545-1800.*** London: Clarendon Press.

Rodney, W. 1986. ***How Europe Underdeveloped Africa.*** London: Bougle L'Overture Publications.

Ross, M. 2003. Natural Resources and Civil Conflict: Evidence from Case Studies. ***International Organization*** 54:35-67.

Ross, M. 2004. What Do We Know About Natural Resources and Civil War? ***Journal of Peace Research*** 41(3): 337-356.

Sorenson, D. S. 2008. ***An Introduction to the Modern Middle East.*** Colorado: Westview Press.

Stride, G. T. and C. Ifeka. 1980. *Peoples and Empire of West Africa: West Africa in History, 1000-1800.* London: Thomas Nelson and Sons Ltd.

Smith, R. S.1978. *The Lagos Consulate, 1851-1861.* London: The Macmillan Press.

Smith, R. S. 1989. *Warfare and Diplomacy in Pre-Colonial West Africa.* London: James Gurrey.

Soysa, I. and E. Neumayer. 2007. Resource Wealth and the Risk of Civil War Onset: Results from a New Dataset of Natural Resource Rents, 1970-1999. *Conflict Management and Peace Science.* 24(3): 201-218.

Taylor, I. 1998. China's Foreign Policy Towards Africa in the 1990s. *Journal of Modern African Studies.* 36(3): 443-60.

Taylor, I. 2006. *China and Africa: Engagement and Compromise.* London: Routledge.

Taylor, I. 2007. Governance in Africa and Sino-African Relations: Contradictions or Confluence? *Politics.* 27(3): 139-46.

Taylor, I. 2008. *China's New Role in Africa.* Boulder Co: Lynne Rienner.

Thompson, A. 2004. *An Introduction to African Politics.* London: Routledge.

Todaro, M. and S. Smith. 2004. *Economic Development.* Singapore: Pearson Education.

Udo, E. A. 1980. *Who Are the Ibibio?* Onitsha: Africana-Feb Publishers Ltd.

Uya, O. E. 1992. Nigeria: The Land and the People. In: *Contemporary Nigeria: Essays in Society, Politics and Economy.* EDIPUBLI S.A.

Uya, O. E. 2005. *African Diaspora and the Black Experience in New World Slavery.* Calabar: Clear Lines Publications.

Index

A

Abacha, Sani, 232
Abasiattai, Monday, X, 221
Abessole, Paul M'ba, 148
Action Group, 230, 231
Adamawa Plateau, 111, 115
African Development Bank, 137, 149
African World War, 85
Ahidjo, Ahmadu, 113, 114
Akan, 29, 181, 195, 197
Ake, Claude, 66, 67, 68, 307
Akpan, Otoabasi, Ii, X, 37, 40, 54, 55, 63, 82, 102, 105, 163, 197, 201, 223, 230, 235, 271, 272, 273, 291, 301, 305, 307
Akuffo, Frederick W. K, 199, 200
Alafin Of Oyo, 42
Alliance Des Forces Democratiques Pour La Liberation Du Congo-Zaire, 124
Alliance Of Cocoa Producers, 187
Americo-Liberians, 218
Anan, Kofi, 202
Anglo-French Conference Of 1890, 64
Ankrah, Joseph A., 199
Arabia, 19, 24, 295
Asante, 29, 30, 31, 38, 41, 42, 183, 198
Asantehene, 31, 41, 42, 198
Assyrians, 62
Atakpame, 251
Atlantic Ocean, Xi, 16, 25, 47, 48, 65, 119, 131, 145, 167, 175, 211, 217, 237, 243, 245
Awka, 22, 77
Awolowo, Obafemi, 230, 231
Azikiwe, Nnamdi, 230, 280

B

Babangida, Badamosi Babangida, 232
Balanta, 211
Balewa, Abubakar Tafawa, 230, 277
Banjul Island, 191
Barlavento, 175

Bashorun, 33
Bata, 139
Baule Kingdom, 183
Bemi Hills, 221
Benin, Vi, Ix, Xi, Xii, 15, 16, 32, 33, 34, 35, 38, 42, 46, 65, 86, 141, 151, 166, 167, 168, 169, 170, 171, 172, 173, 182, 223, 226, 228, 235, 251, 253, 269, 272, 276, 277, 278, 289, 290, 293, 302, 309
Berlin West African Conference Of 1884 – 85, 158, 161
Bight Of Biafra, 16, 151
Bijagos Archipelago, 211
Biya, Paul, 114, 267
Bordeaux, 21, 260
Brazzaville, 104, 131, 134, 135, 206, 283, 290
Britain, 16, 21, 31, 45, 48, 50, 52, 59, 66, 84, 102, 103, 117, 127, 129, 142, 170, 189, 191, 193, 202, 227, 228, 234, 253, 266, 288, 294, 295, 304
Buah, F.K., 38, 47, 48, 50, 289, 308
Buhari, Mohammadu, 232
Bureaucratic Bourgeoisie, 69
Burkina Faso, 32, 167, 181, 182, 195, 251, 269, 271, 272, 293
Bushmen, 160
Busia, Busia, 199
Byzantine, 17

C

Cabinda, 65, 84, 131, 133, 158, 164
Calabar, 35, 36, 44, 221, 223, 226, 227, 229, 307, 310, 311
Cameroon, V, Ix, Xi, Xii, 15, 86, 104, 107, 109, 110, 111, 112, 113, 114, 115, 116, 117, 122, 131, 139, 145, 146, 151, 223, 267, 269, 272, 290
Cameroons, 29, 56, 109, 111, 112, 113, 230
Caminha, Alvaro, 153
Cao, Diego, 122, 133, 147, 160, 161

Cape Blanco, 16
Cape Lopez, 16, 147
Cape Palmas, 16, 218
Cape Three Points, 16, 50, 201
Cape Verde, Vi, lx, Xi, Xii, 16, 46, 49, 51, 52, 57, 59, 86, 96, 101, 151, 166, 175, 176, 177, 178, 179, 212, 214, 239, 269, 293
Caribbean, 20, 169, 187, 234
Casablanca, 186, 283
Casamance, 16, 237, 241
Castro, Fidel, 297
Central African Customs And Economic Union, 137, 150
Central African Economic And Monetary Community, 137
Chakossi, 251
Christiansburg, 198
Cima, 175
Cold War Diplomacy, 98, 99
Congo, Xi, 16, 84, 85, 99, 100, 107, 109, 119, 121, 122, 124, 128, 131, 158, 163, 296
Congo Free State, 53, 57, 121, 123
Congo River, 53, 119, 120, 121, 122, 128, 131, 133, 158
Conte, Lansana, 208
Cote d'Ivoire, Vi, lx, Xi, Xii, 15, 16, 29, 30, 85, 86, 94, 95, 102, 166, 181, 182, 183, 184, 185, 186, 187, 195, 204, 217, 219, 251, 252, 269, 272, 283
Crioulo, 176, 211

D

Dada, Idi Amin, 97
Dahomey, 42, 167, 169, 170, 171, 173, 253, 277
Dan Fodio, Usman, 112, 226
Dapaong, 251
De Gaulle, Charles, 148, 296
Democratic Party Of Guinea, 207
Diagne, Blaise, 239
Doe, Samuel Kakan, 97, 219, 220
Dutch Disease, 84, 85, 233

E

Economic Community Of West African States, 172, 234
ECOWAS Monitoring Group, 220
Efik, 29, 35, 39, 122
Eka, Sylvester, X
Elmina, 46, 51, 198, 227
Ethiopia, 65, 99, 102, 119, 268, 283, 290, 297
Executive Outcomes, 247

F

Fante, 31, 41, 195
Fernando Po, 46, 47, 51, 52, 139, 141, 142, 143
Finer, S.E., 97, 309
Firestone Tyre And Rubber Company, 220
Forest Region, 204
Fouta Djallon Highlands, 204
Freetown, 145, 243, 245, 246
French Fifth Republic, 206, 207
French National Assembly, 134, 239, 253, 298
Fulani, 111, 112, 169, 176, 183, 189, 191, 195, 204, 205, 211, 237, 244, 251
Fulani Jihad, 183, 191

G

Gabao, 147
Gambia River, 46, 51, 189, 191, 209
Gambia River Zone, 51
George, Susan, 73, 89, 96, 235, 275, 278
Germany, 17, 45, 53, 56, 65, 86, 113, 119, 209, 228, 255, 266, 290, 298, 303
Ghana-Guinea-Mali Union, 201, 209, 272
Gnassingbe, Faure, 97, 254
Gold Coast, 16, 22, 44, 45, 46, 51, 54, 195, 197, 198, 199, 202, 229, 246, 253, 279, 280, 282
Golden Stool, 30, 31, 198
Gowon, Yakubu, 231, 232, 287
Great Depression, 59
Great Lake Regions, 99

Green Sea Of Darkness, 48
Greenville, 219
Grunitzky, Nicolas, 253, 254
Guinea Highlands, 217
Guinea-Bissau, Vii, 15, 16, 51, 59, 173, 176, 177, 178, 204, 211, 212, 213, 214, 215, 237, 293, 296

H

Hausa, 22, 30, 65, 195, 197, 225, 226, 277
Heavily Indebted Poor Countries, 72
Hebrews, 62
Hispanophone States, 59
Hopkins, A.G., 17, 18, 19, 20, 22, 106, 309
Hottentots, 160
Hutu, 65

I

Ibibio, 29, 34, 37, 39, 42, 44, 58, 122, 141, 225, 226, 310, 311
Ibo., 29
Ile-Ife, 32, 165, 307
Indian Ocean., 99, 122
Indians, 62
Indirect Rule, 53, 54, 56, 199, 230, 246
International Court Of Justice, 40
International Security Studies, X, 274

J

Jammeh, Yahya, 192
Janowitz, Morris, 97, 98, 309
Jawara, Dawda Kairaba, 192
Jolof, 238

K

Kabbah, Ahmad Tejan, 247
Kanem-Borno, 112, 226
Kanuri, 111, 112, 225
Katanga, 84, 85, 123, 124, 126, 129
Kèrèkou, Mathieu, 167
Khoikhoin, 160

Kimbanguism, 160
Kimbanguists, 122, 131
King Henry, 48
Kinshasa, 120, 125, 129, 288, 290
Kodjo, Edem, 254
Kokomba, 251
Koroma, Jonny Paul, 247
Kumasi, 30, 31, 42, 195

L

Lake Chad, 110, 112, 113, 224, 226
Lake Kivu, 120
Lake Tankanyika., 122
Lansana, David, 208, 247
Le Parc De Korup, 116
Lesotho, 65, 269
Libreville, 145, 147, 148
Lissouba, Pascal, 135, 136
Lokoja, 228
Lugard, Frederick, 59, 223, 228, 229, 236
Luis Carneiro, 175
Lumumba, Patrice, 100, 123, 124, 201
Lunda-Chokwe, 159
Lusophone, 16, 59, 66, 92, 179

M

Maga, Hubert, 171
Malabo, 139, 142
Mali, 63, 99, 169, 181, 182, 183, 191, 197, 201, 204, 205, 206, 209, 212, 218, 226, 237, 240, 269, 272, 283, 285, 287, 293
Malinke, 181, 189, 191, 204, 205, 206, 207, 211, 218, 237, 244
Mambilla, 224
Manchester, 21, 260, 309
Mande, 181, 191, 195, 197, 218
Mandingo People, 176
Mandyako, 211
Mano River Union, 102, 209, 221
Marseilles, 21, 260
Marshall Plan, 295, 300
Mauritania, 182, 197, 237, 238, 268, 272, 287, 288, 290
Mbini River, 140

Mbwiti Cult, 141
Mediterranean Sea, 25
Mende, 29, 218, 244, 245, 249
Mestico, 151
Mesurado River, 219
Middle East, 17, 18, 19, 25, 66, 78, 88, 94, 225, 267, 293, 296, 310
Military Committee For National Recovery, 208
Mills, John Atta, 200
Mitterrand, François, 101
Momoh, Joseph Saidu, 247
Monrovia, 97, 217, 221, 283, 284, 285, 286, 290
Monsengwo, Archbishop Laurent, 124
Moscow, 98, 99, 297
Mount Kilimanjaro, 64
Movement National De La Revolution, 135
Mozambique, 46, 151, 269
Multilateral Debt Relief Initiative, 72

N

Nachtigal, Gustav, 253
Ndongo Empire, 160, 161
Neo-Colonialism, 69, 70, 201
Neto, Agostinho, 162
New World, 20, 44, 46, 62, 100, 103, 212, 288, 311
New World Order For Africa, 100
Nganguela, 159, 161
Nguema, Macias, 141, 142, 143
Niger Coast Protectorate, 35, 229
Niger Delta, 16, 29, 30, 44, 46, 50, 51, 63, 84, 141, 223, 224, 225, 227, 228, 253, 308
Niger Valley, 223, 239
Nigerian Stock Exchange, 233
Nkrumah, Kwame, 69, 94, 97, 196, 197, 199, 201, 202, 253, 273, 280, 282, 310
Nok, 23, 38, 225, 235, 308, 310
Non Aligned Movement, 150, 155
Non-Alignment, 165, 201
North Africa, 17, 18, 19, 47, 121, 186, 197, 225
Norway, 86, 119

Nova Scotia, 245
Nri., 37

O

Obudu, Jos, 224
Oguta, 37
Oil Rivers, 227, 229
Ojukwu, Odumegwu, 231
Okpara, Michael, 231
Old Calabar, 35, 36
Olympio, Sylvanus, 253, 254, 290
Onitsha, 37, 44, 311
Opoku Ware, 30, 31, 41, 183
Overseas Reform Act, 184
Oyo Empire., 31

P

Paleolithic Period, 121
Palm Kernel Oil, 22
Pan Africanism, 102, 201
Phoenicians, 62
Pidgin English, 141
Porto Novo, 167, 169
Preventative Detention Act, 94
Private Military Companies, 83
Pygmy People, 121

Q

Queen Amina Of Zaria, 226
Queen Mother, 35

R

Ranger, T.O., 58
Republic Of Biafra, 231
Republic Of Namibia., 158
Roberts, Joseph, 219
Rodney, Walter, 44, 46, 62, 67, 216, 310
Rombos-Grande, 175
Royal African Company, 191
Royal Niger Company, 228

S

Sanha, Mallam Bacai, 214
Santiago, 46, 175, 176, 179
Sao Paulo De Luanda, 158
São Tomé, Vi, Ix, Xi, Xii, 16, 46, 47, 51, 57, 59, 85, 86, 107, 139, 141, 145, 147, 151, 152, 153, 154, 155, 161, 177, 269
São Tomé And Principe, 139, 151, 153, 155
Seko, Mobutu Sese, 100, 121
Senegalese Democratic Party, 240
Senegambia, 29, 38, 46, 211
Senegambian Confederation, 241, 272
Senghor, Sedar, 92, 239, 240, 288, 298
Serekunda, 189
Seventh-Day Adventist Churches, 152
Shagari, Shehu, 97, 232
Sharia Court Of Appeal, 233
Sharp, Granville, 21
Shaw, Flora, 223
Shonekan, Ernest, 232
Sierra Leone, Vii, Ix, Xi, Xii, 15, 16, 29, 38, 45, 46, 51, 54, 84, 86, 92, 102, 103, 140, 142, 166, 173, 191, 217, 218, 219, 221, 229, 243, 244, 245, 246, 247, 248, 249, 269, 272, 276, 279, 283, 287, 288, 289, 291, 302
Sirleaf, Ellen Johnson, 220, 221
Slave Coast, 16, 141, 142, 170, 253
Small Arms And Light Weapons, 80, 82
South African Defence Force, 154
Southern Zaria, 23
Sovereign National Conference, 124
Stevens, Siaka, 247
Strasser, Valentine, 247
Suez Canal, 25

T

Takoradi, 195
Tamberma, 251
Temne, 29, 244, 245
The 1 Plus 4 Presidency, 125
Tijaniyah Brotherhood, 239
Togolese Youth Movement, 254
Toure, Sekou, 94, 183, 184, 205, 206, 207, 208
Transnational Corporations, 74
Trans-Saharan Trade, 17, 19, 20, 30, 32, 34, 47, 183, 252
Trans-Saharan Trade, 17, 112
Treaty Of Tordesillas, 49, 50, 141
Tristao, Nuno, 212
Tropic Of Cancer, 167
Tutu, Osei, 30, 31, 42

U

Udosen, Charles, X
Uganda, 97, 119, 125, 127, 128, 268, 272
UN General Assembly Report Of The Panel Of Governmental Experts On Small Arms, 82
United Gold Coast Convention, 199
United Kingdom, 86, 244, 248, 280, 288, 289
United Nations Development Programme, 261, 275
United Nations Mission In Sierra Leone, 247
United States Of America, 24, 172, 177, 179, 209, 217, 245, 248, 294
University Of Uyo, X
Upper Benue River, 110
Uya, Okon, X, 18, 39, 44, 236, 311
Uyo School Of Historiography, X

V

Veira, Joao Bernardo, 214
Voinjama, 217
Von Bismark, Otto, 53
Voodoism, 169

W

Wade, Abdoulaye, 240
West Africa, Xii, 15, 16, 17, 18, 20, 29, 38, 51, 53, 54, 65, 81, 82, 99, 112, 167, 171, 183, 184, 202, 204, 206, 209, 217, 221, 239, 242, 244, 246, 251, 259, 271, 272, 277, 279, 280,

282, 283, 284, 285, 286, 288, 289, 290, 291, 293, 298, 302, 303, 307, 308, 309, 311
West Indies, 20, 142, 245
Western Sudan, 17, 18, 47, 63, 183, 189, 191, 196, 205, 218
Wilberforce, William, 21
Wolof, 22, 189, 191, 237, 238
World Bank, 73, 74, 84, 86, 100, 101, 105, 129
World War II., 221

Y

Yamoussoukro, 95, 181

Yancy, Allen, 219, 222
Yaounde, 113
Yoruba, 22, 29, 30, 31, 32, 33, 34, 35, 39, 42, 58, 63, 65, 169, 170, 225, 226, 251, 277, 289
Yoruba Union, 32

Z

Zabarema, 195
Zambia, 65, 119, 128, 158, 269, 272
Zenega, 238

www.ingramcontent.com/pod-product-compliance
Lightning Source LLC
Chambersburg PA
CBHW050336230426
43663CB00010B/1878